NORWAY

Changing and Changeless

BY THE SAME AUTHOR

Essays and Travel

DENMARK, KINGDOM OF REASON

FINLAND, THE NEW NATION

SWEDEN, THE LAND AND THE PEOPLE

IMAGES OF EARTH: GUATEMALA

OUR COMMON ROAD

THE HOUSE OF FRIENDSHIP

A GARDEN ROSARY

THE ROMANTIC SHORE

CAPE COD NEW AND OLD

THE OLD COAST ROAD FROM BOSTON TO PLYMOUTH

NEW ROADS IN OLD VIRGINIA

CENTRAL AMERICA AND THE SPANISH MAIN

SOUTH AMERICA, THE WEST COAST AND THE EAST

Novels

THE HOUSE BY THE WINDMILL

THE HIGH ALTAR

INTO WHAT PORT?

A Play

MISS COOLIDGE

(Some of these titles have been published under the name of either Agnes Edwards or Agnes Edwards Rothery.)

NORWAY

CHANGING AND CHANGELESS

BY AGNES ROTHERY

1939

THE VIKING PRESS · NEW YORK

THE PHOTOGRAPHS IN THIS BOOK ARE BY HARRY ROGERS PRATT

DL
409
R le

FIRST PUBLISHED APRIL 1939

18249

TO

ELLA AND PHIL

Contents

Contents

Illustrations

Illustrations

Part I

THE CHANGELESS
NORWAY OF
THE EYE

CHAPTER ONE

Whither, O Splendid Ship!

WHOEVER travels to Norway from the Continent, from England, from America, must travel thither over the sea. Only where her eastern border adjoins the western border of Sweden, only where—beyond the Arctic Circle—she touches Finland for a few hundred chilly kilometres, has she land connexion with any other countries. For the rest, she thrusts her headlands into the Atlantic and Arctic Oceans. She strews her islands on the North Sea. The Gulf Stream penetrates the water of her fjords.

It is fitting to approach this sea kingdom by the way of waves and wind, through foam and gales. For it was over these very waters, under these very stars, through mists and storms like these, that the Vikings steered their trading-vessels and their slim longships with carved and gilded dragon prows; sailed them to Greenland and Iceland and the Faeroes, to the British Isles, to France and Italy; sailed them to the undiscovered continent that was to be America. Cæsar's galleys worked their way along the coasts of Spain and Gaul, from headland to headland, rarely out of sight of shore. The Norsemen, without compass, headed across the open ocean. Having sighted a new world, they turned around and sailed home without a stop, to return again across the uncharted wastes to the selfsame landing-spot.

Only the Phœnicians can be compared, as navigators, to those Norwegians—and where are the Phœnicians now? The Norwegians, a thousand years after their Viking hey-day, are masters of the fourth largest merchant fleet in the world. Less than three million people, with a country a little larger than Great Britain and Ireland and a little smaller than the state of California, possess shipping tonnage surpassed only by Great Britain, the United States, and Japan.

The journey by fast steamer of less than seven days from New York, or of eighteen hours from Newcastle to Bergen, carries whoever would come to an understanding of this people, not only forward toward present-day Norway, but backward into history—a history that shaped the Anglo-Saxon world and stamped it with an impress unobliterated by eleven centuries.

If it is phenomenal that a small country nearly one-half of whose length (500 miles out of 1080) lies in the polar regions, and three-fourths of whose area is mountains, lakes, marshes, and glaciers, should hold such eminence in current civilization, the phenomenon is enhanced by its duration, losing nothing of its color and movement through the telescope of time.

The Swedish and the Danish Vikings have their own chroniclers. Although the currents of the three Scandinavian nations criss-cross at intervals and intermingle in the sagas, modern scholars have more or less channelized them, so that now the layman can follow the first eastward across the Baltic and to the Dnieper through Russia down to Constantinople, and the second southward to Germany—via the Frankish Empire—

to England and as far south as the Spanish coast to the Mediterranean. The Norwegian Vikings—for whom the term Norsemen is popularly reserved—while they joined their activities
with those of the Danes in the Mediterranean, on the Continent, and in England, went west, and are distinguished by
their discovery of the North American continent and their
influence and activity in the British Isles.

The Icelandic sagas, vividly explicit in so much of their
detail, are not definite as to the exact dates of the Viking
period; perhaps because it had no fixed beginning and no
definite ending. Historians today usually confine it between
the ninth and eleventh centuries, although nearly up to the
thirteenth century Vikings from the islands of North Britain
were raiding and burning, and Swain—the so-called "Last of
the Vikings"—died in the reign of Henry II of England. As
early as A.D. 790 a party of these yellow-haired marauders
landed in Dorchester, England, and when the sheriff ques-
tioned them, they promptly slew him. So possibly this could be
set down as their initial appearance upon the shores of Britain.

These first invaders were neither explorers nor premedi-
tated conquerors. They were a band of violent adventurers
who, sailing, sailing, sailing, their "sea steeds over the waves
high prancing," found the shortest way around the north of
Scotland. They held on through Pentland Firth and then
turned south to the sea islets of the western coasts. There lay
Ireland with its rich churches. There, along the Irish shore,
lay empty estuaries. The churches offered booty; the estuaries
tempting bases for the fleets. Into the estuaries they sailed.
Through the churches they swarmed and looted.

They drew up their ships on the seashore or on the banks
of a river, and threw up earthen barriers to protect them—

crude fortresses, some of which became seaports and some of which grew into towns. The present cities of Cork and Limerick, Waterford and Wexford, all originated in Norse defences on the shore. In the capital city of Dublin, which they founded, their language and customs prevailed until the English conquered it in 1171.

Ireland with its gold was irresistible to freebooters for whom buccaneering was a career and whose young sons were taken along as part of their education. Olav the Holy was raiding up and down the North Sea at the age of twelve. But the small islands were equally valuable, not because of their portable treasure but because they were convenient headquarters. The Orkneys and Hebrides, the Isle of Man and the Isle of Thanet, and the Scottish Isles—they overran them all. Sometimes they took wives away from them and left children behind in them, and sometimes they left wives behind also. In Ireland and the Hebrides and the Isle of Man they intermarried and produced a mixed stock, but for years the Orkneys remained a colony of pure Norse blood and the chief rallying-point of Norse power outside Norway. The Icelandic sagas give an almost complete account of this earldom, which spread through the Shetlands and through large areas of Scotland and into Ireland.

Neither did they confine themselves to Ireland, Scotland, and small islands. Olav Tryggvason "sailed to England and harried far and wide in the land. He sailed right north to Northumbria and harried there: from there he went north to Scotland and harried there." His ships were in the fleet that assailed the English coast, and he took a leading part in the victory over the English army at Maldon. When his first cousin (Olav the Thick) left East Anglia, "red with blood was Ringmere Heath while the host piled up the heavy heap of corpses

Over these waters the Vikings steered their dragon-prowed vessels.

No dust will ever sully this crystal water; no pollution taint this air.

from the ships." This Olav sacked Canterbury and out of eight
thousand he massacred all but "four monks and scarce eight
hundred of the inferior class of people." To make it good
measure he also sanctioned the murder of Alphege the Arch-
bishop. King Olav "rode right up under the [London] bridge,
put ropes around the piles which supported the bridge and
fastened them: and all the ships rode downstream with all their
might. The piles were dragged along the ground until they
were loosened under the bridge . . . and when the piles were
broken away, the bridge burst asunder and many men fell into
the river," and London Bridge came falling down with a
vengeance. It was no mere rhetoric when the monks prayed,
"From the fury of the North Men, deliver us, O Lord."

D. P. Capper, in his thoroughly delightful and scholarly
book, *The Vikings of Britain,* locates sites which these invaders
set up for their councils and courts of justice. Some of these
may still be seen at Tynwald Hill in the Isle of Man and in
Dublin and possibly on the Isthmus of Stenness in Orkney. In
Lerwick, Shetland, the most northerly seaport in the British
Isles, Yuletide is still celebrated with a festival obviously surviving from Viking days: a long war galley of painted canvas
and paper, with helmsman and gorgeously attired earl on
board, attended by a costumed escort and followed by two or
three hundred "quizers" carrying lighted torches, is borne
through the streets. When she reaches the shore the torches
are flung on her, ships' sirens shriek and fireworks blaze, and
—a floating bonfire—the galley makes her one brief and flaming
sea voyage. After that the celebration moves indoors, and probably most Shetlanders do not connect this rite with Viking
days any more than most boys and girls connect the Christmas
mistletoe with the mistletoe arrow that slew the god Balder.

8 The Changeless Norway of the Eye

Whoever would follow the deeds and misdeeds of the Vikings in England cannot do better than to turn to Capper's book and read how Olav the White was made King of Ireland; how London and Rochester were invaded; how the Isle of Sheppey and the Isle of Thanet were used as wintering bases by these barbarians who plundered first for pleasure and then for profit.

Their energy was inexhaustible. While they hammered Britain with one hand, they pounded Spain, Morocco, and the Balearic Islands with the other. They sailed up the Rhone to Valence (860) and grabbed Pisa and Luna in Italy (861). They swarmed up the Seine and the Loire (862). They battered Constantinople (865) and struck terror to Cologne, Bonn, Coblenz, and Metz (881). With seven hundred vessels and thirty or forty thousand men they beat the Seine into foam and besieged Paris (882). They took a whack at Flanders, Brabant, Picardy, and Louvain. Neither did they omit attention to Frisia, Hamburg, and the banks of the Rhine.

In the year 982 Eric the Red discovered West Greenland, but before that (in 900) Rolf, the son of a Norwegian earl, received a fief from the French king and founded the dukedom of Normandy and his bones rest in the capital he founded—in Rouen Cathedral—to this day.

Here one can take breath for a moment in the blood-letting and recall that, if the Vikings were bold navigators and brave fighters, they were also able administrators. At the end of the eleventh century Normandy was the best-governed country in Europe. Paradoxical as it may seem, the Vikings had a code of honour and moral behaviour, and M. du Chaillu has found this worthy, both in substance and style, to merit translation into blank verse in *The Viking Age*.

If it is difficult to distinguish the Norwegian Vikings from the Danish Vikings among the invaders of England at the end of the ninth century, to the Norwegians belongs the most spectacular achievement of that period—the discovery of America.

It was Bjarni Herjolfsson—son of a Norwegian colonist in Iceland—who, blown off his course, was the first white man to sight (in 986) the wooded hills of what was to be called North America. Bjarni Herjolfsson was not interested in America. He was seeking for his kinsfolk who had migrated from Iceland to Greenland and he did not even pause, much less anchor, on the unknown shore but turned directly back toward Greenland. But his report of the country he had glimpsed so excited young Leif Ericson that he bought Bjarni's boat and in the year 1000 or 1002 set out with thirty-five men to find that country again.

Christian Krohg's huge picture of this adventurer, in his yellow blouse embroidered in Norwegian colours, with his golden belt and sheath knife, surrounded by his long-haired companions, hangs in the National Gallery and gives an idea of how these first explorers must have looked. And Gudmundur Kamban's thrilling novel *I See a Wondrous Land* sets forth in vivid freshness the whole story of those years when the Norwegians were voyaging back and forth between Greenland, Iceland, Norway, and the New World. For Leif Ericson was followed by his brother Thorvald, who was the first white man to be buried in the wondrous land, and by Thorfinn Karlsefni and his wife Gudrid, whose son was the first child to be born in it.

Kamban's novel, founded on the sagas, tells of the early Norse settlements and attempts at colonization; of trading and fighting with the Indians; and of the daughter of Eric the Red, Freydis, who organized her own expedition, killed men and women alike with her own battle axe, and returned to Greenland at last to end her days in tranquillity.

For two centuries after this extraordinary communication between Norway and North America, the oceans of the world were white with Norwegian sails. Viking raiding had prepared for Norwegian trading, and in the twelfth and thirteenth centuries the ships of Norway were busy visitors in Dutch and English and German ports.

Then sails were slowly furled. Smoke, not canvas, was white above moving vessels. Prodigious, indeed, was the effort for a country as poor as this to meet the change from sail to steam. But the effort was made, and by the beginning of the Great War once again Norwegian keels held third place among the fleets of the world.

When that war strewed danger upon the sea, the Norwegian ships weighed anchor and continued to carry their cargoes, not only across more distant, safer routes, but also over the exposed English Channel, the North Sea, the Mediterranean, and the Atlantic. When unrestricted submarine warfare was proclaimed and all vessels were ordered to remain in the ports where they then were, the Norwegian ships—quite alone at first—defied all proclamations and proceeded methodically about their business.

This defiance cost them dear. Upon those far-flung watery highways more than two thousand of Norway's seamen met their death and her merchant fleet suffered a greater percentage of loss than that of any other nation, neutral or belligerent.

And yet today, unhelped by government subsidy of any kind, unsupported by any colonial empire, and with a standard of wages, accommodation, and maintenance for her sailors higher than that of any other country—with the possible exception of the United States—Norway has regained her prewar position. Adapting herself to changes in technique, in world-trade routes and commercial policies, at present she possesses not only the fourth largest but the newest merchant marine in the world—almost half of it in ultra-modern motorships.

Across the Atlantic ply the Norwegian-American liners, led by the *Oslofjord*. Across the North Sea skim the lovely transports *Vega* and *Venus, Black Prince* and *Black Watch*. Up the Norwegian Sea to the Arctic Ocean cruise the *Stella Polaris* and the *Meteor*—exquisite motor-yachts. Along the coast, into a hundred harbours and up and down countless fjords, glide fishing-craft, ferries, and local steamers, while into the Oslofjord steam the floating whaling-factories from Antarctica. All these are but a fraction of Norway's fleet, for 75 percent of it never comes to Norway and nearly one-half of it is in tank ships carrying oil. From San Francisco to the Far East, from the Gulf to the Argentine to the Dutch East Indies—to every country and every port go Norwegian tankers, freighters, and tramps. The largest privately owned merchant marine in the world is that of the Wilhelmsen Steamship Line.

Running side by side with the subsidized fleets of other nations, these independent vessels not only hold their numerical rank and prestige, but make money. They *must* make money, for the Norwegian Government does not regard Norwegian shipping as an industry needing protection but as a source of revenue. In order to survive, ship-owners and seamen of the twentieth century must gather their energies, strain their endurance, and perfect their skill as their ancestors did in the seventh. The same necessities and the same conditions that bred the Vikings breed their descendants.

The tradition of the honourableness of a seafaring career has not changed in a thousand years. But the conveyors of that tradition have changed. Those slim war galleys with their high prows carved and gilded, those sturdier trading-vessels with their sails of purple and red and black—all the Viking craft that tossed upon the waves a thousand years ago have sailed over the horizon of time and vanished from sight. Long after they had disappeared, their reflections burned in such clear outlines and vivid colours that whoever read the sagas imagined he had seen a Viking ship. Such "gold-mouthed, high-masted beasts, all painted in gay colours" were as real—and as unreal—as the Ark. But never again, mourned men through the centuries, would such vessels be seen in actuality.

That which was denied many generations is granted to our own. Buried in the earth for hundreds of years before they were discovered, lifted out of the blue clay which had so miraculously preserved them, reassembled in their original forms, placed in the permanent drydock of their own museum —today in Oslo may be seen three original Viking ships.

Gazing up at them from the floor, or down at them from the galleries, one realizes that not all the sagas, not all of Snorri's detailed descriptions, not the paintings of artists or the sketches of archæologists, have ever portrayed the strength of that deli-cate shallowness, the breathtaking lift of those rearing stems. No reproduction, however skilful, has simulated this actual structure. No model on a lesser scale, even if its proportions are correct, produces the effect of these precise dimensions.

The first of the three to be seen when one enters the hall— the Oseberg ship—was the last to be discovered (1903), and its several thousand fragments have been so skilfully fitted together and supplemented that it is the most complete of them all. The articles found in the burial chamber—although many had been stolen and others damaged by pressure—were so much more numerous and in so much better condition than any previously discovered grave-goods that they are given their own exhibition room.

The Oseberg ship is clincher-built, about 70 feet between the stems and about 16 feet across at its widest part. It was so well preserved within its mound, under a stone cairn, sealed in blue clay and under a hermetic layer of peat, that it was possible to collect its timbers, cross-beams and ribs and keel of oak; its planking, floor boards, masts, and thirty oars of pine; and steam—or boil—them until they could be bent back to their original shape and fastened, for the greater part, with their old rivets. Both the stems, intricately carved in relief by the best artists the age could produce and the court could engage, are of specially selected oak. The serpent figurehead is a replica, and frankly so, of the original, which could not be remounted.

The Oseberg ship was not built for heavy seas, but for short journeys in quiet water and was, therefore, quite suitable to carry a queen upon the brief, calm journey to eternity.

The queen was laid in the burial chamber with a bondswoman to bear her company, and their bones tell the tale that one was young and the other was old and palsied and stiff with rheumatism. Quilts and pillows and blankets furnished the beds, and on the posts of the Great Bed carved heads with open jaws and protruding tongues guarded the sleeper. Tapestries decorated the walls of the chamber, and chests furnished it; one of them was stocked with lamps and scissors and balls of

yarn. Looms and flax-beaters and flax-combs were thought-
fully included, and all kinds of utensils for cooking and tools
for building and gear for the ship. There were stakes and ropes
for the fifteen horses and chains for the four dogs and the ox
which were sent along. In chests and buckets ripe wild apples,
grains of wheat, cress seed, and woad (a vegetable dye used before indigo) testify that the burial took place in the autumn.

But in whatever season the queen was to reach Valhalla, she
could drive or sleigh across it in a vehicle that would put to
shame any rival royalty she might chance to meet.

The semi-circular body of the four-wheeled cart is so intricately carved that it is actually a fretwork. Gunnar in the
Snake Pit decorates the front, the horseman and attendant figures of the Hiadnings saga the side. The wooden pieces that
join the shafts to the axle are a maze of restless design. The
ends of the trestles are heads of men. The great wheels of
beechwood might jounce the royal occupant, but doubtless
pride in her so elegant conveyance would soften the discom-
fort. If it were a sleigh and not a cart she needed, why, she had
not less than four, with shafts and runners and bodies elaborately chiselled. (One of these sledges was put together from
1068 fragments, and the restoration took a year. The working
sledge with shafts is a copy.) In preparation for every exigency,
a saddle was also included. Thus, with clothes and furniture
and food and animals and utensils, her retainers fitted out the
Oseberg queen, no more aware that they were preparing a
historical testament than were the Egyptians who laid King
Tutenkhamon in his tomb.

The Oseberg ship is so convincingly complete that only
specialists in boats or students of history will examine the dif-

fering details of the Gokstad ship which was excavated nearly
a quarter of a century earlier. It is somewhat larger, its burial
chamber was more carefully built, and it was a better and
swifter sea boat. Indeed, its seaworthiness so fired the imagination of young Magnus Andersen that he built another precisely
like it in equipment, dimensions, and decoration, and sailed
in it across the Atlantic. With a crew of twelve, he left Bergen
on April 30, 1893, and arrived in New London on June 12,
and from there the *Viking* was taken to Chicago, where it still
stands in Lincoln Park.

Since there were left twenty-five of the black and yellow
shields that once hung upon the shield-racks of the Gokstad
ship, it has been possible to reproduce the full number of
sixty-four and lash and overlap them in the manner characteristic of the period. Such warlike equipment was suitable for
a ship that carried the burial chamber of a chieftain—a tall and
powerful man laid upon his bed in his finest raiment and with
all his weapons. It carried three smaller boats and all kinds of
gear, even to boards for playing games and even—besides the
usual horses and dogs—a peacock, whose fragile bones bear
evidence that the chieftain knew other climates and creatures
than those of Norway. How highly he valued this rare pet may
be surmised from the fact that the horses and dogs were placed
outside the ship but the peacock was found inside.

The Tune ship, which was the first of the three to be found
(1869), is broken and decomposed beyond power of reconstruction. It lies in its special hall, very much as it lay in the
earth for centuries, oar-holes and shield-rack and much of its
planking rotted away, its mast a mere stump, its few grave-
goods—a handspike, a wooden spade, bits of carved wood, and

some beads; the burnt bones of a human being and those of a horse that was buried standing—telling what story they can to the archæologist.

The three ships, seen together, infuse sudden reality into one's nebulous conception of the Viking Age. One sees the differences between the slim longship, which was primarily intended for inshore work in fjord and estuary, and the sturdier deep-sea vessels, and understands why Olav the Holy, on leaving England in November, "let his longships lie behind," and shifted his men into trading-craft. One understands the earl's reply to a Norseman who was preparing for the Faeroes: "You cannot go in longships thither, but I will have two merchant ships made for you." While it is a little difficult to grasp the five separate classes of longships—all of somewhat similar mould—the distinction between them and the traders is quite clear.

By studying these three actual ships in connexion with the sagas, it is easy to appreciate how the Vikings could have "great armies but no land," for a warship was, actually, a piece of battlefield. Two hostile vessels, with masts down and sails stowed, rowed to within striking distance of one another and shipped their oars. They lashed the bows and sterns together until both vessels made one compact mass. Not until everything was fast did the war horns sound. Then "they alone who were in the stems could get near with their blows. Those who were in the forehold thrust with their spears, and all those who were further aft shot with barbed spears and darts. Some cast arrows and stones, and those who were abaft the mast shot with bows."

The fighting went on until the vanquished ship was boarded

and cleared of men. Then she was cut adrift by the conquerors and captors, and floated away with her dead and dying. Even when whole fleets fought, the method was the same. Grapnels and grappling-irons were important, and there was no attempt at ramming. The weapons for such hand-to-hand combat were the straight sword and broad-bladed axe, bows, arrows, slings, pikes, and javelins. The minor and major changes in this offensive and defensive armour can be traced in the quiet glass-enclosed cases in museums: the short single-edged sword that was easier to handle than the mighty double-sided, two-handed blade; the plain rectangular crosspiece of the swort hilt that lengthened to form a guard. As for the shields—sometimes round, sometimes oval, with a hide covering clamped by an iron ring to a wooden backing—when warriors on land locked such shields as these together they made a movable rampart. During a sea fight, a circle of locked shields around the mast offered a protective screen and also a rallying-point.

Enough of ships and shields and weapons are left to show the methods of warfare. But the zest and gusto of that primitive fighting can be imagined only by recalling that these oars were pulled and these sails were raised not by galley slaves, to whom the outcome of any fight meant merely a change in masters, but by freemen, each one with his teeth set and eyes flaming, fighting for his own benefit and his own life. A chieftain did not hesitate to take his seat on the thwarts. A king or an earl was ready to grasp the tiller. This did not imply that he was demeaning himself, but that they were all men together. Under the udal system—the opposite of the feudal—the landowner was an absolute freeholder and the smallest freeholder was a petty chieftain. A Frankish envoy who sent word he wished to treat with the leader of a Viking expedition, received the answer: "We have no leader. We are all equal!"

Such methods of seamanship, such customs of fighting and trading, such democracy of intercourse, intensified every Viking instinct. And the same methods, prevailing to this day, create the same type of seaman.

The Norwegian ship is still a piece of battlefield, although in the twentieth century there is only one weapon permitted against its rivals—the weapon forged of good service and good seamanship and sound merit. Judging by the status of the fleet, it seems to have been sufficient.

The traveller to Norway on a modern liner may find the Atlantic foggy in June, the North Sea rough in July, and the Arctic Ocean ice-strewn in August, and he may wonder how it was possible to navigate small open vessels over such seas, not only in summer, but in winter. For sentiment pictures the Vikings on ships the whole year through, exploring new coast lines, discovering new countries, and attacking those already established. As a matter of fact, two-thirds of the year they and their craft were ashore. At the end of the summer, longboats and trading-ships were beached. Figureheads, masts, oars, and all portable gear were lifted out. "The beasts of the sea" were dragged or rolled into winter quarters and lay "in the boat house until spring, with heads bent low."

During the dark winter the mariners were tame householders, carpenters and blacksmiths. In the spring and autumn they were farmers and fishermen. At home, when they sat around the fire, they were saga-tellers, repeating, and without doubt enlarging upon, their exploits. When they wintered in distant colonies, or camped behind earthwork fortresses, they planned campaigns of conquest. But at home or abroad, they were land-bound in winter.

By spring the mountains of Norway, the narrow fjords, the restricted valleys, pushed them out. They had to escape that oppressive confinement. The encircling ocean received them, and taught them endurance, independence, democracy. But as the winter storms darkened, the fjords and the valleys and the mountains drew them home again. They were world-rovers but home-lovers.

Thus twisted and turned and tossed between the two opposing forces, all superficialities were ground away and the essential individual was left. Climate and topography produced the Viking character. Climate and topography produced the Norwegian people.

When the fifty-four-foot sloop, *Restaurationen,* sailed from Stavanger (July 24, 1825) carrying fifty-two men and women to America, preachers and pedagogues, patriots and politicians tried frantically to combat this "emigration madness." Vainly they tried to cure "the most dangerous disease of our times" and to argue away the force which was propelling Norwegians from Norway to "lend their strength to others." But although they called it "economic pressure," it was the selfsame necessity of escape that had driven forth the Vikings. The mountains are high, and on many of them snow lies throughout the year. The fjords are barriers, and into some of them the sun can hardly reach even in summer midday. The broadest valley is narrow and frost comes too soon. "Economic pressure" is created by topography and climate.

Over the ocean to that new world which Bjarni Herjolfsson sighted, have sailed, in the last hundred years, eight hundred thousand Norwegian men and women, for they are world-rovers. Over the ocean which we traverse today many Norwegians and their American-born children and grandchildren have sailed back, some to visit and a few to take up life in Norway. For they are home-lovers.

The ocean not only holds Norway as a matrix holds a crystal; it not only cuts between her mountains and penetrates far up into her very fields; it also beats in the blood and directs the life of her people.

As we enter the harbour of Oslo—the Oslofjord—we see high-set upon Ekeberg Hill a large and handsome granite building, flat-roofed with a square tower at each corner and with an arcaded façade. It is the Navigation College, where future officers, having already had three years at sea, are being further trained in the rigorous discipline and exact knowledge that keeps the Norwegian standard the highest in the world. In every branch of its courses and every detail of its equipment the college merits its eminence. Furthermore, the institution has been judged worthy of having one of the foremost artists, Per Krohg, decorate the interior walls with frescoes that are the pride of Norway.

There is no other seaman's school in any country so built, placed, and decorated; there are few schools anywhere directed in such a manner as to impress upon their students the seriousness and dignity of seamanship as a career. To the incoming visitor this college symbolizes the fact that the sea is the arena of Norwegian history and the determinant of Norwegian character.

CHAPTER TWO

To the North Cape

IF NORWAY had no cities, no streets, no towns; if she did not contain a house or a human being, she would still possess a kingdom, nor have to seek one to come. She would hold sovereignty over a changeless realm that changes with every shift of light and is rebuilt with every rising sun. Sailing northward, we approach those cities whose streets are of water. Entering the fjords, we pass into that kingdom whose walls were not made with hands.

The trip along the Norwegian fjords to the North Cape and the Midnight Sun was once available only to those who were wealthy enough to have their private yachts, or fortunate enough to have such yacht-owners for friends, or hardy enough to stomach the motion and odours of primitive coastal steamers. Now it is taken by those yearly increasing hundreds for whom travel agents and steamship companies make straight their paths before them, across the Atlantic, up from the Continent, or over the North Sea from England.

Perhaps, after a few more revolutions of the wheel, when everything will be prescribed for our greatest good—whether we want that good or not—only a selected few will be granted passports for a trip which surpasses the spectacular to become

21

an emotional experience. A novitiate of purification will be obligatory before one is allowed to enter upon this pilgrimage of pleasure.

But the dictators will—and not for the first time—be putting the cart before the horse. The cruise along this coast, where the elements are transmuted before one's eyes, where light becomes colour, and the solid rocks melt, thaw, and resolve themselves into a dew of sea and sky, is in itself a purification.

Ocean liners take the cruise nowadays, the largest of them floating, foamlike, past headlands which in turn float floamlike to the clouds. The slim motor-yachts *Stella Polaris* and *Meteor* can slip between the islands and the shore and slide down corridors walled with rock and curtained with waterfalls, where sound is a profanation. The small coastwise steamers chug along their daily routes, occupied with the practical business of mail and cargo and passengers, no more impressed by the awful heights than a milkman by a familiar skyscraper. The ferries go gossiping between islands whose only communication with the world is by boat, and up and down the fjords between hamlets as isolated from the world and from each other as any islands. For the mountains which lie between them have been traversed only by the winds and their dizzying trails have been marked only by the footfall of the snow.

There are fjords accessible by boat, and other fjords discovered only by the eider duck and the eagle. There are fjords whose walls are treeless precipices, and others where the forest slopes from crest to coast. There are fjords whose floors are strewn with islands and islets, and others whose margins are broken platforms of stone, and still others which widen into harbours or shelve back into terraces or flatten into pastures. There are the great fjords piercing the land for a hundred

Svartisen Glacier flows with imperceptible urgency into the sea.

American-born Norwegians sail home to visit or to take up life in Norway.

miles, and the thousand and one branch fjords fraying out
from them. There are famous fjords and nameless fjords, and
the glory of the famous is one and the glory of the nameless is
another. There is one glory of the narrow and one of the
broad, for one fjord differeth from another fjord in glory.

The extraordinary complexity of coast line is such that
Puck, putting a girdle around the earth in forty minutes,
would have to allow twenty of them for this particular section.
For, actually, a coast that measures a little over a thousand
miles by a straight line drawn from its north to its south, measures half the circumference of the globe when that line follows
the inlets of the fjords and the shores of the large islands.

Neither is this coast a mere margin of successive bays and
beaches. The sea cuts between mountains that rise abruptly
to the clouds, and it penetrates into fjords as deep as those
mountains are high. Only sailors and sea gulls can trace the
intricate channels among these rearing headlands, along these
convoluted waterways, whose names change and multiply and
differentiate themselves with each twist and channel and diverging branch. The sun itself is lost and unable to find a
way into some of the narrowest crevasses.

As one leaves the skerries of Bergen for the cruise northward, it is like slipping out between infinitely articulated fingers of rock—æsthetic fingers tapering into tips of green. They
stretch westward from a hand with a ruffle of foam-lace around
its wrist. They let us go, these fleshless digits. They have let
such multitudes of boats slip through their rigid grasp in their
thousands of years. They have let such multitudes of boats
slip back between them to the safety of the harbour, which is
the hand's palm.

Bergen shuts itself away behind closing hills and pulls down a curtain of rain. Docks and harbour, city and suburbs disappear. We do not even notice our dismissal, for our faces are already turned toward the Sognefjord.

The Sognefjord is a great arterial channel confined by precipices and diverging into lesser channels. Isolated cabins cling like wasp nests high on the face of its crags, or on the utmost tip of a treeless promontory brace themselves against the elements. Here a half-dozen houses, with hayfields, potato patches, and a thimble-spired church, scatter themselves at all angles and at various elevations, according to the contour of the clearing toilfully won from the forest. Yonder a town, which has squeezed itself into a crack between the cliffs, pushes its main street, its pier, and its hotel down to the water's edge. Between some of these settlements there is a connecting road, cut out of the face of the mountain but forced to tunnel in certain places and to overhang the water in others. Between many of them the only communication is by boat.

But whether it is only a solitary cabin set so high, so sheerly up, that it must lower its harvest by a cable, or whether it is Balestrand itself—that pridefully regarded resort, extending its long hotel and bathing-houses and pier along the beachlike front—nothing of man's handiwork, nothing of man himself, seems important against mountains whose peaks are in the clouds, whose feet are set in prehistoric time, and whose sides are scored and whitened by tearing waterfalls.

At Vangsnes a statue of Frithiof stands on its pedestal against the sky. Frithiof was one of those eighth-century heroes whose love affairs led to an unconscionable confusion of bloodshed and, it must be confessed, a good deal of confusion in recording as well. Tegnér wrote Frithiof's saga and Longfellow was one of the first to translate it—in part at least—into English,

and Kaiser Wilhelm of Germany thought enough of the rover
who became a king and a temple-builder to give this statue of
him. But against that sky Frithiof seems no more significant
than Longfellow or Kaiser Wilhelm; no more significant than
his father-in-law, King Bele, whose cairn mound is pointed out
at Balestrand.

The Sognefjord thrusts its profound waters for more than
a hundred miles inland. It is the longest of all the fjords of
Norway, and boats are busy up and down its highways, which
are four miles across in certain reaches, and up and down its
byways, which are the width of only a few hundred feet. Brown
and white herring boats, gold and white motor-boats, draw
their white strakes across the dark blue surface. Ferry boats
come alongside each other in midstream and transfer passengers as prosaically as do buses or trams. What effect have the
wakes of any or all of these vessels on water that sinks down
four thousand feet?

And now the pencillings of snow lie in a web on the diapha-
nous domes. Nothing static in paint or prose can capture that,
the essence of which is tender and malleable. Alas, that essence
can hardly be recalled by the most sensitive of all reproducing
machines—the imagination. For such a fleeting moment creates
itself in conjunction with the senses, and severed from that
conjunction it does not exist in full-dimensional completion.
When we are far away, and time and distance have dropped
between us and Balestrand, we shall wonder: are they still
there, those blue and green fjords, with sunlight sifting on
their undulating walls and glinting on their deep, deep water?
Impossible! For they were composed not merely of their own
substance but of our vision, and their terrestrial bodies gathered radiance through the lens of our delight.

One travels to the southern countries—to Italy, Greece, and Egypt; to Mexico, Guatemala, and South America—to see the monuments men have made: monoliths dragged from great distances and carved into forms and engraved with decorations and inscriptions, pillars raised to uphold roofs that have disappeared, pavements laid for processions that have marched into oblivion. One travels to Norway to see monuments that are the sum of a million monoliths: stones that have been carried thousands of miles, not by slaves but by glaciers, and engraved by the elements with alphabets and calendars only geologists can decipher.

Not all the fjords are so dedicated to majesty. Nordfjord grants more indulgent concession to humanity. Pushing inland fifty miles from the sea, it ravels out at Loen under a gentler air and warmer sky. It lies meekly in shallow waters that meander through tidal marshes. The mountains enclose but do not constrict the village, and their wooded slopes open widely to the sky.

The English, who have long been spending holidays in Norway, used, in the 1880's, to take a week or so travelling by pony cart and boat to get from Bergen to Loen. Nor did the journey seem too long in those days when overnight stops were made in farmers' cottages and when all the native girls wore white blouses, embroidered bodices, and full pleated skirts to their ankles, and their hair in two long braids. Now buses, with tops specially constructed so that the passengers can see the mountains and waterfalls, and private motor-cars with tops folded back, bring tourists every day, and during the height of the summer season there is a seaplane covering the distance from Bergen in less than an hour.

Methods of transportation change, but the tides of Nord-

fjord continue to mark their slight variation along the edge of
the piers, and half a century more or less is but a watch in the
night to valleys that hold relics of the Bronze Age. Regardless
of foreign intrusion, the farmers methodically plant potatoes
and cultivate them in patches by the roadside and terraces on
the mountain. They cut their grass in their sloping meadows
and hang it on fences to dry. The herring boats come and go,
and in the spring the cattle are driven up to the pastures on
the mountains and in the autumn they are brought down
again. The village church, overlooking the fjord, has, however,
made a concession. It is an octagonal church built of logs, clap-
boarded outside, and painted white inside and out. During
July and August the Lutheran gown and ruff give place to
Anglican cassock and cotta, and English visitors hold the services of the Church of England under the votary sailing-ship
model suspended from the ceiling and before the reredos
painted in a design of complicated simplicity in true Norwegian reds and greens and blues.

Although Loen lies so far north that the Jostedal Glacier,
which is the largest in Europe, thrusts a snowy arm almost to
its border; although ice grottoes, with their peculiar blue radiance and honeycombed surfaces, melting and building up,
touch the air with a chilly vapour, there is something sugges-
tive of the tropics in this region. Perhaps it is because the wild
peaks are so thickly wooded, perhaps because the flowers are
taller than elsewhere and the garden benches not wholly a
mockery. Perhaps a solitary cottage, tinted a pink more often
seen in sunnier climes, contributes to the illusion.

Even the local catastrophes partake of tropical savagery. For
the mountain slide that killed sixty-nine people in January
1905 was swift as a volcanic eruption, and the tidal wave thirty-

one years later was similarly violent. The farms, which had grown fat beside the protected Loen lake, were lying tranquilly beneath the stars of the September dawn when a great mass of rock tore itself from the mountainside and crashed into the lake, pushing up, instantaneously, a tidal wave two hundred feet high. In four minutes this thunderous wall of water had rushed the full seven-mile length of the lake. The sleeping people leaped from their beds as the first wave struck their cottages. As they strove to open their doors, a second wave tore away roofs and sheds. Those who escaped from the swirling wreckage were washed by the third wave to the opposite shore, where they clung until, hours later, boats could reach them. Farms and farmers, boats and buildings, plump ponies and planted fields—the very soil itself—were engulfed and dashed to destruction.

So deep is the lake that the broken-off rock mass is not visible, but sterile stones lie where once were fertile fields. A white scar glistens on the mountainside and the waters of the lake are still whey-coloured from the monstrous churning. And eyes still fill with tears as a mother tells of seeing her son torn from a floating timber and carried away, or a father of finding the body of his little daughter far down the fjord.

> My love lies in the gates of foam,
>   The last dear wreck of shore:
> The naked sea-marsh binds her home,
>   The sand her chamber door.

Norway is not a conjurer guaranteed to produce a rabbit out of a hat for anyone who pays the price of admission. If she were to be classified with necromancers, it would be with the Hindu yogis who create a growing mango tree which those under the spell can see, but which simply does not exist for those who come at an unpropitious moment, or who sceptically disprove it with a camera. There is no country more dependent upon imponderables: the weather, the mood of the spectator, and not only his transient mood but his appetite for visual provender, which, like other appetites, fluctuates with time and circumstances.

Sognefjord and Nordfjord are mango trees best seen from the water. But Geirangerfjord should be approached from the land. One must climb up the back way to Grotli and to Lake Djupvasshytta, three thousand feet above the sea, where the white sky without boundaries merges with white mountains without substance. The icy lake lies above the tree line—the floor of that very temple, whose inverted dome is hung with cloudy trophies, and where "Veil'd Melancholy has her sovran shrine." And one descends from this aching pleasure by steps of appropriate pain.

For from Lake Djupvasshytta the road unwinds like a thread pulled from a bobbin revolving on a monstrous machine. Around and around, and down and down, the Geiranger Road turns and twists and returns upon itself in half a dozen hooks and curves. So sharp are many of them that the buses, although short, must stop and brake and back and cut before they can start again and make the corner, during which interval they pulse upon the brim of eternity. Around and around, and down and down, with waterfalls splashing above and below and the rowan trees crowding to the edge to display their clusters of white blossoms or red berries. The road, although admirably graded, surfaced, and balustraded by rock, is so narrow that when two cars meet, there must be backing and filling and edging to the nearest cutback and then a cautious sidling past each other. The passengers hold their breaths, and even the violas, pressing forward in an eager host to see the fun, shudder and turn away their horrified faces!

Down and down, and around and around, and then, quite suddenly, at Flydalsjuvet, the mountains draw back like curtains on either side with a theatrical flourish. Nine hundred —nearly a thousand—feet below, the Geirangerfjord pushes its way through a steep and rocky channel, spreads out and comes to a motionless end. Across the glassy water, between the mountains, a white boat moves like a dragonfly. And all the precipitous distance between Flydalsjuvet and Merok is hung with houses and strung with waterfalls.

The snow-topped mountains with the patches of farms upon their sides, the twisting fjord—dark blue where the mountains shadow it, pale green where the sunlight sifts across it through parted peaks, white where waterfalls foam into it—this is the Norway every traveller expects to see!

This is the scene our grandparents marvelled at in old steel engravings or woodcuts in the monthly magazine. This is the view those few fortunate friends who were able to take such an adventurous journey described to our parents. This is the photograph on the picture postcards our contemporaries have been showering upon us ever since North Cape cruises have made Geirangerfjord accessible for anyone with modest holiday funds and a few weeks' vacation. This is the coloured film that will be exhibited next winter in a thousand parlours by a thousand moving-picture amateurs. It is precisely what every traveller anticipates. Even the octagonal black and white church, framed by the black and white trunks of the birch trees; even a village girl in a white blouse and a scarlet handkerchief; even a farmer in blue, scything a patch red with

clover and yellow with buttercups. And yet it is not less striking because of its oft-portrayed familiarity. A masterpiece is
not drained of virtue because it has delighted successive generations. An individual does not find the rapture of first love
hackneyed because it has been experienced before by the majority of the human family.

On their tilted plateaux and irregular terraces, the most
accessible of the mountains which enclose Geirangerfjord accommodate farmhouses, hayfields, and gardens. It is a long
zigzag climb up to them from the water's edge and a long distance between neighbour and neighbour. But since these skyey
ledges catch more sunlight than those further down, it is comprehensible why men have chosen to live on them.

But there are other mountains whose sides are bare except
for waterfalls and whose tops are naked except for snow—wet
and rearing crags over which the birds fly and in whose crevices
they build their nests. Surely these were never intended for
human foot—much less for human habitation. And yet, on
what appears from the fjord below to be an absolutely perpendicular cliff, is stuck, by some reversal of gravitation and
common sense, a cottage. One—two—three—half a dozen—a
dozen—in as many miles.

Between the sky and the water the farmer lives.

His front gate is a tumble of seaweed and boulders at the
edge of the fjord, and there he leaves his boat. His front walk
is a series of toe-holes in the cliff and his front steps a ladder
five hundred feet long, whose crazy rungs are slabs of slippery
rock. His side yard is a little better. It is a bit of cleared land
hanging practically at right angles to the horizon, like a table
cover on a clothesline. But the land is fertile and the grass that
grows upon it is rich. There is room enough for him to raise

his winter's supply of hay and potatoes, and that is all he expects to do. His wife tethers the baby by a cord and does not worry lest unexpected guests drop in for tea. For entertainment they can see from their window the Seven Sisters, letting their hair stream down in seven parallel waterfalls, and a rainbow transforming every filament of the Bridal Veil into prismatic tissue. Although they are near enough heaven to read by the stars, they have electric light. Obviously these comforts and opportunities are sufficient, for farmers have persisted in these eyries for generations, and nothing less than a snow avalanche, which annihilates the house and everyone in it, or a rockslide which is equally effective, has dislodged them. And then, not permanently. Like the vintners on the slopes of Vesuvius, like the citizens of St. Pierre, like the riverfolk along the Mississippi, as soon as the cataclysm of nature is over, the survivors creep back to build again upon the site of their disaster.

From the deck of a passing cruise ship these faraway homesteads do not reveal all their secrets. That one, like a bit of brown lichen gripping a rock, is not only an airy summer pied-à-terre, but it is a profitable farm. For from one hundred and twenty-five goats, one can sell eight hundred kroner's worth of cheese a month from April to October, and after that there is a market for goat meat. Such a farmer may well be content in the evening to see his herds come stepping down, one after the other, from the heights where they have been feeding.

For the thrifty folk who hang their hayfields on the walls of a fjord, who clap a turf-roofed cottage the size of a cup on an island the size of a saucer, and who, inch by inch, win a farmstead from the virgin forest, do not live by vistas alone. Those who are isolated as the moon can fish and farm, and those who draw together in closer constellations engage in all the activities of a town.

Such a town is Molde, protected by a line of islets, like a breakwater, and with its main street marching as straight as it can between quite an array of wooden shops and offices, cafés and cinemas. On the hill, which slopes up from this comparatively flat waterfront, the roads make no pretence at regularity, but accommodate themselves to the plain painted homes—some of them with a "look-out" or widow's walk on the roof—which, like the homes of seafaring people in Nantucket and in Cornwall, turn their faces toward the water whence come their menfolk and their livelihood. Lanes edged with hawthorn jog past cottages whose gardens are bright with currant bushes and fragrant with box and sweet peas.

And such a town is Aandalsnes, with its streets at different levels, trailing off in different directions, in the sturdy unconcern characteristic of such settlements. Life gravitates to the waterfront, where herring boats and private yachts are anchored, and where cruise passengers come ashore to take a motor trip up through Isteidal—a side valley of the Romsdal —zigzagging around mountains and whirling past waterfalls, or merely to stroll through the streets redolent of freshly caught fish and freshly cut timber.

But fishing and farming, shopkeeping and schoolteaching, printing a local newspaper and shepherding the souls and doctoring the bodies of the parish, are not the only activities in such towns as these. The hotel-keepers are as intrepid as any fishermen and toil as doggedly as any farmers.

Where a chasm drops down into a fjord, where a cleft opens up to a wilderness of peaks, upon sites calculated to meet the requirements of every type of lungs, legs, and photographic lenses, the hotel proprietor hopefully arranges accommodations. His father, his grandfather, and possibly his great-grandfather had an inn of sorts upon this very spot, catering to the English who long ago discovered Norway as a vacation land, and to those most faithful holiday habitués—the Norwegians themselves. During the winter it is the family home. During the summer it is a hotel.

The enterprising twentieth-century proprietor refurbishes the old inn. (Sometimes he makes the mistake of covering the original log walls with panel board to make everything fresh and new, but doubtless his son will take off the panel board and make everything old again.) He adds a cocktail bar, a bathroom—perhaps two. Whether he obtains a government subsidy or not, he collects remarkably adequate equipment, considering the shortness of the season, and charges reasonable rates, considering the 10 percent government tax which he must add to every bill and out of which he profits nothing but the complication of bookkeeping. He enlists his sisters and collects village girls and trains them to be waitresses and chambermaids. He arranges with his neighbours and the local garage-owners for motor-cars for excursions. One brother is a porter, another a guide, and the mother is chief cook and housekeeper. He plants lettuce and tomatoes for those strange Americans who, like the goats, are eternally poking about in the most unpromising places for a bit of fresh green provender, and he polishes up his English, French, German, Italian, Spanish, Swedish, and Danish.

Then he looks at the sky, consults the barometer and the thermometer, turns on the radio for weather forecasts, and then—sometimes for weeks on end—he laments without ceasing.

For despite the vaunted Gulf Stream—despite perfervid tourist literature—despite all laws of probability and all cycles of recurrence, the weather in Norway is no more certain than in old England or New England. It may rain all day every day, or some of the day every day. It can drizzle, it can shower, it can pour. It can be uncomfortably cold and even unexpectedly warm. All vacationists are disappointed and some resent it as a personal grievance. But to the hotel-keeper it is a calamity. He assures his guests, almost with tears, that it is a most unusual season. He buys meteorological instruments and sets them up in a conspicuous place in the garden. If he does not consult the entrails of slain animals for propitious prophecy and raise altars to conciliate Balder and mollify Jupiter Pluvius, these are the only rituals he omits.

The officials on cruise ships regard glum skies more philosophically. They politely assure their passengers that the sun will shine again. Experience has taught them that the mirror which was misty yesterday and may be cloudy tomorrow will not only reflect but intensify the proper morning of today.

When such a morning now dawns, it is so radiant that if one caught it in words they would burn the paper as light concentrated by a prism.

The coast floats by, hour after hour; the mountain tops, curved, jagged, folding away in vistas, and each one tipped with an incandescence that consumes the corruption of melancholy as flame consumes a moth-fretted garment. Upon the translucent green of the hills the sunlight lies in lemon rays as in regions beneath the sea. In such blanching purity the Fear of Hell is swirled away in the Hope—in the conviction—of Paradise. And whoever has feared that Paradise might be monotonous has only to drift through this celestial scene, changing with every ripple of air and unchanging through the ages.

In future summers, when heat bakes the pavements and dust blows down city streets, when drought parches the grass and kills the very trees, no dust will sully this crystal water, no foliage decay upon these hills. Pollution will never taint this air. Young eyes are not surprised at this wonder. They have been expecting their brave new world to be like this. But older eyes gaze at it with thoughts that lie too deep for tears. For their faith had forsaken them and they had no longer believed that there could exist a scene so unspotted by the world.

There seems no need of man, his movements or his habitations, in such a universe as this. The widely scattered settlements shrink to nothing. On an isle without a tree a cabin quivers like a mote in a sunbeam and is lost. Not a figure moves, not a hand is waved, from the distant shore.

Such hours of brilliance, slipped between days of lesser light, make compensation by creating not one such universe but two, for the duplication in the water is as vivid as the object it reflects and of a luminousness to radiate through many a future mundane month.

In this real and unreal world, what substance have the large white wooden buildings, the monuments and docks of the city that now solidly spreads itself beside Trondheim Fjord? The streets of Trondheim are wide and its ancient stone cathedral the most splendid in Northern Europe. But the traveller, bound for the North Cape and the Land of the Midnight Sun, cannot direct his attention or fix his humour on any man-made town. He must come back to Trondheim, as every book on Norway must come back to it. Today its royal history is but an unheard sigh and its Gothic spires like the fabric of Prospero's palace.

Far more in tune with the tranced progression northward are the broad level acres, green to the edge of the Trondheim Fjord, and the towers of the Castle of Ostraat, gloomy enough against the gaunt mountains. Here, during the dark period of the sixteenth century, lived Fru Inger Ottisdatter, "the best born, wealthiest, and ablest woman in Norway," and if the Lady Inger of Ibsen's play is more a creation of poetry than of history, the setting is true to them both.

And still the boat heads northward.

When it reaches the place where the long narrow map of Norway is frequently chopped in two to make it fit a page, does it hesitate for a moment on that perilous crack? When one can hardly distinguish the sky in the air from the sky in the water, it is well to take precautions lest visible and invisible also exchange positions. The Polar Circle, across which we pass without a tremor, assumes momentary definition, and once across it on the other side everything is reversed as on the other side of Alice's looking-glass.

The very sun behaves contrariwise to the sun we have known before. It begins to set at the normal hour, but instead of sinking below the horizon, it gathers up all the sunsets that have ever been lost and unfurls them in one supreme sunset. Every broken fragment is completed and magnified. The most gigantic formations become tender and the most evanescent tints overpowering.

Sunset over the fjords, beyond the Polar Circle, mounts to an intolerable crescendo and is prolonged and increasingly intensified like a savage ceremonial. It is held until we are as satiated as the lover glutting his sorrow on the morning rose, but still we cannot look away. What was natural becomes supernatural, for at eleven o'clock the sky is swept with streaming flares and at twelve o'clock the crimson disk is held above the horizon and then is slowly raised.

It seems almost a profanation to gaze too fixedly at this up-lifted host with its incense of burning clouds, while all the ambient is shaken with vibrations not of sound but colour. But it is not the sacred symbol of Christendom. It is not the gentle Nazarene who walks with sandalled feet over these cliffs of fire and ice, but Balder, the Norse Lord of Light. We are not absolved from sin, but we are forgiven for faint-heartedness and for doubting if the sun would ever shine again in Norway.

In the Land of the Midnight Sun—which is, in actuality, an all-night sun—hours of sleep become erratic; perceptions become taut and fancy plays strange tricks.

Is this Svartisen Glacier, flowing with imperceptible and ir-resistible urgency down to the sea, actually a river of ice? Is it one of the largest glaciers in Europe? And the only one which empties directly into the ocean? At all events, the sun is shin-ing on its snows, "shining with all its might. And that is strange because it is the middle of the night." But it is not the middle of the night. It is the pleasant mid-afternoon and everyone is going ashore to stroll across the moss whose springy resilience is unpressed by the passage of the ages. Everyone is stepping over streams that are clearer than melted crystal and breathing air that is more exciting than champagne, and everyone is gathering gentian and buttercups, violets and heather. The birch woods slant away in shadowy aisles,

> And then the air, that lies above,
> Can with a hundred pale blue eyes
> Look through the leaves and find

its love.

In regions where no sound of a railway has ever been heard, one
travels by leisurely horse and carriage.

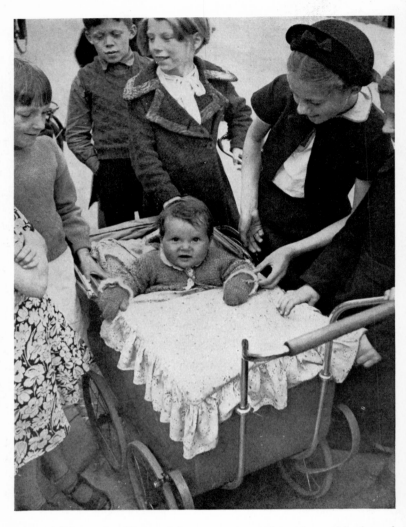

The children in Hammerfest are scoured and scrubbed and
stuffed with vitamins.

It is all mixed up and perfectly logical, like an extraordinarily vivid dream. Now we are actually standing on the glacier edge and looking into its glittering crevasses. Here is "that sunny dome, those caves of ice," of which Coleridge cried, "Beware! Beware!" and, "Weave a circle round him thrice." But those were in Xanadu, "Where Alph, the sacred river, ran through caverns measureless to man," and this is behind the Looking Glass.

But at least there is no doubt at all who these little people are, standing in the shadow of the birch woods, clad in parti-coloured costumes with long-skirted jerkins belted about their waists. They are the Old Men of the Mountain looking for Rip van Winkle, or perhaps the Seven Dwarfs—with their numbers augmented—seeking for Snow White.

As a matter of fact, the Lapps may soon be almost as legendary as these others. For although there have been Lapps in Northern Norway since the beginning of that country's history, there are only about twenty thousand now and the number grows steadily smaller and their racial traits less and less distinctive. For not only do physical characteristics alter with the inevitable intermarriage, but the habits and customs of a primitive people cannot escape modification in a world of motor-cars and motor-boats and telephones and radios. The Lapps who learned that a mud hut was more comfortable than a tent are now persuaded that a frame house is even better. And when one has moved into a frame house, it is not easy to fold it up and pack it on a sled and take it and the kitchen kettle and all the family and follow the reindeer as they move south in the autumn and north again in the spring.

There are still nomadic Lapps—perhaps a thousand of them. There are fishing Lapps and farming Lapps, and in Finmark

District there are plenty of them who have never seen a stranger. But there are, in increasing numbers, tourist Lapps, such as those at Lyngen, not far from the Svartisen Glacier, who set up their encampment and don their costumes when a tourist boat comes in, and keep a few reindeer on hand as exhibits. While sociologists are arguing whether the Lapps should be taught to farm or should keep to their reindeer-herding and -raising, the tourist Lapps are carving knick-knacks out of reindeer horn and bone and investing in postcards to sell to the next shipload of Americans and English. With the approach of the big boat they are galvanized into action; with its departure they sink back into slow movement and speechlessness.

Since they are far from stupid, they know a good deal more about the tourists than the latter will ever know about them. Doubtless, as their association grows, they will assume the virtue of cleanliness, although at present they know it not. And doubtless they will lose something of that queer kinship with natural forces and powers which has given them the reputation for wizardry. As the sewing-machine has already supplanted the needle of bone and thread of sinew, so they will rely upon warnings from the weather bureau instead of trusting to a mystical tying up the wind in three knots which, as they are loosened, blow greater strength into the gale. If, more and more frequently, erstwhile orthodox Laestadians, whose religion forbids them to have their pictures taken or even to look in a mirror, lest they blasphemously create an image of the Creator, permit (for half a crown) the tourists to snap them with the camera—well, they will not be the first to have compromised between God and Mammon.

In this region, in this age, where the Lapps are oscillating between the shadows of a culture that is passing and the illumination of a civilization that is approaching, there is a legend which, swinging ever more faintly with every turn of the tide, has not even yet quite faded into the common light of day. Where the water races in a narrow channel at Bodö, there still bubbles the maelstrom which whirled into its vortex the imagination of Edgar Allan Poe. At a certain turn of the tide, with a certain direction of the wind, it is well to avoid the "Saltströmmen." But as boats have grown larger, the centripedal force of this phenomenon has grown proportionately less. In fact, no one has seen that furiously spuming inverted funnel since the young Virginian peered down into its horrid depths. The maelstrom is still there. "An opiate vapor, dewy, dim" still "exhales from out its mystic rim." The maelstrom is still there, but its opiate vapour condenses most headily on the printed page.

On the printed page exists also the symbolic farm whose physical counterpart is northeast of Bodö. Sellanraa is more than a high patch of ground to which Isak—a lumbering barge of a man—carried his axe and cooking-pot and to which Inger, with brogues on her feet and a calfskin bag slung from her shoulders, led her solitary cow. It is more than the great farm with its fields and cattle, and Isak and Sivert sowing and harrowing, and Inger and her daughters tending to barn and kitchen. It is the genesis of all Norwegian farms, the visible alliance between man and nature, the history of a microcosm, the actual "Growth of the Soil."

Travelling northward—northward—through a night that is light as day—the land becomes merely an undulation of form, and time a fluctuation of light. And fact undulates into legend and fiction into actuality. Wings of fire unfurl across the sky and fold themselves away in cloud. Can one paint the wings of the morning? Or the air that is ruffled by those wings?

For travellers in such a mood, the city of Tromsö is a banner blowing in the wind toward the North Pole. It is to Tromsö that all the Arctic explorers come to fit out their expeditions, and one of the most famous, Roald Amundsen, stands in bronze looking out over the harbour. Here the whalers and sealers and trappers, bound for the Arctic, gather their equipment and provisions, and here they return with their sealskins and bearskins and fox furs and whale blubber. Colliers run like shuttles between here and the coal mines in Spitsbergen. Here is a museum, unique in its latitude, filled with shells and stuffed birds and the skeletons of the animals of the Arctic, with artifacts from the Stone and Bronze Ages: keys without locks and bells without tongues. Here also is an observatory for the study of the Aurora Borealis, terrestrial magnetism, and atmospheric electricity.

For the people in the provinces of Northern Norway, the little town on the little island, with its rowan trees and wild cherries and silver birches, is a city of smartest shops, prodigious activity, and the gayest society, not only urban but suburban. To the tourist it is a springboard from which leap the devotees of the Arctic, lovers whose lips, having touched those of a frozen Belle Dame sans Merci can never be appeased by a milder embrace.

Beyond Tromsö, the air is so pure that, like ether, it gives one light-headed fancies. Those mountains, for instance, which were somnolent hulks in the sun, are now, in the mist, metamorphosed into playful pachyderms, padding in a procession, one behind the other, around the watery forest clearing whose floor is edged with foam.

There is no doubt about it. Everything is different on this side of the Polar Circle. It is possible that all the earth is not apple tart or that all the sea not ink, but what about Hammerfest, lying on the mainland of Norway, and yet inaccessible by land, but only by water or air?

Like a harlequin, the most northerly city in the world is clothed half in black and half in white, for unmitigated darkness lies upon it during the weeks of winter and unwinking daylight during the nights of summer. The hottest season is not hot enough for a fan. The coldest is not cold enough to freeze the water in the fjord. Except for a handful of wind-blown trees, its only orchards are wooden racks, planted between shore and street and bearing for fruit tons and tons of split and drying stockfish. A granite shaft at latitude 70° 40' 11.3" and topped by a copper dome announces itself as nothing less than the northern end of a measurement made by the geometricians of three nations to determine the form and size of the earth. The southern end, marked by a similar column, is at Ismail on the Danube.

Despite all these possessions, Hammerfest, in true storybook style, disguises itself under a cloak of commonplaceness. It does not look in the least like a harlequin. Seen from the water, it is as bleak and bare as lead-coloured houses with roofs of cold grey slate can make it. Seen from the street, it is just as forbidding. But the people contradict this drabness by their cheerful faces. Children, scrubbed and scoured and stuffed with vitamins—for that dull building which looks like a factory is really a fountain of codliver oil—laugh and shout and chatter in English as well as Norwegian. Chunky horses clatter along pulling chunky carts. On the sills of white-curtained windows bloom begonias as big as cantaloups and in the churchyard, where lie the Olavs and Annas, the Kristines and Johans of a hundred and fifty years, phlox and lupines, hyacinths and forgetmenots are hurrying to push out all the bloom they can before frost.

In the stark frame cottages are unexpected comforts of plenty of warmth and plenty of light. In the larger wooden houses are unexpected elegances. Series of drawing-rooms hung with portraits open into a billiard room on one side and a dining-room on the other, with silver and glass shining on the polished sideboard. Such rooms are the scene of a social life by no means dull, for there is both time and money for entertainment and an inclination to set it forth with the proper formalities.

There is plenty of contact with the world outside. The big modern hospital on the hill serves all of Northern Norway. To the big school come boys and girls from all over Finmark. Down in the harbour are fisher boats from France and in the town a Roman Catholic church for French fishermen. Fish and hides and fur and oil go out on the ships, and radios and pianos and sewing-machines and automobiles come in, and the four thousand inhabitants look down on the water and up to the mountains and nod their heads approvingly and consider that this is a favoured spot indeed and that they are fortunate to find themselves in it.

After Hammerfest the mountains discard all verdure and stand forth like the resurrected on the Day of Judgment, clothed only in their bones.

On one such cliff, its stratified courses giving it resemblance to an Aztec temple, are cut rude galleries and slanting platforms open to the sky. Upon these platforms sit a thousand gulls and guillemots, auks and puffins. In the ledges of these galleries perch ten thousand more. The splintered pinnacle that serves as a watch tower is empearled with them. Down by the water's edge broken terraces, carpeted with brown sea-weed, are drifted as if with snow. In a cave hollowed at the base of the cliff, an ancient Merlin—feathered instead of bearded—succumbs to the witcheries of a web-footed Vivien. As the great strange bird, which is a boat, draws near this sanctuary, there is a whir of wings and the air is filled with flying particles. The birds, whose colour is one with the whitecaps and the clouds, whose movement is that of the sea and the winds, shriek and soar away, disappear, return, and settle once again.

Northward and northward, along a naked, sterile coast to where a horn of rock projects from the forehead of a cliff as if to guard a Plutonian entrance.

On and on, to where the winds whistle and the mists rise and the North Cape turns its bleak and haggard profile to the Pole.

Like midges attracted by a lamp, the people from the boat begin to swarm about that lightless sphinx. Well-shod Sard Harkers, they find a foothold on those motionless shoulders. They crawl across that iron brow. They stand upon the top-most height and blink at the Midnight Sun. And, even as they look, the "hollow fires burn out to black." The flames are thin-ner than a shrivelled leaf and the clouds are cold as cinders at the earth's core. . . .

The Sard Harkers who climbed up must now climb down. The Sphinx-Medusa stares stonily across the sea. So will she stare through many a summer sun, nor close her eyes in the void of winter night.

After one has seen the Midnight Sun, after one has climbed the North Cape, what has he done?

What he has done can be measured only by what he has felt. In that passage, of the glory and the freshness of a dream, "the muddy vesture of decay that doth grossly close us in," is temporarily washed away. Only the purified projection of sense is left.

"The world is too much with us," sighed Wordsworth. "Getting and spending, we lay waste our powers: Little we see in Nature that is ours; We have given our hearts away, a sordid boon!" But it was not Norwegian Nature that he meant. And this world, apparelled in celestial light, redeems the sordid boon and replenishes the wasted powers.

O ask ye no more of me. Were I to tell you more . . .
Ye would burst your bonds: no roof nor door could restrain
    you.

CHAPTER THREE

A Piscine Calendar

THOSE mountains which reverse themselves into the waters of the fjords seem to indicate that there is a duplicate universe where height is depth and where sound is silence. In such a reflected universe one imagines the only reality to be swaying shadows, drifting motion, and colours melting into colourlessness.

There is indeed another world below that glassy surface, but it is not a world of dim duplications. The deep waters of the fjords, the shallower ones of the shores and island banks, are pulsating with swift motion and sharply darting shapes. Like an endless chain whose strands are beyond computation, the fish swirl around and around the coast, in and out of the fjords, up and down the rivers. According to season, and according to place, the chain thickens and tangles and changes from silver to bronze to platinum and to all the metallic glints of blue and black and brown and red and grey. Millions of fish! Billions and trillions of fish! Mountains of fish! The leaves upon the trees, the blades of grass in the pastures which the water reflects, are as nothing compared to the glittering infinity of finny forms darting through and below those reflections.

As the chain slips rapidly by, as the glittering links break through the water, now in the south, now in the north, the fishermen rush after it with nets and seines and hooks and sinkers and floaters and flies and spinners and every kind of tackle.

The pursuit, although fast and furious, is not far when herring are the prize, for, having spent the first years of their lives in the fjords before going out to sea, the herring return to seek their old playgrounds in the fjords. Like the fish which rose to the hook of Peter carrying a piece of money in its mouth, they come to the fisherman instead of forcing him to distant pursuit. That is, when they come at all. For all years are not good years, even for herring, and in some seasons the money-bringers are so few that the fisherman is hard put to it to find not silver but common bread for human mouths.

But in good years, when the watcher on an island or on the banks of a fjord sees the gulls hovering above a distant herring school, he gives a cry of warning, and then every man and boy, woman and child, rushes out to push the boats from the shore.

The boats are ready and so are the nets, and well the fishermen know how to chase after and seize the precious catch. Two small boats accompany the larger one and between the two former a net is set which is, when full, drawn in over rollers, pouring its slithering mass directly out into the large boat. There are whole fleets of these herring boats and with them goes a hospital ship, for sudden storms may bring disaster not only to vessel and gear but to men. On Sundays, when no fishing is permitted, the hospital ship becomes a church.

When the herring are plentiful, the nets are set again and again, and no matter how many times they are emptied there is a market for the catch. Home buyers will take some of the fresh herring, Germany and England much of the iced, Russia a large portion of the salted, and the United States most of the canned and kippered. What is left of the three or four million hectolitres will be made into herring oil, the best grade to be refined for margarine and the second grade used for industrial purposes. Heads and bones will be manufactured into herring meal for stock-feeding.

Great herring, which appear from January to the middle of February; spring herring, which come at the end of March; fat herring and small herring; North Sea herring and herring from Iceland waters—these six different catches may yield as much as a million and a quarter dollars in a single season, and before that season is over, the cod-fishing begins in the north around the Lofotens.

This wild and barren congeries of islands—unnumbered if not numberless, lying not far from the mainland in miles but centuries away in tradition and custom—becomes from January to April the most concentrated fishing-area in the world. All the year round tiny boats are bobbing about the islets and inlets and out at sea in the mist of morning and the darkness of night. But when the cod is in season, thousands upon thousands of boats from every part of Norway come crowding to the harbours.

Your true Lofotener is a fisherman and a sailor and nothing else. He refuses to plough; he cannot swim; he has never been to the mainland; he may never even have left his own island to visit a neighbouring one. At the age of six, he is splicing ropes and rowing like a man. At the age of sixty, he is sliding down rocks and jumping into boats. His glance is direct and his words are few. There is hardly a family that has not lost a husband, a father, or a son, but few gravestones tell their story, for the sea is their churchyard. Men and women look death in the eye without a change of expression. Their faces, weathered and stern, reveal acceptance of inevitable fate.

Few trees grow on the Lofotens, and the precious wood imported for building and for fires is handed out with niggardly anxiety, and although certain of the islands are green with what looks like Kentucky bluegrass, not cattle but birds—millions upon millions of them—are their visitors.

In culs-de-sac among the rocks are tiny villages with nets hanging in the yards and boats drawn up on the beaches and, during the summer, everywhere the rocks are white with codfish bleaching as on some vast perpetual wash day, drying like a gigantic harvest of hay, and tended and turned and gathered by the women and children, according to the custom of hundreds of years.

For in this limited area, within this limited season, forty million codfish may be caught. In one memorable week thirty-six million pounds were brought in. About thirty-five thousand tons of these are usually dried and salted (*klip-fisk*) and exported to the Catholic countries of Spain and Portugal, France and Belgium, South America and Cuba. Those which are not salted but merely cleaned and split and hung up to dry (*stock-fisk*) are chiefly shipped—sixty-five thousand tons of them—to Italy and West Africa. The roe is salted and canned —five or six thousand tons of it—making a savoury pink caviare which France has long appreciated. A thousand years ago London was receiving shipments of codliver oil from Norway. Popular respect for vitamins has given the grade-A product an added value, and science has found veterinary and industrial uses for grades B and C.

Svolvaer, the capital of the Lofotens, a network of wooden

bridges connecting flecks of rock, is, like Jonah, swallowed up
by fish, by factories making codliver oil and fertilizer, factories
canning caviare, factories packing *klip-fisk* and *stock-fisk*. During the season the population of two thousand is engulfed by
ten thousand visiting fishermen, and along the shores the boats
are crowded so close together, it is a miracle how they can
escape collision when, in the early morning, a gunshot gives
the starting-signal, and they all leap forward at the same in-
stant. Most of the fleet is motorized nowadays. Only a few
sailing-boats from the Faeroes, manned by two or three men,
recall the days which Johan Bojer describes so movingly in
The Last of the Vikings.

Although there are many islands which the inhabitants
rarely leave, except to go out to sea, and which the tourist
never visits, sometimes cruise ships wind their way between
the fjords, past the steep red-roofed thirteenth-century church
at Trondenes and stop for a few hours at Harstad, a substantial
and pretty town with its fish factories and shops near the quay
and its snug houses along the lanes and up amid the hayfields
and on the hillsides.

Before the boat has docked, the children have gathered upon
the pier. Yellow-haired, brown-haired, black-haired, chestnut-
poll, and brick-top; little girls in cotton dresses and gaily embroidered knit coats; little boys in bright-coloured shirts;
babies in white—there are four thousand people in Harstad,
and to the dazzled eye, three thousand of them appear to be
children. The boys swarm over the quay like midges; the little
girls wave. Perambulators and go-carts crowd into the thickest
of the press, wheeled by grandmothers who look like mothers
and mothers who look like older sisters. The herring catch

may be poor and the codfish a disappointment, but the crop of sturdy smiling human youngsters shows no signs of petering out.

To stroll through Harstad is like strolling through the pages of Hamsun's *Segelfoss Town,* the community which grew from a few cabins to a thriving centre, with its schools for adults as well as for children, with its shops displaying silk underwear and bananas, and with not weekly but daily steamers. This must be the familiar apothecary's shop and that road must lead to the office of the telegraph operator. The doctor's office is on this corner, yonder is the harbour master's house, and up on the hill is the roof of the cottage a retired sea captain has built for his declining years. There are hayfields and potato patches and granite quarries. Poppies and anemones, asters and phlox, line the path to the tiny Catholic church with its blue and white walls and its seven pews for visitors from Latin countries.

Although the craft of the forty thousand fishermen who hurry through January storms up to the Lofotens have changed in the half-century since *The Last of the Vikings,* the islands themselves, except for a few towns where larger steamers stop, have altered not at all. The Lofoten Wall, which from the Vestfjord seems to be an unbroken mountain barrier, still lifts its peaks sharply from the sea. The widely scattered hamlets, with what look like doll houses surrounded by toy boats, still cling to the bare rocks, encircled by fish drying in the sun— or, more accurately, in the wind—each tiny settlement more isolated, more forlorn, more appealing than the other.

The women wash and work in houses so near the water that an inadvertent step will be their last, for who can learn to swim in water which, although it never freezes, is always numbingly cold? The bearded men still carry, in gaily painted wooden casks, enough bread and margarine to keep them alive during their fishing-trips and, with the same matter-of-course foresight, tags to identify them if they meet with the all-too-frequent fatality. They still fish, wordlessly, through the night and through the fogs, and wordlessly spread their catch upon the rocks in some far inlet, and compose themselves in silence to wait until it dries. If the storms spare them, they return in time to that cranny where they were born, to remain there until the next trip, scorning the mainland and all its ways.

Cod, with the codlike coalfish, haddock, tusk, and ling, is the principal catch around the Lofotens.

Mackerel—that ichthyic delicacy the salted export of which met disastrous curtailment when prohibition put an end to "free lunches" in the United States—is caught in the warmer south where, in May, they "tumble joyfully through the water, waving their fins and splashing their tails," until the "rosiness of the bay breaks into ripples."

Whoever reads *Markus the Fisherman* by Gabriel Scott will henceforth associate this prosaic commodity with the excitement of a wild-boar hunt. For Markus, looking out from his hut in the mountain cleft, sees the mackerel coming in such abundance that the sea is fairly boiling with them, making a din that can be heard a long way off. The shoal keeps to the shore and the fish hold their snouts glued to the surface so the foam stands around them like feathers. They bring life to the harbour, and the people are seized as if with a fever and throw down whatever they have in their hands and get into their boats. "The mackerel draws them all like a mountain of gold. Birds and fishes come in from the ocean, and people come in hordes from inland. Such hustling and bustling as ever you saw in your life, beating of oars, struggling with sails, and in between shouting and swearing, so that it echoes among the holms." In the outer harbour, the mackerel remain day after day. "They dance in and out among the holms there and stay and spawn in the bay and seem to be quite at home. Now and then they behave as if they had got a fit and drive wildly between the sounds . . . one chasing the other, till the water foams and froths. Look, the leader has already reached the island over there. Immediately a net is put out. They do not get time to stop: they cannot even if they wanted to, for the others are heaping up behind for all they are worth. There is not even room to turn. They can feel their neighbours' fins pricking them in the side and the nose of the one behind prods them in the tail. They are so tightly packed that they tickle each other. There is nothing for it but to try and get through, it looks as if they could manage, there are holes and openings everywhere. And in this way the whole shoal goes straight into the net, and in less than no time it is quite full.

"As they get the net in, wealth rolls thickly ashore, fat glistening autumn mackerel, shining with all the colours of seaweed and like cold metal to the touch . . . a golden shimmer of sea-green and silver which darkens in the light and changes colour to mother-of-pearl, copper and blue. The mountain shines far off in the sunlight, spreading a kind of whiteness in the air. And as every minute passes the white and shining mass grows in front of one's eyes and takes up more and more space. It rises over the rocks and heaps itself up in a wet pile, which slithers about on all sides, like a playing fountain of fish that comes silently out of the mountain, rushes forth and glides away in an incessant stream."

Markus the Fisherman is the story of the excitements and

Beyond the fjords lie the valleys with new roads connecting once-
severed hamlets.

There is work on the farm for everyone, and plenty of it.

disappointments, the humble triumphs and humble defeats of one simple man, drifting about "in his tiny vessel day in and day out between two vast elements," which leave their "mark on his mind and touch something in the bottom of his soul."

This book is the unique guide to the cycle of the fisherman's year. Such an earnest and persuasive figure is Markus that the most indifferent non-fisherman will never again look at a lobster pot without seeing the little man bending the juniper sticks into rings, "just big enough to get his hand through, a couple for each lobster pot. Then he spins over the whole framework and covers it from end to end with big meshes of coarse thread. He keeps on turning it in his hands, while the needle flies in and out like a spider." Now comes the pocket, which "must not be too pointed or too shallow, nor must it stand up in the middle of the net or be too high up under the top. The tying up is very important too. To make the whole a success it must tighten with one single thread and that only happens if it is in just the right place and put there by a skilled hand . . . the stone must also be just the right size and shape, a thin flat flake. . . . If the pocket is a bit too deep, or the lobster pot too short, it is equally bad; then the lobster dare not even go in, it sits in the pocket like a parrot in its cage and helps itself as it pleases." The grass rope is easily made, "but the floats are not quite such an easy matter, for not every one has cork, and then they must find light pine wood, which will not sink when it carries the ropes." These "are planed all over and painted white with a carved M on them filled in with a most beautiful pink." When finished "they lie inside his shed in rows and look like the daintiest basket work: light and strong at the same time, nicely shaped and with a wonderful finish." Those that are for deep-sea fishing are "fitted on to a sort of sledge with a piece of wood fixed across to steady them when the sea swills over the shallow part."

Markus sells his lobsters and buys net and thread and rope in town, wondering whether he dare risk the money it takes to make such a big net. For "while the huntsman has changed his tools for guns and other weapons, while the huntsman has moved with the times, the fisherman has kept to his twine, as his forebears have done thousands of years before him. He makes his nets today as they did in the time of Christ, and sets them in the same way as the disciples did in the Sea of Gennesaret."

Markus sits in his little house twisting and tying as hard as he can. "The small room is full of net: it hangs on the wall, it hangs from the roof, it lies on the table and benches, and runs crosswise from peg to peg. And in the middle of it all sits Markus and spins and spins until he almost spins himself in. His fingers flew, his hands turned, the needle ran backwards and forwards, and the meshes fell quietly away. They fell like tiny oblong squares and joined themselves together diligently and busily. They fell down over his knees, on to his shoes and the floor, on to his rug, and spread and increased from day to day. It is mostly in the evenings he works, the lamp humming on the table, while the thread runs silently through his fingers, soft, greasy and good to touch."

Markus knows all about fish. He knows when the cod are free from worms and "do not go about with a swollen head and dried up body like an idiot." He knows the habit of the eel, the fat silver-eel with its pointed head, and the broad-mouthed frog-eel with its golden-skinned stomach. The townsman knows nothing about eels. "He looks at the size, asks the weight and the price," but the fisherman knows, and the frog-eel which he will not touch himself, unless he is very hard up for food, he sells in the town.

It is worth reading *Markus the Fisherman* because it gives an idea of how the vast fishing industry is built up of individual fishermen. "It may seem a small thing to lie by the quay and sell mackerel, but what [each fisherman] is really doing is helping to maintain the life of the country, and that is indeed work of the greatest importance, work which cannot be rated too highly. He is part of the nation's housekeeping, an important and very essential part, on which the country depends."

The simple life of Markus is repeated in nearly two hundred thousand similar lives—lives very close to destitution when the luck at sea is poor. For although some of the fishermen have other and additional occupations, fishing is the chief source of income for most of them, and the only source for many.

The majority of Norwegian fishermen are their own masters and either owners or part owners of their craft and tackle. To be sure, there is a union—the Fishermen's Association of Norway—and there are many small independent groups, working in a kind of co-operative system, each member contributing to the cost of the boat and tackle and each receiving his share of the profits. Although inspectors from the office of the Government Director of Fisheries grade all fish that is to be exported, and although the government has established a Deep-Sea Fishing Fund to assist in the purchase of deck boats for coastal fishing where there is no protective chain of islands, the Norwegian fisherman remains an individualist even when his numbers are sufficient to man a fishing-fleet of over twenty-five thousand registered vessels (1936). The greatest number of these are motor-boats. Sail and steam come next, and there are, in addition, about fifty-five thousand open boats, including dories.

Herring, cod, mackerel—and then in June comes the brisling, that silver morsel which, when put down in oil and packed in cans, appears as a Norwegian sardine on the hors-d'œuvre tables and in the picnic baskets of the world.

The brisling, which is not an immature herring but a fish that, when full grown, is still small, must be 90 percent fat to be of first grade, and there are strict regulations to ensure that this standard is maintained. He made his initial appearance in 1892 when Mr. Angus Watson arrived in Stavanger in a top hat and frock coat. Mr. Watson had come from Newcastle, England, and after careful deliberation decided to try his luck with a hundred cases of Norwegian sardines. He thereby became the founder of the canning industry in Norway. He lived long enough to appreciate the magnitude of what he had started and what he describes in his autobiography, which is not bad reading. But even he could not foresee between two and three million gallons of brisling being netted out of the fjords in a single season, and factories making cans to hold them and steamers making trips to carry them until the brisling industry has mounted to more than two million kroner a year.

The fishermen in dories, in sailboats and small motor-boats, draw herring and brisling and mackerel from the coastal waters. From off the banks and out of the sea, with net and line they draw cod and halibut and ling. They gather lobsters, shrimps, crabs, and prawns. Altogether they may catch two billion pounds of fish in a year with a value of more than eighty million kroner.

Besides this army in oilskin—this fleet of fishing-boats—there are other Norwegian vessels far from Norway pursuing not

schools but single prizes—whalers who bring back to the home-
land an annual income equal to that from the fisheries.

There is something about the mightiest creature of the deep,
the largest mammal that has ever lived, which is fascinating to
human speculation. From the infant that may be half a hundred feet long when it is born and increases at the rate of two
hundred odd pounds a day until it is three or four years old
and then tips the scales at a hundred and twenty-five tons, to
the adult with a mouth twice as high as a man, to the carcass
which produces hundreds of barrels of oil, it staggers the imagination.

It is not only its gigantic size, which seems as fabulous as that
of a dragon or as incredible as that of a dinosaur in a world
where mythology has given way to zoology and the prehistoric
is overlaid by the news reel; it is also its streamlined shape,
bluntly pointed in front and tapering to tail fins behind; it is
its vast journeyings, its mumbling and grumbling up and down
the parallels and meridians of the wildest and most frozen
wastes of the globe. Into the twentieth century, where all sizes
tend to standardization and all motion to mechanization, the
whale comes rolling and blowing in uninterrupted majesty
from the days of Jonah and Job.

Merely to mention him confers a grandeur upon the speaker
and has done so ever since the psalmist chanted: "There go the
ships; there is that leviathan," and Job queried: "Canst thou
draw out leviathan with an hook?" until Herman Melville
wrote the acknowledged classic of American literature, choosing for his sublime theme the sublimest protagonist he could
imagine—a white whale. Even F. D. Ommanney, distastefully
examining whale carcasses and embryos in a marine biologi-
cal station in South Georgia, comes near to writing another

classic in *Below the Roaring Forties*. Although he is determined to be as revolting as the censor will allow, his subject
gets the better of him. He is lifted above his ingratiating flip-
pancy and swept into sonorous stateliness in spite of himself.

Of all the nations in the world, Norway leads in whaling, and
those others which engage in this specialized industry employ
mostly Norwegians on their ships.

The hunt is no longer carried out as in the days of *Moby
Dick*, with men leaping like goats from the mother ship and
rowing in small open boats over the hills and hollows of the
sea, until they are near enough for the harpooner to hurl his
dart into the fleeing monster, and near enough to be capsized
in the bloody churning and engulfed in the wallow of the
death throe. Stub and Starbuck, Tashtego and Flask and the
others—eighteen of them—toiled hour after hour to tow the
inert colossus back to the *Pequod* and many hours more to strip
the blubber from the body, which was left lying in the water
by the ship's side. To turn that dead mass so that the blubber
could be spiralized off it, as an orange is peeled, required that
some men should work a windlass from the deck while others,
ten feet below the level of that deck, inserting a hook in the
prodigious carcass, were forced into a dance with death as they
balanced themselves on the slippery, revolving treadmill, with
the sharks ravening about it and them.

In modern whaling, a man still stands aloft in the crow's nest
to sight the scattering puff of vapour that betrays the distant
quarry, and he gives the immemorial cry when this is seen. But
the small boats that set out from the mother ship are motor-
driven, and the harpoon, which is a grenade, is shot from a gun
instead of being flung by hand, so that fewer men are lost and

many kinds of whales which could not be approached by the old methods can be captured by this newer technique.

Nowadays, the stupendous corpse is slid directly up upon the deck of the whaling-ship, which is built with a hatch (which may be closed) cut into the stern, and with an inclined slipway to receive such cargo, leading from this hatch to the deck, while machinery manipulates the gigantic bulk.

In the days of the *Pequod,* except for a steak or two, only the blubber was salvaged, and the flensed body, changed in colour but not perceptibly smaller, was cut loose and left to float away. Today there is no such squandering of the precious booty. Every particle is saved and utilized: the oil—thanks to improved refining processes—is used for soap and margarine. The meat is made into food for domestic animals. The very bones are ground into fertilizer. Certain explosives cannot be made without whale oil, and certain delicate machinery requires sperm oil for lubrication.

On the *Pequod* the blubber was cut into small pieces and boiled down in iron pots with their fires fed by the shrivelled scraps. The oil was then casked. Today the blubber is still boiled down in iron pots, but most of it is hardened into tasteless and odourless fat for easier transportation. Neither does the interior of a modern whaler resemble the old crude and malodorous shambles. It is called a whaling-factory, and from its ship-shape butcher shop to its laboratory-like boiling-rooms, it is genuinely a factory in efficiency, cleanliness, and economical management.

But although steam or Diesel engines have taken the place of sails, and although there are moving pictures and newspapers and three hundred men or so on board such a twenty- or thirty-thousand-ton floating factory, there is still a special excitement and romance about whaling. The very duration of the trip— about six and a half months, with half of that in intense activity —sets it apart from ordinary fishing. The great distances they must travel, passing through temperate and tropic zones to reach the frozen Antarctic, impart the glamour of adventure. There are new methods of harpooning and improved technique, but the wild fury of the chase and the substantial value of the catch remain. It brings to Norway an annual income approximating eighty million kroner.

Although Norwegian whaling originated in the Arctic, since 1904 the bulk of it has been carried on in the Antarctic where (in 1939) a royal proclamation claimed one million square miles to be used for whale hunting by Norway, but not closed to other nations. While there are stations outside Bergen and Tromsö to take care of those smaller whales that are caught around the Lofotens, Northern Norway, and Spitsbergen, the pelagic method—by which all the operations are carried out on board ship—is the one now chiefly used. Since the fishermen prevailed on the Storting to prohibit whaling off the Norwegian coast, as they believed it detrimental to the herring fisheries, one can cruise up and down Norwegian waters for many days and never see a whale and only an occasional small whaling-boat.

But the big Antarctic whalers are not uncommon sights. They come steaming up the Oslofjord in the spring with their season's treasure and go steaming out in the autumn with fresh provisions. In recent years the number of Norwegian whaling-companies has decreased, but the size of the floating factories, the number of their catching-boats, and the efficiency of their equipment have developed.

Having learned its lesson in the Arctic, Norway is working for proper regulation of the industry in the Antarctic. At present, all the interested nations, except Japan, have agreed as to the limit of the time of the catch and the number of tons of oil. This quota in the southern seas for all nations amounts to something over four hundred thousand tons, of which 45 percent is Norway's.

To Sandefjord and Larvik, and to Tönsberg, the home of Svend Foyn, who inaugurated modern whaling-methods, come whalers from other nations to get equipment and hire Norwegian crews. In such a town is ending up his days many an elderly man who once lived in the Polar Seas "as prairie cocks in the prairie," who has known what it is to be so long away from land that when he came "to it at last it smelled like another world, more strangely than the moon would to an earthsman."

And here is growing up many a young boy dreaming of the days when he will hide among the waves of Antarctica and climb them as a hunter climbs the mountains; and of the nights when "with the landless gull that folds her wings and is rocked to sleep between billows," he will lay him "to his rest, while under his pillow rush herds of walruses and whales."

CHAPTER FOUR

Ploughshare and Harvest

BEYOND the fjords, between the mountains, lie the valleys, and in the valleys the cycle of springtime sowing, summer growing, and autumn harvesting repeats itself generation after generation.

To be sure, there are farmers tucked into and onto every odd corner of Norway. No island, apparently, is too barren to grow potatoes in a crack between the rocks, even if the soil must be brought thither a handful at a time. On cliffs that seem too steep to hold a bird's nest, on hilltops that seem utterly inaccessible, grass is growing, cows and sheep are feeding. In suburban back yards, at seaside resorts, are garden plots.

For not only do fishermen and lumbermen supplement their earnings and occupy their slack seasons by a bit of farming, but clerks and clergymen, mechanics and merchants salvage, when they can, a few square metres from the congestion of a city block, and find time to plant and tend a garden.

But the farms which not only supply the family but support it, the farms which occupy over three hundred thousand of Norway's approximate three million inhabitants, are mostly in Tröndelag, and in Troms Districts; in Hedmark and in the valleys in Central Norway; and in the fertile regions of the south and within a hundred-mile radius of Oslo.

One often hears that only 3.5 percent—or possibly 5 percent —of the country is arable. But after a day's travel between Oslo and Trondheim, it seems as if all Norway must be under cultivation for some kind of crop, or used for grazing, or preserved and carefully managed for lumbering. The Dovre Railway runs through an interior where many farms have been in the same family for hundreds of years—a few of them able to trace their descent for a thousand years. The Viking was a farmer as well as a fighter and a navigator. "Swain had in the spring hard work and made them lay down very much seed and looked after it himself. But when that toil was ended he fared away on a Viking voyage and harried about among the Southern Isles and Ireland, and came home after midsummer. That he called the spring viking. Then he was at home until the corn fields were reaped down, and the grain seen to and stored. Then he fared away on a Viking voyage and then he did not come home until the winter was one month off and that he called his autumn viking."

Nobles and peasants alike worked in the fields—one reason why they were both to prove good colonists in Iceland and Greenland, Normandy and the British Isles. And just as on the Viking ships each man was a free man, so on the farms each man was a freeholder. He still is, to a large extent. Of the 264,-784 registered farms in Norway, 94 percent are owned by their occupants. Tenancy has never been popular in this individualistic and democratic country.

The first part of the trip from Oslo along the shores of Lake Mjösa—the country's largest inland water—is not unlike a trip along the shores of certain lakes in Northern United States or

Southern Canada. There is the same clear mirroring surface, occasionally cut by the keel of a small steamer or a canoe. There are the same green hills. The same rolling meadows are broken by an outcropping of granite rocks, presenting the well-known challenge to the fortitude and to the weary back of the farmer. Tansy and clover, sorrel and yarrow, thistles and ferns, brambles and berries are as familiar as the hemlocks and birches, pines and cedars, scattered or clumped on the cleared hillsides or growing more densely on the hilltops. Telegraph poles and wires run alongside the track. Cows chew their cuds in the shade or meditate by a brook. Chicken wire encloses fowl identical with those whose chicks make surprised entry upon the Easter breakfast tables of Christendom. Like the face of the people, the face of the country is entirely comprehensible to Englishmen and Americans.

Stone walls or fences of rails or slats or wire outline the fields of grain, potatoes, turnips, and beets; white picket fences or hedges mark the boundaries of the yards and paddocks. The red wooden barns upon their stone or concrete foundations are large and substantial. The houses—smaller—are also of wood, painted white or brown or grey or yellow, most of them commonplace enough. Only the roofs, which even on the smallest houses and sheds are of heavy slate cut in squares, oblongs, or elliptical shapes, or left in natural irregularity, and the casement windows, with an ornamental finish around the frames, distinguish them from farmhouses in any North American region where wood is cheap.

For the rest, during the first few hours after leaving Oslo, one might be travelling along the shores of Lake Champlain with the Adirondacks in the distance, were it not for one unfamiliar feature. The first crop of hay—two crops are gathered here, with enough of a third for grazing—is not piled in cocks. In this land where the sun is uncertain and showers are capricious, after the grass has been cut, it is hung, a handful at a time, upon wires stretched between posts. There are four of these wires, the top one about shoulder-high, and when the hay is arranged neatly upon them all, they look like well-kept hedges, first green and later golden. Since they do not enclose anything, but lie in parallel rows across a meadow, or are stretched singly wherever there is room, perhaps rather than hedges they resemble from a distance formally planted parterres. These racks of drying hay lend to the rural scene a pattern and a light and shadow which is peculiar to Scandinavia.

An hour passes; two. Hamar, which was an ecclesiastical centre in the Middle Ages, is, from the train, merely a modern wooden town. The cathedral ruins at Storehammer, on the banks of the lake, are not visible. Neither is the outdoor museum at Lillehammer, preserving the various types of old log buildings which once made each of these valleys different from its neighbour and all of them delightful. These places must be returned to and visited at leisure. For a general survey of the farming regions, it is best to push on from Lillehammer into the Gudbrandsdal Valley, the most luxuriant and longest in Norway, and watered for its entire length by the snow-fed river Laagen.

Now the painted farmhouses, similar to those in the American Middle West, begin to give way to those age-stained buildings which, grouped around a central court, are traditional in Norway. Now come the low brown log houses and sheds with turf roofs, thick with grass and with daisies pied, the architecture of which, of all others, best blends in form and colour, in material and construction, most pleasingly with the Norwegian landscape.

Log houses, log barns and sheds, even log churches—whether the logs are squared or left in the round; whether they are darkened by stain or only by the weather of passing centuries—there has never been architecture more suitable to a land of many forests and of cold winters, and it is hard to believe that there will ever be. Wood is not only cheaper than stone but, when stoves and fireplaces are the only means of heating, it is warmer. The very shape of the logs, their sizes carefully graduated, and their corners fitted with greatest nicety, seems to enforce pleasing proportions and a snug substantiality never obtained by panel board.

As the painted frame houses grow fewer in the Gudbrandsdal Valley and as the log buildings grow more frequent, the whole landscape deepens in individuality.

The foaming, curvetting, twisting river, which draws its greenish tints from dissolving snows, long ago found the lowest if not the most direct route and has channelled it still lower. The railway follows the river on one side and the highway on the other, and the farms edge themselves in where they can: along the water's edge if the bank is not too narrow, upon a hillside if it is not too steep—each farm a collection of nut-brown buildings. There is always the original and principal building holding the chief place with sometimes a dower house for the owner's parents at right angles to it, and always the storehouse standing above the ground on four legs to protect it from rats and winter snows. Sometimes there are a number of these storehouses and sheds with a farm bell on one of them to send the labourers to work and call them back to meals.

Whether the farm presses itself close to a forest or shelves itself upon a plateau, it looks earnest, determined, sufficient. Most of the farms in Norway are small. It is generally stated that 90 percent of them are of twenty-five acres or less, of which 35 percent is ploughed land and 65 percent is partly cultivated meadow. But there is nothing of the doll's house or the temporary camp about them. Their sober hue, and sound and simple construction, all speak of adults grappling with the necessities of making a living.

And they do make a living. Wheat and rye, barley and oats, peas and maize, fruits and berries, and, of course, hay and potatoes. Hay and potatoes, hay and potatoes—to the non-agrarian eye it seems as if practically every planted field were devoted to one or the other; that there must be enough hay raised in Norway to feed every animal descended from the Ark and enough potatoes to put Ireland to shame. If vegetables seem non-existent—certainly in any variety—the illusion is strengthened by a survey of hotel menus. Perhaps it is just as well, for the monotonous succession of carrots and cauliflower, cabbage and peas, are all doomed to extinction by drowning, the only culinary treatment of vegetables known in Norway, while the meagre salad-green stuffs are set forth reluctantly as garnishes, no more to be eaten than the decorative design of a wallpaper edging.

If the area given over to hay and potatoes seems disproportionately great, and that for vegetables microscopic, the apparently small grain allotment is deceptive. For, thanks to scientific methods of fertilizing and cultivation, since 1900 the amount of home-grown grain has increased 32 percent. In the boyhood of men who are now middle-aged, Norway had to import most of her grain and foodstuffs. Today she ranks fifth

among the countries of Europe in yield per acre and is exporting farm produce.

Whether the farm is very small and gives only a part of his
livelihood to the owner, who must work in the woods or elsewhere for the other part, or whether it is large, it produces a
mixed and not a single crop. And it is mixed not only in grains
and grasses but in livestock.

The Norwegians are fond of animals and have a knack with
them. Whoever remembers a chunky brown rocking-horse
with a thick fair mane, or whoever has loved a sturdy buckskin
pony, will feel a gush of childhood affection at sight of the Eastland and Westland horses, hirsuted to one or the other of these
colour schemes, easily pulling ploughs through the heavy earth
or clattering down a country road, drawing a two-wheeled cart.

Flocks of sheep make a shifting design upon the hillsides.
Goats, standing sidewise, peer down from the overhanging
rocks, wagging their beards and winking wickedly, while in the
farmyard children are playing with a puppy and a pet lamb,
and a woman, holding a leggy kid in her arms, looks up at the
passer-by. But while the colt flings himself after his mother in
the pasture or trots beside her as she carries her master to
town, while cows and calves amble across any road at any time,
or a goat asleep in the roadside dust scrambles up and paws its
way to the top of a bank, these are only a few of the farm animals.

Most of the cows and goats and sheep are out of sight, grazing in upland pastures where the grass is rich. This custom of
sending the cattle into the mountains for the summer, with
dairymaids and shepherd boys to look after them, has created
the *seter*, which is such a distinctive feature of the Norwegian
landscape, life, and literature. The mountain meadows are

The genesis of all Norwegian farms: the *Growth of the Soil*.

The grass is cut and hung, a handful at a time, upon wires
stretched between posts.

common land, with their property rights vested in the State, but every farmer is permitted the use of them, and is allotted a certain tract. This is an extension and an integral part of his farm in the valley, a fact that is not taken into consideration in the statement that 90 percent of the farms are only of twenty-five acres or less.

Many of the tiny habitations one glimpses from the fjords or valleys on distant heights are seters, although the majority are completely hidden by distance and the folds of the mountains. To climb up to one of these seters is to climb Jack's beanstalk ladder and re-enter the realm of the nursery tale. It is, quite properly, a long climb.

The faint path that winds into the forest beyond the farm is hardly more than an indication of passed footsteps and, as it begins to ascend, the uninitiated cannot see it at all. It goes around half-sunken boulders; it wades through streams tinkling down to join the river below. It leads into shadowy copses and out of them into marshy clearings where the white silken wool flower is blowing. Its trace is obliterated on the springy moss, but is caught again on the bank beyond. Up and up, twisting with every slope and declivity of the ground; picked out with pink everlasting and orchids the size of a finger nail. Up and up, until it opens after one hour—or two, or three, or five—out on a sloping plateau, where a miniature log cabin, with a blue door and blue window frames, is enclosed in a rustic fence precisely like an illustration from Mother Goose or the cottage that Hänsel and Gretel stumbled upon.

Far below is the curve of the village road and the spire of the village church. It is hard to tell the green turf roofs of the faraway farm buildings from the green fields around them. But despite the distance of the diminished scene, the sound of the farm bell floats up in the unstirring air. The seter has been elevated and set apart from the mundane activities below, but who can resist looking down over the tree tops and tracing out the boundaries of the meadows and trying to distinguish one roof from another?

The log cabin, whose blue door is about high enough for a gnome, is not alone in this upland clearing. Near by is the shed where the cheese and butter are made, and another—the byre—where the cows are stalled at night. Although of toy size, everything is quite complete. It may be that there is no human being, or even an animal, in sight, for the cows and goats and sheep are grazing still further away, and the dairymaids with their knitting may be chatting together at some other seter and the shepherd lads sitting cross-legged on some point of vantage, keeping an eye on their scattered charges.

But the key hanging outside the door invites the visitor in, and the door handle, which is a knot of a tree, twisted, carved, and polished, turns to give admission. The door is so low and the room is so small, it is like squeezing into a doll's house. The chairs are tree stumps or tree roots, ingeniously shaped and rubbed to smoothness. The corner fireplace is stone naïvely carved; the table scoured white. In the still smaller adjoining room the built-in beds are covered with hand-woven quilts and quite obviously intended for Goldilocks and the three bears. Each simple object—the bouquet of wild flowers, the touch of painting on the hanging shelves, the hearts and roses cut out of the cupboard doors, the shining copper utensils hung beside the fireplace—speaks of sunny morning hours when the solitary occupant burnishes up and embellishes her pied-à-terre; of Saturday nights and Sundays when her sweetheart, after tramping "up the airy mountain and down the rushy glen," sits by the fire or on the doorsteps and hollows a spoon-holder out of a bit of burl or whittles a lock or a latch from a piece of wood.

If all dairymaids are not young and pretty, a sufficient number fulfil these specifications to give verisimilitude to the folk songs of long ago and the romances of today and, when they leave the village on Midsummer Eve for their summer sojourn, to give gaiety to the farewell festival. The dairymaid may be the farmer's daughter, or his young wife, who takes the smallest children with her, and to the seter the rest of the family may come on holidays. Here the invalid may convalesce, the lovesick girl or the brooding boy find solitude, and many a Norwegian writer, painter, and musician has found in one of these skyed retreats, where the silence is disturbed only by the sound of a distant cow bell, the perfect studio.

It would seem that more than a million cows and a still greater number of sheep, that the third of a million goats and three million poultry would account for the principal products of the farm; and it is true that Norway, which, a few years ago, was importing butter and eggs as well as meat, is now exporting them—a result not only of increasing numbers but of improvement in methods of feeding, so that the average cow gives two hundred more litres of milk yearly than she did formerly. So healthy are the horses and cattle, sheep, goats, and pigs, in a land where the foot-and-mouth disease is rare and where tuberculosis among domestic animals is almost non-existent, that the rearing of livestock is part of the activity of every farm. In the mountain districts and northern regions, it is often the principal activity.

But these mild creatures, which graze in the pastures and come home at night to be milked or fed, are not the only animals. Unlike the grazing cattle or the roly-poly horses, the silver fox makes no public appearance, either at the seter or in the valley pastures. He lives behind a wire enclosure in privacy and seclusion and darts back nervously into his house at the approach of strangers. Ten years ago there were only three thousand of these shy, lustrous little creatures, divided among less than three hundred owners. Today there are half a million on twenty thousand farms, where, like the other livestock, they are bred and fed and tended. They must be tended well if their fur is to bring a good price, and tons of whale meat supplement the fish and goat meat and the occasional titbit of chicken. It costs money to feed a fox for the five years which are necessary if the breeder's ambition is for a pelt like the one from West Norway which sold for eleven hundred kroner.

Norway was one of the first countries to start systematic fur production and is now the leading fox-farming country in Europe. Silver foxes, blue and red and white and cross-breed; nutria, fitch, martens, and mink are being raised. Breeders' associations, fairs and exhibitions, a research farm and veterinary clinic at Oslo all stimulate an industry which furnishes one-fourth of the world supply of silver-fox furs and represents an annual turnover of about thirty-five million kroner.

Gudbrandsdal Valley, up and down whose length traffic has moved since the Neolithic Age, is not only the longest valley but the richest. It takes the train four hours to cover the ninety-five miles from Lillehammer to Dombås, but there are other agricultural regions which cannot be seen from the train window: upland regions which have never been penetrated by rail or contaminated by smoke; low-lying regions where life is as isolated as on an island in the sea. A sportsman who strayed into one such valley and was given a night's shelter returned two years later to find that in the interval not another stranger had been seen. It is possible—and not infrequent—to be born, grow up, and die and never once cross the enclosing mountains of one's native valley. It is rare that the traveller in Norway finds his way to such districts, not because they are necessarily far from the beaten track according to mileage, but because they are separated from the world by difficulties of terrain.

Now, with the extension of good roads and the penetration of motor-buses, narrow valleys whose names are unknown to the road map have been discovered, and new highways, paralleling the inevitable watercourse or zigzagging along the mountainsides, draw a thread of communication between the once severed hamlets.

Such a settlement may be hardly more than one or two farmhouses with their aggregation of barns and sheds and storehouses and their topless corridors of drying hay. But a waterfall gives motion to its setting, and its activities, spilling out into the road, give life to all the scene.

The farmer drives his two-wheeled cart to the blacksmith's shop, and beside the buckskin mare a buckskin foal canters like a little rocking-horse. In the local sawmill, run by power from the waterfall, half a dozen men are making those boxes which are so shallow they will hold herring and brisling without crushing. The shoemaker and shopkeeper can be seen through their open doors. Children are going to the woods to pick cloudberries and blueberries. In the yards by the houses are drying the hand-woven rugs, the hand-knitted socks and stockings, the hand-embroidered pillow covers and curtains which are the pride of the country housewife. In the yard by the church the gravestones are facing east, as the preacher does on Sunday. And all along the roadside are potato patches and hayfields and plots of turnips and beets, and the swish of the scythe is more often heard than the clack and whir of the mowing-machine. Here and there the thread of rural road knots into the comparative congestion of a town and, when a finger of a fjord pushes inland to the heart of the land, the town crowds itself between it and the road.

Such a town is Sandane, which, although tourists come to its inexpensive inns, and three hundred students to its college, and fox-breeders and furriers to its exhibitions, nevertheless remains tranquil.

In Sandane, on a wedding day, the floor of the church is strewn with flowers, and the priest in his black cassock and white ruff stands before a bride in a golden crown with brocaded streamers hanging down behind. When bride and groom leave the church, they are preceded by two fiddlers, either on foot or in a pony cart, and all the village follows.

In Sandane, a road winds up a hill and white cottages face it, currant bushes crowd close to it through the palings, and cherry trees lean over it by the front gate. There are hawthorn hedges and vines trained over front porches and cats washing their faces on front steps. In the light of the summer evening, a small boy is performing his nightly chore of carrying the firewood to the kitchen, and his older sister is selecting a ribbon to tie around her hair, for she is going down to the pier to see the bi-weekly boat come in after its eighteen-hour trip from Bergen.

In Sandane, no one of the thousand inhabitants is very rich and no one is at all poor. There is a co-operative store for the natives, and there are walks and drives for the English visitors who have long been coming here for quiet holidays. They can stroll to the small Folk Museum on the hill, or they can drive to Eidsfossen, where the cows graze at the foot of the waterfall and snow lies on the mountain tops the year around. They can drink their afternoon tea in the front yard of the inn, looking out at the street, or on the veranda at the rear overlooking the fjord, or before the fireplace in the living-room. Innocency of entertainment is not only encouraged but enforced by such surroundings, and sufficient stimulation is supposed to be derived from looking at the reflection of the snow-topped mountains in the fjord. For near-beer is the only purchasable potable.

Agricultural Norway is not confined to the central interior. Down in the warmer south and southeast the crops are fuller and more varied. Most of the fruit comes from here and it is even possible to grow tobacco in the regions of the Hardanger and Sogne Fjords, north and south of Bergen. Up in the north, past the Polar Circle, besides the ubiquitous hay and potatoes grow barley, certain vegetables, and some of the hardiest berries.

North and south, east and west, all over Norway, the number of farms increases.

Since the Great War, more than thirteen thousand new farms have been developed and this "home colonization," as it is called, is proceeding at the rate of about two thousand new homesteads yearly. For although it seemed at one time that the entire limited area of arable land was utilized—which was one reason why between 1880 and 1890 so many immigrants came to the United States and Canada—it is now believed that Norway can double the area of her fields and meadows. More forests can be cleared, more marshes drained, more rocks cleared away.

Such labour demands not only physical strength and pioneering courage but capital, and those who would be homesteaders frequently possess only the two former. The Government has recognized this and has founded a Colonization Bank from which a homesteader of good character and agricultural experience can not only get a loan to establish himself on new soil, but also a subsidy for buildings and (if he has no other income) a certain sum per acre for clearing the land. He may, furthermore, obtain a grant of working credit to buy necessary machinery, implements, seed, and fertilizer.

The Ministry of Agriculture directs a hundred and twenty-four schools and a number of experimental stations. The Government subsidizes colonization with part of the profits from the State liquor monopoly, and the Storting gives annual grants to the Royal Norwegian Agricultural Society, the Norwegian Peat Society, and the New Soil Society.

These three societies are private in their organization but public in their aim. They are non-profit-making, the members paying a nominal fee, voting on all business matters, and receiving magazines, bulletins, and so forth.

The Royal Norwegian Agricultural Society, which is more than a century old, encourages the co-operative movement among farm producers and consumers. (There are five hundred co-operative creameries and cheese factories; there are joint slaughter houses and societies for the sale of eggs and butter. There are six co-operative societies with a combined membership of seventy-five thousand for the joint purchase of fertilizers, concentrated cattle food, farm machinery, and so forth.) It also works along the lines of the New Soil Society to buy and drain tracts of vacant land and colonize them suitably. The Norwegian Peat Society, as its name implies, surveys and examines peat moors, so as to best utilize some for fuel and to drain others for farms or forests.

Besides these public and semi-public organizations, the farmers have their own societies: the Farmers' Association of Norway, with a membership of fifty thousand, and the Small Farmers' Union. These busy themselves with all types of problems, from the colonization of new land to co-operation in marketing and consumption. They get no Government grants and ask for none, as they prefer to be entirely independent and free to fight for what they want without political fear or favour. Since 1935, the Agrarians and the Labour Party have to some extent been in a political alliance which was a factor in determining the present Labour Government. The Norwegian Federation of Labour, and the Norwegian Employers' Association are both strongly organized. Although the compulsory arbitration law of 1927 was repealed in 1929, both respect each other's strength and settle their disputes by arbitration.

Thus, public, semi-public, and private agencies are constantly increasing the arable area and also combating unemployment and emigration. While agricultural wages are still lower than industrial, they have been increasing since 1935, and the prices of agricultural products have, since 1930, increased more than those of manufactured articles.

To travel through rural Norway is to read the lives of over 25 percent of the Norwegian people and to realize that although they do, indeed, make the country, the country, in its turn, has bred them. It has bred them to frugality, self-respect, providence; in kindness to animals and family tenacity.

The farmer whom the nineteenth-century romanticist idealized and the twentieth-century realist debunked, the farmer who was once called a radical triumphing over bureaucracy and is now considered a conservative and a bulwark against

Bolshevism, permits novelists and politicians to call him whatever they choose. He does not indulge in volubility. He raises hay for his cattle and potatoes for his family. He sells eggs and milk and cheese and butter. His numbers are greater than those in any other industry and they produce a larger aggregate income.

If the Government recognizes the value of the farmer, the farmer does not underestimate his own worth, nor does he shrink from the weight of his labour.

He works. He must work. Everyone on a farm must work. The man must heave stones, hew trees, build bridges, guide the course of streams and waterfalls, plough and harrow, cultivate and harvest. The woman must work in kitchen and cowshed, at the river's edge with her washtub, in the evening at her loom or with her knitting-needles. The children must work shepherding the flocks and gathering berries, and men and women and children must all work together at haying-time, hanging the still green grass in handfuls on the long drying-wires.

There is work for everyone and plenty of it. Work that must be done if human beings would hold onto existence on these sloping farm lands in this sparing climate. They must hold on as the durable rocks hold on. They must dig in stubbornly if they would endure and not perish as the flowers which bow before the breeze and vanish with the frost.

CHAPTER FIVE

Hark, the Waterfall!

THE fjords lie between the mountains of the coast. The valleys lie between the mountains of the interior. Three-fourths of the surface of Norway is crumpled into mountains that are wreathed, draped, and looped with waterfalls.

The crash of their mighty downpouring, the clatter of the stones they loosen or churn around in pot holes, the sibilant whisper of their spray, is the voice of Norway.

They leap down gigantic stone stairways, and slide through polished channels. They hang in perpendicular, thousand-foot streamers from the top of a cliff to the bottom. They fray out in double and triple and quadruple cascades and unite in curtains of melted crystal. Some of them dry up in the autumn, many of them freeze in winter, most of them overflow in the spring, and all of them pulsate in volume during the summer. They are the movement, the rhythm, the inhalation, and exhalation, of Norway. No static picture can convey their animation. What looks like a chalk line in a photograph—or at best a streak of snow—seen in actuality is like an inverted fireworks, pouring white light and rocket trails and sparklets, not up into the sky but down into the water.

They are fed by the melting snow, whose greatest fields are on the mountains of Hardanger, Jostedalsbrae, and Jotunheim, and, in their turn, feed the multitudinous rivers, the longest of which is the Glomma.

The rivers—short and rapid when they run westward, accelerating in force as they run eastward, swelling to power in the coastal rainfall—are almost as lively as the waterfalls. They prance in tandems and spans through ravines and lope peacefully through green valleys. They cavort over rocky rapids and come to rest in those deep lakes which, although small individually (except Mjösa), together cover more area than the present area of cultivated land.

The sternness of the mountains is softened by these playful cascades, the seriousness of the valleys redeemed by the romping streams and rivers.

Thus Norway is not only almost surrounded by the sea, but is interlaced with inland waters.

The rivers are too short and too broken by rapids and falls to be useful as waterways for boats, although they serve to carry logs from forest to factory and from the mountains to the sea. The lakes are utilized for storing and regulating the river flow. But the waterfalls, myriad in number and distributed all over the country, are "white coal"—the source of power, heat, and light to all the urban and to more than half the rural population.

Norway is the richest country in Europe in potential electric energy, and although she has as yet developed only a little over two million out of her available fifteen million horsepower, she nevertheless generates 20 percent more current in proportion to her population than any other nation in the world.

Plentiful and cheap electric light changes the whole character of the long winter and the whole character of common living. To the remotest cabins as well as to villages, to isolated farms as well as to city blocks, it brings light, warmth, and service. Every Norwegian, worthy of the name, knows how to ensnare the wild cataract which pitches past his window, to make it captive, and convert it into the most docile of household slaves. Every hamlet can have its small power station and every town its large one. At present, about 10 percent of the power is developed in Government stations, about 30 percent in municipal, intercommunal, and county electric works, and about 60 percent privately.

The value of such easily available and widely distributed power to industry can hardly be overestimated. Practically every factory in the country is run by electricity, and industry occupies about one-third of the population. The traditional and fundamental industries—based upon the forests, ore deposits, stone quarries, and minerals, and on fisheries—have been so expanded, varied, and specialized in less than a century that 75 percent of her total exports are industrial goods (only a quarter of these are raw material), and Norway now considers herself an industrial country.

While over half of the electricity generated is used for general purposes of lighting, heating, cooking, and miscellaneous minor services and industries, the second great power consumer is the large-scale electro-chemical and metallurgical industry. Although this ranks only ninth in the table of thirteen groups based on the value of production, it absorbs 40 percent of the country's electrical power, obtaining this, with few exceptions, from its own power stations.

It seems fitting that electricity, whose substance is invisible as spirit and whose speed is as swift as thought, should be as-

sociated with an invention which, speaking scientifically, is
the most brilliant in Norwegian technical history and which,
speaking scenically, is embodied in almost fantastically dramatic setting.

One must travel to the province of Telemark, into the interior and up into the wild and lonely mountains, to see the
world's largest nitrogen factory. Immense, apparently impreg-
nable, and wellnigh inaccessible, the mighty Rjukan works
dominate a strategic site like the stronghold of a medieval
robber baron. But the modern robbery that is plotted here
and put into execution is beneficent. From the Rjukan waterfall—the largest and most powerful in all Norway—it takes two
hundred thousand horsepower, and from the air, by means of
an electric cannon, it takes nitrogen. Combining this with lime
and other ingredients, it manufactures wall-saltpetre, an excellent artificial fertilizer.

In many countries, for many years, men have wrestled with
the problem of how to manufacture a synthetic product which
could be used in place of Chilean nitrate. It was a Norwegian
professor, Olaf Birkeland, who hit upon the astonishing idea
of milking nitrogen out of the invisible atmosphere and who
invented an electrical cannon to do it. The explosions separate
the nitrogen from the air very much as lightning does. Out of
this principle grew an industry which has its factories throughout the world and whose value must be reckoned not only in
monetary returns to the manufacturers but in an enrichment
of the farms which can hardly be calculated. The early method
has been improved upon and the original product multiplied
into a variety of products. There are now many fertilizers,
each with a different composition, for specialized uses: for the
soil, for gardens, for orchards, fields, and forests. Gases and

chemicals are also manufactured, and while in some years the company produces half a million tons, the waterfall does not run dry and the air is not exhausted.

Samuel Eyde was a civil engineer who organized the Norsk Hydro and developed the Rjukan waterfalls, but the first factory—which was also the first of its kind in the world (1905)—was not at Rjukan but at Notodden. Now the Norsk Hydro owns three saltpetre factories in the province of Telemark: one in Rjukan, one in Notodden, and one in Porsgrund, which is on the coast. From Rjukan to the sea, along the Skien waterway, the Norsk Hydro has developed electric energy of four hundred and fifty thousand horsepower, while other companies, building their stations and factories for paper, lumber, carbide, rayon, metal products, and so forth, along the same waterway, use another hundred and fifty thousand electric horsepower.

Telemark, once purely agricultural, now knows the good and evil of industrialization. The electro-chemical industry, producing over three hundred thousand tons of nitrate of lime annually, strikes the imagination because of its priority in industrial history and its impressiveness of site, and its obvious value to a country endeavouring to increase and improve its cultivated area. The fact that the electro-metallurgical industry consumes 40 percent of the electrical current of the country indicates its scope and importance.

But industry is not concentrated in a few companies or in a limited region. Since many of the waterfalls are along the fjords facing the sea, a factory which places itself conveniently near its source of power may also be near ships and cheap transportation. This has led to a healthful decentralization.

Norway is not poor in minerals and metals. She has the

world's largest zinc-producing works and holds first rank in molybdena and titanic iron, and is second only to Spain in sulphur pyrites. Besides iron ore, she mines copper, nickel, lead, and silver, and quarries limestone, quartz, marble, and granite. In fact, mining of ores and metals employs her greatest proportion of workmen and yields the largest value of production and is the oldest export industry she has.

Although the agrarians bewail the growing industrialism, a visit to one of the many manufacturing centres which now mingle their smoke with what was once unvitiated forest ozone, and their sounds with what was once the silence of a fjord, is reassuring.

Such a town is Höyanger at the end of a branch of the Sognefjord. In 1916, there were thirteen farms in this cup hollowed from the forest. A hundred and twenty souls completed its census. The great waterfalls—one of thirty-seven thousand horsepower and one of sixteen thousand five hundred horsepower—roared their unobstructed way from mountain top to water and the quiet clouds lay upon the crags or drifted into the quiet sky.

Now three thousand people work and play, sleep and discuss politics, in a closely built and exceedingly attractive town. A large aluminum smelter and manufacturing plant belch yellow breath into the air. In research laboratories scientists bend over their crucibles and test tubes. Boats bring ore from Greece and Italy to be made into aluminum by a secret Norwegian process, and boats carry away the mountains of cans which will be used in the ever-expanding fish industry.

If it is something of a shock on rounding a curve of the fjord to be suddenly confronted by this congestion of roofs and murk of smoke, it is extraordinarily interesting to examine their

The whisper, the crash of the waterfall, is the voice of Norway.

The widely scattered hamlets shrink to nothing in such a universe.

Reflection makes duplicate glory as the waterfall reverses itself into the fjord.

Only cycles of geologic time will alter the icy profiles of the
mountains.

cause at close range. The factory cannot be seen by the usual visitor, but the town can be, and a heartening sight it is. For it has been laid out with an open square around its good-looking clubhouse and entrance gates, with broad streets passing the large dwellings and offices along the waterfront and well-kept roads curving between picket fences and hedges among cottages, which, without suggesting regimentation, complete the effect of a harmoniously unified village.

The company architect planned and placed most of these delightfully proportioned small homes, which accommodate two, four, and six families, and also the larger apartment houses and the spacious modern hospital. But employees are helped, by easy terms of amortization for over ten to fifteen years, to buy and own their homes, and the community has been encouraged to buy and take over the clubhouse and the hospital. It has independent shops, as well as a co-operative store.

But even after the buildings have passed into individual ownership, the company still donates the services of gardeners, so that these cottages are not the unshaded shoe boxes usual in most new Norwegian villages, but are set among lawns and shrubbery. Vines are trained over their front porches—another rarity in a land where the average cottage is bare not only of any ornamental planting but of a porch or even a covered doorstep. Most gratifying of all—at least, to the visitor—is the company's gratuitous donation of paint, both to the tenants who rent from it and to freeholders. Since this paint must conform to the general scheme worked out by the company architect, Höyanger, instead of being sombre red, drab, or grey—the predominating house colours elsewhere—glows like a basket of fruits in rich orange, henna, green, coral, and lemon, tobacco-brown and cinnamon, while the trim, in contrasting shades, picks up the motif and completes the pleasing effect.

Höyanger was not built primarily to please the eye of the tourist, but to accommodate in comfort and at a price they can afford, the six hundred employees. About thirty kroner a month will cover the rent for a family. Every cottage has its bathroom—by no means a common feature in rural Norway—electric current is cheap and plentiful, and people are assisted, by easy terms, to buy electric stoves. Not an indigenous village, but an admirable example of progressive standards and good taste, this and similar industrial centres offer persuasive argument for certain material advantages of industrialism.

Industrialism needs all the arguments it can produce, for the man who, like his ancestors for a thousand years, was an independent farmer, frequently inclines to be a difficult employee, expressing in political discontent his anger and humiliation at his loss of individual freedom and authority and instinctively craving the cycles of activity of fishing, farming, hunting, and trapping, in preference to the regular hours and mechanized employment of a factory. It was this discontent which fed the revolutionary undercurrent in those days when Norwegian labour, after the Russian Revolution, left the International Federation of Trade Unions to join with the Red International. Labour has gradually retreated from its extreme radicalism, although sporadically its impatience flares up with those leaders who advocate policies of too great moderation.

All the factories are not manufacturing aluminum or electro-chemical products. There are two hundred paper and pulp companies, many of them owning several mills, and the largest of them—with branches in Sweden, Austria, and the United States—with ten thousand employees and a daily production of two million pounds of paper and pulp.

Where Norway's largest river, the Glomma, thunders over the Sarpsfoss, generating sixty thousand horsepower of electric energy, this company, the Borregaard, has its head offices and mills, its laboratories and headquarters for its civil engineers. One-fourth of the world's supply of sulphite pulp, for the manufacture of rayon silk, is furnished by Borregaard, and one-third of the world's supply of pulp comes from Borregaard and other Norwegian mills.

Six hundred large lumber and sawmills (besides hundreds of small ones) take care of the forest industries in which Norway was a pioneer.

One-fourth of the total area of the country is dark with forests: with pine and fir and birch in the southeastern and central parts and with fir in the far north. A great majority of the farms (80 percent) have forest land attached to them, producing timber and firewood not only for the farmers' use but also for sale. But in spite of the multitudes of small owners, this actual and potential wealth is not permitted to be dribbled away or squandered. Like the other Scandinavian countries, Norway long ago graduated from the era when individuals or companies could wastefully deforest tracts which, if properly conserved, would continue to give employment to woodsmen and factory hands and to swell the country's exports.

Individual farmers own 65 percent of the forests; the State, provinces, or municipalities own 20 percent, and large private corporations, such as paper and pulp companies, own 15 percent.

But no matter whoever owns the forests, inspectors, in the joint service of State and municipality, protect them from being mishandled. As a rule, the owners and the public timber inspectors co-operate willingly, the former being only too glad

to let the latter take over the responsibility and labour of mark-
ing the trees which are suitable for cutting. Those individuals
who might injure their wooded property by unwise or avari-
cious cutting are controlled by law.

The State Forestry Service, dating from 1857, with nurseries
for the sale of trees and drying-rooms for forest seed and experimental service stations, is by no means the only agency for
protecting this important national resource. There is the semi-
public, non-profit Norwegian Forest Association, which has
(since 1898) planted almost four hundred million trees, besides
draining marshy land to make it suitable for more tree-
planting. This is the association which has brought practial
policies of conservation into the public-school curriculum.
For not only are there courses in forestry in all the agricultural
schools, but also every spring school children, under the direction of the association's inspectors, plant about three million
trees on either publicly or privately owned land, and are educated to understand that trees are part of the country's wealth
and that the forests contribute to the livelihood of many thousands of people. A hundred years ago, Henrik Wergeland, Norway's greatest lyrical poet, "was in the habit of carrying his
pockets full of the seeds of trees, ever and anon strewing a
handful of these about him in his daily walks." It is such
individual co-operation as well as an intelligent conservation
policy which, despite all the cutting and logging, has yearly
increased the wooded wealth of Norway.

The forest-owners and timber-buyers have their own associations. There is a Mutual Forest Fire Insurance Company and
a Peat Society, all working together for the formulation and
enforcement of a constructive forestry policy.

This is merely sound common sense, for the raw material

from the forests brings in annually about sixty million kroner, and the finished products, such as lumber, pulp, and paper—accounting for 40 percent of the export trade and going chiefly to the western part of Europe, South Africa, South America, and Australia—brings in about two hundred million.

The farm's close association with the forest, and the relation between forest products and industry, and the inclusion in industry of so many diverse branches—from mining to manufacturing—explain the oft-stressed statement that today industry fills the most important place in the national economy, with about seven hundred and seventy-five thousand people engaged in it.

As the forest area can be greatly enlarged by planting, so can water power, which converts forest products into manufactured goods, be tremendously augmented.

Thousands of vagrant waterfalls, which, like truants on a holiday, tumble and romp where they will—the little ones leaping out at the passing train as if to trip and splash it, the larger ones crashing down as if to engulf it—can be brought to heel. And after they have permitted their flow to be regulated by dams and impounded in lakes and led through conduits and pipes to power plants, after they have turned wheels and applied their energy to creating electric current, they will still have plenty of impetus left to careen and pitch down hills, to whirl into rapids in the rivers, and to drop like plummets over the sides of the fjords.

Like the elves of folklore, these invisible agents cook the food and illumine the rooms and do the washing for the womenfolk. In the weaver's room they turn spindles, in the carpenter's shop they hammer and plane and saw, in the secret laboratories of twentieth-century wizards they convert air into food for plants. Then, like the elves, they dash off to whirl in eddies in the river current and somersault down the cliffs. If some of them are held and sentenced to such hard labour that they have little vigour or none left for frolic, they will hardly be missed.

As long as there are mountains in Norway, and the snow falls upon their summits, and the sun shines, there will be waterfalls. They will pour from the eternal crucibles above the clouds, separate into parted strands, and join again in floating, falling fabric. "There is no speech nor language where their voice is not heard"; no air that is not freshened by their flow. Their splash and crash is the music of Norway.

> And hark! is it the music of the pines?
> Is it the lake? Is it the waterfall?
> 'Tis something sadder, sweeter far than all.

These white-limbed Mænads, who "flow like meteors through the night," are, many of them, already enslaved. More are due to be broken into captivity. But "some we knew, the loveliest and best," will be free to "float upon their way."

They will be left unpent to fling their streamers "through the boundless element" and deeper than did ever plummet sound to plunge their echoes into the waters of the fjords.

CHAPTER SIX

According to Season

SUMMER visitors to Norway, although they may admire the snow-tipped mountains in June and exclaim at the snow tunnels along the Bergen-Oslo Railway in July and even—for novelty's sake—stage in August a snowball fight when the train stops for a few moments at Finse, can hardly visualize the thickness of that muffling envelope in winter. For months it seals the pastures away from the cattle in the country and piles up against the walls of buildings in the towns. One can hardly imagine what it costs, in money and in labour, to clear the city streets, to shovel individual paths, to protect highways and railways from dangerous drifts, to build roofs which can withstand the weight of winter's accumulation. Even if the magnificent glittering transportation provides painters with scenes they are expert in portraying, it might seem that these billions of tons of snow, which block the roads and impede trains and maroon communities, were, from an economic point of view, a nuisance and a dead loss.

But people who turn enchanted waterfalls into industrial power, who harness capricious rivers to the task of carrying timber, who extract from the invisible air itself material which fertilizes the soil, have thriftily converted this other apparently non-utilitarian element of Nature into hard cash—as well as into health and international good feeling.

The snow has helped the Norwegians to become the foremost ski-ers of the world. Together with the terrain, it has made Norway the headquarters for exhibitions attended by competitors from many countries.

It was natural that in such a sparsely settled and hilly land skis should have long been commonly used for getting about in winter. Just how long depends upon what credence one gives the special goddess of ski-ing—Skade was her name—mentioned in Norse mythology, or a more tangible bit of evidence in Frognerseteren outside of Oslo. In a unique museum, dedicated entirely to skis, with its walls hung and its cases filled with more types and styles than the astonished layman knew existed in the world of sport or in the imagination of sportsmen, is exhibited a bit of wood from Telemark, tagged "circa 2500 B.C.," which makes it more than four thousand years old. It is part of a ski whose age throws the fragment found in the Tune ship into the class of practically snappy new models.

Skipping a few millennia, authentic history records that in 1206, during a time of civil war, two ski-ers of the Birkebeiner party carried the infant son of the king thirty-seven miles across the mountains from Lillehammer to Rena. It is in commemoration of that feat that the Birkebeiner ski race, in which many hundreds participate, was started as an annual event.

Covering the ground on skis was an obvious and practical method of travelling, and the Norwegians thought of it as exciting fun long before it was an organized sport. In pairs and parties and in solitary flights, they flew over the fields and down the mountainsides, the "yellow skis like flames on the white snow."

Everyone knew how to ski, although it is said it took Nansen to make it fashionable. This is not strictly accurate, since there were ski meets at Grorud and Trysil in 1862 and in Tromsö the following year, and twenty years later a ski exhibition in Trondheim. By 1879, when the first ski jump was held on Huseby Hill near Oslo, followed by a ski exhibition, those contests had begun which have been held annually on Holmenkollen Hill ever since, with two or three hundred jumpers and as many as seventy thousand spectators watching the event.

It was a Norwegian who initiated Wilhelm Paulke into the sport, and Paulke introduced it into Germany (1883), and the same year a Norwegian traveller presented a pair of skis to the monks of St. Bernard in the Swiss Alps. Although it takes a bit of imagination to visualize the sandalled, long-robed monks flying over the hills on "flames on the white snow," nevertheless, shortly afterward, there were dozens of pairs in the monastery and races were being held. The sport gained in popularity throughout Switzerland, which organized its first ski club in 1893, although nearly a decade was to pass before the first ski meet was held (in Berne, 1902).

It was a Norwegian, again, who is given credit for having introduced skis into the United States. In 1856, when John A. Thompson began to carry the mail the ninety miles from Placerville to Carson City, California, the track of his skis was the only line of communication between these two points. "Snowshoe Thompson" maintained his mail route for more than twenty years, often travelling after dark, a unique figure in America's history of overland transportation. Finally, it was a Norwegian who, at the first ski competition held in Red Wing, Minnesota (February 1887), introduced ski jumping to Americans.

Before the days of ski jumping as a sport, the competitive form was "slalom"—the first syllable of which means "sloping evenly" and the second (*laam* in Norwegian) meaning ski road or track. The slalom obliged the ski-er to jump fences, negotiate precipices, and find his way through forests while speeding downhill. It was a common enough feat to ski down-grade fifty or sixty miles an hour with a bowl full of ale without spilling a drop, but to make several loops, or "Telemarks," so that one's tracks crossed themselves in the speed of a slalom, was respectfully recognized as an art.

Today the great Hovedlands meet takes place at the end of the season, each year in a different district, and the sloping framework of ski jumps is seen in widely separated regions.

When the churches could no longer ignore the fact that the majority of their congregations were out on the hills all day Sunday during the winter, they did not waste time scolding the few who came to service for the defection of the many who did not. Instead, they built small wooden chapels near the ski jumps and have had the satisfaction of seeing them filled by sportsmen—which, of course, means sportswomen as well—during those brief intervals when they can pause in their strenuous slaloming.

The undulating mountains, which are freer from avalanches than the jagged Swiss Alps, are bright in sunlight for fifteen hours a day in March and for twenty hours by the beginning of May. From December to April the white hills and fields are animated by brightly clad figures recalling the passage in Johan Bojer's *Life:* "The skis glided of themselves: the feet moved but only to yield, not to work. It was like a voluptuous dance across a floor bounded by infinity itself, beneath a dome whose height none have measured. The mind is filled with rhythm and one looks about smiling."

After ski-ing comes skating—figure and distance—and in this Norway also holds the leading place. The country which produced Molla Bjurstedt Mallory, to win nine championships on American tennis courts, produced another girl, Sonja Henie, to win consecutively ten world and three Olympic championships on the ice. At the Olympic Winter Sports of 1936, Norway won seven gold medals and all the world records.

If these two spectacular sports were all Norway had to offer, her attractions would be limited to winter and to a specialized class of athlete. But with her usual foresight she has managed to spread her sporting season over the whole year, luring other visitors with more years and less energy, who are content with the exercise of casting a hook and reeling in a trout or a salmon.

A grey day, a rainy day, a chilly day—it is all one to the angler, who, with rod and reel, saunters out from the small red clapboard hotels, in the valleys from Telemark to Dovre, to the lake lying conveniently near. In the lakes along the south coast, in the ponds and tarns along the west coast, and in the lonely mountain plateau of Finnmarksvida, trout are gamy enough and abundant enough to meet every requirement. They are also of an exceptionally delicate flavour for those who are base enough to regard them as food, not fun. On Hardangervidda, fresh water trout often weigh four pounds, while the migrating or sea trout, which ascend hundreds of large and thousands of small rivers, can reach a weight of over thirty.

As for salmon—it is so plentiful that the old story of the servants who stipulated that they should not be fed it, except on certain days, can still be appreciated. The majority of innumerable rivers and the two hundred thousand lakes and tarns contain fish of the salmon species. Although it has been caught and sold commercially since earliest times, salmon-fishing as a sport is comparatively young and began when the English visitors of a few generations ago started fly fishing.

There are pike and perch in the southeast lowlands and forest regions; there are red char and grayling. Not only along the coast, but even in the innermost branches of the fjords, are tunny of great size, so that big-game fishing is now attracting the sportsman.

In a country the length of Norway, the angling season varies in different sections. From June to September there is good fishing somewhere. And in a country as practical as Norway, all regions, seasons, and regulations are carefully scheduled. Of late years these regulations have been somewhat tightened, but there is still plenty of sport, accessible or remote, to suit every taste. Many hotels own their own fishing rights, and these are free for guests. The fee for foreigners fishing on crown lands is reasonable and the fixed daily licence, as a rule, extremely moderate.

While the visiting angler with his expensive tackle bulks large, the clerk with a fortnight's holiday and the man of wealth, with his summer log cabin beside a lonely lake, are equally followers of Izaak Walton. All summer long the shop windows in the towns are crowded with hooks and flies and rods and reels and with handbooks for the fisherman. And with guns for the huntsman.

The posters in the railway stations, depicting faceless ski-ers in blue, whizzing down hills made of rising dough, are balanced by others showing hunters' camps garlanded with dead fish, dead birds, and the carcasses of elk and hare. These scenes of "still life"—so very still and so entirely lifeless—indicate that shooting is also available under properly formulated and enforced game laws. As the season for geese, duck, and snipe opens in August and ends in March; as there is a short season for elk and red deer in September, for capercailzie, black gamecock, hazel hen, and woodcock from September to December (grouse and ptarmigan until March), and bear from May to November, a determined sportsman can find some target practically throughout the year.

Besides all these professional and semi-professional ski-ers and skaters; besides these anglers and hunters who call a day well lost for a basket of trout, or a hare, or a grouse, Norway is a pleasant port of call for another set of frank—even rank—amateurs.

While some of the ascents, such as those of the Dovrefell, call for skill, and those of the Kjölen Range should be attempted only by experts in rock and ice craft, many people climb mountains, particularly those of the Jotunheimen Range, without any regime of preparation. The Britishers are the most regularly expected mountaineers and there are a sufficient number who return for their holidays every summer to give them a quite definite classification. The Englishman who systematized his climbing so that in his youth he scaled the Lofoten Mountains and in his middle age the Snöwhetta, who plodded up Galdhöpiggen on his sixtieth birthday, and then strolled up the lesser hills for remaining decades, recognizing that as one grows older mountains have a way of growing higher, had imbibed philosophy as well as health from his summers on Norwegian peaks.

Meanwhile, a whole generation has made another astonishing discovery. Walking has become the vogue. There have always been walkers, long before they were called "hikers." Norwegians are as accustomed to walking in summer as to ski-ing in winter, and many are the Scottish and English vacationists who have tramped the valleys of Norway.

But now these ranks of genuine pedestrians, hardened through an apprenticeship of practice, have been augmented. Young things from New York and London have discovered that human locomotion need not be limited to stepping in and out of motor-cars. No longer do American girls in silk stockings and street shoes, and English girls in garden hats, scrabble up the hilly trails. Now no socks can be too thick, no boots too heavy, and handkerchiefs tied under the chin out-Herod the veriest peasant crone's. As the bathing-costume has been abbreviated to shorts and a halter, so the skirt has been lengthened to trousers. The trousers are not always cut to fit the figure. In fact, most female figures are so cut that no matter how cleverly trousered, they are distressing to the spectator. But the intention is there, and the achievement. Doubtless, ultimately, the spectator will cease to be distressed. These boys and girls, these men and women, walk for sport; walk to discover new trails and follow those too rough for any wheel. They walk in preference to riding in a train or in a motor, carrying on their backs rucksacks sprouting reindeer horns and decked with bunches of heather. And in Norway they find, one minute from the hotel, or a day's distance from anywhere, paths aplenty and camps where they can sleep along with those other holiday-makers who have been intrepid enough to attempt these roads and heights by cycle or motor-bike.

Sports, which have for their goal the development of physical prowess, or the slaughter of fish, flesh, or fowl, are popular in Norway. But the supreme sport—the killing of other human beings—is not popular. Like the other Scandinavian countries, Norway not only abhors war but refuses to engage in it. She dissolved her union with Sweden (1905) with no more than an exchange of verbal bullets, and in the bitter and protracted Greenland controversy with Denmark, ink, not blood, was shed.

The Vikings fought furiously during their lusty youth. But, like the philosophical mountain-climber, as they have grown older, they direct their energies to less exhausting physical pyrotechnics.

They not only prefer to spend their national monies on social reform and public health than on military and naval defence (13.2 percent for the former and 12 percent for the latter), but are so convinced of the wisdom of this preference that they have actually succeeded, in a conflict-racked world, and in a country with no forts on its borders, in staying out of war for over a hundred years. The Norwegian Labour Party has gone so far as to include in its programme the abolition of all military forces. This has not been done. On the contrary, military service is compulsory for all men, conscientious objectors being drafted for civil duties.

The naval defence is divided into two branches—the Navy itself and the Coast Artillery. In a country of less than three million people, the size of the Army and Navy is necessarily small. The money appropriation for defence is also small, compared with that of larger nations. But the human material, thoroughly grounded in a highly developed educational system, made sturdy by a strenuous outdoor life, accustomed to the rigours of existence on land and to experience at sea, is of highest quality. Norway acknowledges the necessity of preparedness while resolutely turning away, both in sentiment and demonstration, from glorification of war.

In 1612, some Scottish mercenaries going to Sweden to fight for Gustavus Adolphus landed at the mouth of the Romsdalfjord and came marching through Gudbrandsdal toward Oslo. Colonel Sinclair was in command of the high-handed Scots, who so enraged the peasants that the latter annihilated them and their commander. Three hundred years later the Norwegians erected a monument to mark Colonel Sinclair's grave. It can be seen near Kringen, not far from Otta. But this marker is set in a valley that has long been peaceful. The thrifty, hardworking farmers have enough to do, battling with the elements and providing their children with a proper education and themselves with a decent security for their old age.

They are not unaware that in case of war between Germany and Russia, it might be impossible to remain neutral, and, as Marquis Childs points out, scarcely a winter passes without some sort of a spy scare in the Arctic Circle. Neither are they unaware of the cost of neutrality. They remember that in the World War Norway's shipping suffered greater loss proportionately than that of any other country, belligerent or neutral. But they would rather pay for neutrality than for war.

If they want excitement, they can climb mountains. If they want to exhibit physical fitness, they can ski and skate. And if they want to indulge in the sport of shooting, they have agreed on better game than other human beings.

A grey day or a sunny day is all one to the angler.

Glaciers whose trails are marked only by the footfall of the snow.

CHAPTER SEVEN

Norway Paints Its Picture

COMPOSED out of living rock and living waters, painted with pigment that is light itself, Norway lies upon the canvas of Nature—one of her masterpieces. It is to gaze at these prismatic cliffs and moss-patterned mountains, to admire the waterfalls streaming through the sunlight, the starlight, the moonlight, that most people travel to Norway. There are other Scandinavian countries where co-operatives and adult folk schools and old-age pension systems may be studied. But this is the only one where such grandeur of form is veiled by such tenderness of tint, where the evanescent shifts of light and shadow lie upon such eternal sternness, where winter's snow follows summer's sparkle in a seasonal panorama of such overpowering sublimity.

The casual traveller through Norway—like the casual listener at a concert—may be content with his own impressions. But the visitor who knows enough to feel that he could know more, perceiving this Norway of the eye, instinctively seeks those who have perceived it more variously and more penetratingly and have dedicated to its delineation the passion and study of a lifetime. To this seeker rush in response the whole glorious fellowship of Norwegian painters as mediators and companions of delight.

For the walls of the picture galleries and museums everywhere are brilliant with bold, perceptive, and extraordinarily excellent interpretations of Norway's land and seascapes: elucidations of her moods, visual recordings of her history, studies of the faces of her people.

Vital and fresh-visioned, these paintings by Norwegians of Norway and of other Norwegians are given honoured precedence over the works of foreign artists, so that the National Gallery in Oslo is truly national and the Rasmus Meyer's Collections in Bergen among the most interesting in contemporary Europe, both of them not only depicting the visible scene but revealing the profound affection with which the Norwegian regards every fold of the mountains, every glisten of rain and marsh, every beam of sunshiny warmth.

Escaping until 1909 from the button-mould of an academy, the Norwegian painters have been free to develop their genius with originality and directness. Instead of copying other men from other lands, they have gone forth and painted what they themselves saw, so that their works are a revelation and a refreshment. The large art museums in Oslo and Bergen, the permanent art galleries in Trondheim, Stavanger, and other towns, the frescoes in public buildings, and the oil portraits and etchings in private homes are tonic expressions of artists, many of whom are still living and none of whom dates back much more than a century (Dahl, with whom the newer history of Norwegian painting properly begins, died in 1857), and all of whom worked most enduringly when they chose their subjects from native material.

Edvard Munch has, indeed, overstepped all confines of na-

tionality. The men and women he paints are not merely Norwegians but universal human beings and, more and more, ab-
stracts and symbols of human nature; his mountains rise "wild
ridgèd, steep by steep," his rivers flow from some untrodden
region of the mind. But Edvard Munch, whose name is known
to every man, woman, and child in Norway, to a wide public in
Germany and France, to all critics in England, and to a few
in the United States, is a Norwegian. And as the position of a
star in the heavens is determined in part by sighting it from
various angles, so his signal eminence takes its place in the
brief, vigorous, and highly distinctive history of Norwegian
painting.

That history did not begin until after the union with Denmark had been dissolved. To be sure, there had been artistic
expression before that time, and its testimonials remain in the
antiquities of the Viking ships in the cathedrals of Trondheim
and Stavanger, in Haakon's Hall, and in the relics of the wood
carving and wood painting and decoration of the oldest
churches. Magnus Berg is placed among the best of the carvers
in ivory of the baroque age. But since he lived chiefly in Copenhagen, was in the employ of the Danish king, and died in Denmark (1739); and since he was primarily a craftsman, it is not
his name which holds the initial rank in Norway.

That position is allotted to Johan Christian Claussön Dahl
(1788–1857), who was not only the first in point of time but
who remains first in point of certain merits among the Norwegian landscape-painters. His large canvases of fjords and
cliffs, of harvest fields and sunsets, of girls on seters with dog
and basket looking down on the village below, of torrents and
waterfalls, of a birch tree tossing in a storm, are hung conspicuously in every Norwegian collection and in museums on the

Continent. For although his successors learned that melancholy blues and violets represent not only Nature but feeling, he was the first to express these things in Norway. He was the first to discover the old churches, and while others were idealizing and making heroic studies, he depicted actual people fishing and lumbering, and painted rivers that are real rivers splashing and foaming.

Like the other members of that early school who were trained in the foreign academies of Copenhagen, Dresden, Düsseldorf, and Munich, Dahl studied in Denmark and Germany. But he was never influenced by the German Academy, and however prolonged his foreign residence—he became a professor in Dresden, since at that time an artist could not live by his art in Norway—he continually returned to his native land. The son of a Bergen fisherman, he went back during the summers to the west coast of his childhood. He wandered along the fjords, making his studies of herds of reindeer gazing down into an abyss, of a man on horseback by a waterfall, and, in the autumn, returning to his Dresden studio and teaching with material for his winter's work. His detail is meticulous—the stratification of rocks, the bark of trees—but the whole is not lost in its parts. His period coincided with that of Constable, although he did not know the English artist, and he is an easily approachable guide to lead the novice toward the opening vistas of Norwegian painting.

Dahl's immediate successors did not study with him nor did they learn from him, preferring to sentimentalize their subjects. This was not true of Mathias Stoltenberg (1799–1871), who, although he studied for a short time in Copenhagen, escaped all falsification and empty traditionalism by being chiefly self-taught. Deaf and poor, this unpretentious Nordlander journeyed about the country, chiefly over the uplands, content to get his board and lodging in return for portraits of the country squires, petty government officials, clergymen, and county judges and their wives. Extraordinarily lifelike, these faces, which once hung over the sofas in middle-class living-rooms, now look directly out from the walls of the National Gallery—shrewd, wise faces, which time has graven and character has moulded. Stoltenberg was not a great painter. Too often an awkwardness or an unsophistication confessed his faults. And he was almost forgotten until his works were collected by the Jubilee Exposition of 1914. But he brings close to today the gentry who moved among the Biedermeier furniture that is now ranged in museum rooms. With loving detail he gives the hair of the women, their lace caps and fichus, their brooches and ribbons, flowers and chains; the men in their robes of office. Men and women alike are set forth with such spontaneity and joyousness of colour that, with their clear eyes and mobile lips, they seem as heartily alive as they ever were.

There was one talented pupil and devoted friend of Dahl who may be called his successor. Thomas Fearnley (1802–1841) brought to his art a romantic aspiration, but he nevertheless remained true to his master's teaching and to his example of fidelity to Nature. Fearnley had other blood than Norwegian in his veins. He loved to travel, and some of his Italian studies confirm his confident composition and his response to the southern sun. But his masterpiece *Labrofossen* (National Gallery) is purely Norwegian—a broad and foaming cascade, a dead pine against the sky, dark forests, wet clouds, derelict logs caught in an eddy with an eagle upon them, the only living thing in the sublime waste.

Fearnley's name is linked with Dahl's because he was both

a friend and a pupil, and because, although he brought a southern lyricism to the northern scene, that scene is nevertheless immediately comprehensible. But there was another contemporary who stood quite outside the influence of the father of Norwegian painting. For although Peder Balke (1804–1887) studied with Dahl, his striking idiosyncrasies place him apart from all who preceded as well as all who have succeeded him. His small grey-green marines, his Nordland studies of the most singular individuality—almost Japanese in their suggestiveness —can never be confused with those of anyone else. Although they purport to be scenes from Norway, they are kin to the moor and the sea which Emily Dickinson never saw and whose essence she caught in a line, and to that Noah's rainbow which William Blake approached "on the fiery chariot of his contemplative thought."

Balke's *Lighthouse* (National Gallery), formed of a feathery splash above the "foam of perilous seas in faery lands forlorn," is due to stand firmer and for a longer time than the substantial and detailed interiors and exteriors of Tidemand and Gude, which fill large spaces in every museum and disproportionately larger ones in popular estimation.

Adolf Tidemand (1814–1879) had his message and he delivered it vehemently. But it was the message of the prolific storyteller, gifted with a sense of narrative and a feeling for harmonious composition. Conscientiously, and sometimes dramatically, he depicted the Norwegian peasants—the outside of their clothes and the inside of their cottages—rural weddings, funeral feasts, incidents in country churches, and *The Disciples of Hauge* attending a prayer-meeting in a smoky, raftered cabin. The original of this, which is his most celebrated work, is in Düsseldorf, but there is a replica from his hand in the National Gallery.

The very explicitness of these pictures gives them a value to the historian and archæologist and explains their popularity. But Tidemand's studies, in which he escapes from the German sentimentality of his large finished paintings, suggest that his lyrical vein might have deepened and his taste become more eclectic if he had come in contact with the France of Delacroix, Millet, and Corot, instead of with the fixed formulas of Germany.

Much the same can be said of Hans Gude (1825–1903), who was a friend of Tidemand, a student with him at Düsseldorf, and even a collaborator with him, as in the theatrical tableau *The Bridal Procession in Hardanger* (National Gallery). Gude painted industriously and sometimes extremely well, as in his mountain-heights series (National Gallery), and his mild panoramas, like Tidemand's narrative canvases, are especially admired in Germany.

The Düsseldorf influence, although it impaired the standards of those artists who came under it, could not destroy that native energy and instinct for colour which so conspicuously mark the Norwegian painters. August Cappelen (1827–1852), dying young, escaped from the blight of calculated studio effects, leaving, as in his *Forest Landscape in Telemark* (National Gallery), deeply romantic but not specious landscapes. And Lars Hertervig (1830–1902), the artisan artist of Stavanger, escaped it by madness, forgetting foreign formulas for popularity in his moods of dark, cold melancholy or of luminous ecstasy.

But the others, even if they were infected lightly or seriously, nevertheless pressed forward eagerly, so that along the strong evergreen axis, with Dahl at one end and Christian Krohg, at the other there blooms such a garden full of flowers that it is difficult to select a bouquet. So freshly do the landscapes blow, so naturally do the portraits bloom, that one feels no inclination to criticize and discard, but only to wander among them in delight.

This rich profusion of the early nineteenth century is intensified around the exquisite cultivation of Eilif Peterssen (1852–1929), one of the group who studied in Munich during the time when that city was gathering to itself painters, teachers, collections, and exhibitions from many countries. Highly talented, mature at an early age, Peterssen responded to the highest art of the past. To the solid technique which he acquired, to the sense of form and arrangement which was instinctive, he brought the Norwegian flair for colour. His *Dame Portrait* with the lovely hands (National Gallery) suggests the tone of old masters, not because he was imitating them but because he had been ennobled by study of them. Gracious and winning, Peterssen was not only a painter but a member of juries and committees connected with the National Art Gallery and a tactful force for the practical and public advancement of Norwegian art.

The same aptitude in youth, the same diligence in study, and the same reverence for the art of the past which characterized Peterssen were shared by his friend and comrade, Hans Heyerdahl (1857–1913), who also studied in Munich, also received great stimulus in Italy, and great honour in France. Although Heyerdahl's later work is sometimes too unctuous, his worship of beauty and his light touch did not falter. In his *Portrait of Laura Gundersen* (National Gallery), the austere and delicate face of the actress is executed with a modelling worthy of Holbein.

In this group of Norwegian painters who expanded under the successive influence of Munich and Paris and came back to heap their gifts in the lap of the mother country, glows the sifted light, the voluminous colour, the interiors suffused with personality, of Harriet Backer (1845–1932), Norway's greatest woman painter. No other artist has achieved the effect on canvas of her golden light of summer flowing through the green of leafy trees into a vaulted grey country church, where it envelopes the figures of women kneeling at the rail before the white-ruffed preacher, is shattered against the gilded altar, and sinks away in the corners. No other painter has more coherently captured within doors the precious outdoor radiance. In the National Gallery hang a number of Harriet Backer's immediately recognizable compositions, but she is more fully represented in the collection of Rasmus Meyer in Bergen, where the green-drenched sunlight in the *Opdal Church* and the voluminous delicacy of the *Blue Attic* hang with others of her early interiors and later still-life fruit and flowers.

In her four happy years in Munich, before the ten in Paris, Harriet Backer knew not only Peterssen and Heyerdahl but two other men who have painted so superbly and over so long a period that they immediately assume importance to the foreigner who may not have been familiar with them before visiting Norway. Gerhard Munthe lived to be seventy-nine (1849–1928), and Erik Werenskiold eighty-three (1855–1938), both of them painting prodigiously with ever-increasing gusto through the years, both of them leaders in that group who brought home the inspiration of French nationalism and impressionism.

Gerhard Munthe's two widely diverse styles—in both of which he developed the highest distinction—sprang from the soil and almost the same seed. He was born amid the spacious freeholds, large barns, and tranquil farms of Elverum in Eastern Norway, and as a child he followed the haymakers to the fields, helped round up the horses in the enclosure, sat in blue-painted kitchens, and explored treasures in the old painted cupboards and chests. He knew the seasons and the hours of the country day as country dwellers know them, the agricultural implements as a boy who has handled them. It is this Norway of naturalistic meadows and fields and rivers; of twilight stealing in over a roughly scythed yard, where a horse with a sleepily lowered head stands under a morel tree; of sparkling light of summer, that he caught in such pictures as *A Farm Garden* and *Haymaking* (National Gallery), and *Snow Melting at Hedemarken* and the *Small Fishing Harbour* (Rasmus Meyer's Collections).

But the open farmsteads were surrounded by dark woods. The peasant girls sang ballads of bears and wolves. The chests whose tops and sides were painted in flowers held embroideries of old design. When Munthe chose this stuff of fable and fairy tale for his material, it called for an archaic, decorative portrayal, and his fantasy and jubilant humour fitted itself precisely to this new-old style.

The Rasmus Meyer's Collections have rooms prismatic with his drawings for Snorri's sagas, his illustrations for folk tales, his vignettes and friezes, decorative drawings, and preliminary sketches for the murals in Haakon's Hall. It also shows some of his designs for picture-weaving and wall-hangings. These are of greatest interest, as Munthe, besides being one of the country's foremost landscape-painters, was the revivifier of its modern decorative art. It is tranquillizing to see the farm and the meadow as Munthe saw them through the lens of his boyhood experience and through his mature discrimination. And it is peculiarly fitting, when one is in the land of saga and fable, to see the trolls and dragons, the knights and princesses, as they flitted before the imagination of the child and have been transfixed, motionless, spellbound for ever, in flat friezes and frescoes, by the skill of the artist.

Although Werenskiold was long associated with Munthe, both as a fellow-student abroad and as a co-worker for a national art in Norway; and although his black and white drawings and etchings are of the highest rank (they are well displayed at the Rasmus Meyer's Collections), his portraits are so convincing and the men who sat for them so famous that they seem his most valuable contribution.

If Norwegian scenery offers splendid material to the landscapist, so do Norwegian faces to the portraitist. Those abrupt brows and direct glances, the unposed confidence of posture, the fresh colour of hair and skin and eyes, all fuse in a force which is part of Norwegian physiognomy because it is part of Norwegian character. And the artists have painted themselves and each other and their friends and their enemies with such liveliness that their countenances become as familiar as their canvases.

Werenskiold's portrait of Ibsen hangs in the National Gallery and there is a copy in the Rasmus Meyer's Collections. Against a lightly sketched background of icy spaces, crystalline as his own mentality, the great man stands with his hands behind his back, looking uncompromisingly through his glasses and through the spectator. The mouth is stern as a rock, the frosty hair tossed back from a mountain of brow. This powerful embodiment is Ibsen and Norway.

Björnstjerne Björnson is here, too, as the self-confident professor, the argumentative poet and dynamic founder of a party, broad-shouldered, muscular, his reddish hair turning grey, but with no sign of diminishing energy in his firmly closed lips. He is here again, sitting, white-haired but still rugged and majestic, in the empty auditorium of the theatre he directed, studying the invisible stage absorbedly. Werenskiold's direct, powerful portraits set forth more searchingly than written biographies not only the appearance but also the psychology of the men and women who were created by the fundamental forces of Norway and who in turn have created the art of Norway.

Werenskiold, who was a radical in his youth when (1885) he painted the peasants not as picturesque lay figures but as plain and stolid men and women, as in his *Country Funeral* (National Gallery), grew even freer and bolder with age. His *Logging Scene,* hanging in the same gallery, was painted when he was eighty-three! The Rasmus Meyer's Collections show that intense concentration which led to his development as draughtsman and colourist, animated from first to last by a buoyant love of life.

So vigorous, so vital are the host of canvases by the painters who crowded on each other's heels from the middle of the nineteenth century until past the turn of the twentieth, that for one to overtop them is indeed an achievement. And yet it is generally accepted that after Dahl there was no one to reach his eminence until Christian Krohg (1852–1925), the magnificent painter of a magnificent period.

Krohg's burning social passion, his sympathy with the poor of the city, and his journalistic sense too often determined his choice of subject and too often injected a literary interpretation or proletarian message into his themes. And, too, the immense output of a long life (painting seems to be a healthy pursuit in Norway judging from the mortality statistics among artists) has been uneven. But after these defects have been granted, there still remain his intensity of statement, his intrepid hand and direct vision, his strength and a mastery of finish and tone such as belong to only truly great painters.

His large canvas *Albertine* is an example of his journalistic choice of subject and his absolute command of technique. Krohg—who had defended Hans Jaeger's novel *The Christiania Bohemians,* which had attacked social conditions and landed its author in prison—himself published a novel *Albertine,* the story of a girl of the streets. The book was confiscated and Krohg was fined. However, the public conscience was stirred, and conditions were improved both for victims of the social law and for radical authors. Krohg's book is forgotten, but his painting *Albertine in the Police Court* is properly given a place of conspicuous honour in the National Gallery. Such textures of velvet, feathers, and watered silk, such firm and flowing outlines, have never been equalled in Norway and not often surpassed in other countries. In his portrait of his frail little aunt with the wrinkled hands and the sea-blue eyes, it is possible to affirm that a black dress has never been better painted by anyone, anywhere, at any time.

Krohg's preference for literary themes, while it militated against his highest æsthetic achievement, gave him great popularity. His sailors and fishermen on board ships on stormy seas, his poor seamstress in a garret, his mother by a sleeping child, and—above all—his *Sick Girl* (National Gallery) are master-pieces of realistic painting. Norway was to show no such virtuosity until Edvard Munch.

But before Munch was to come Fritz Thaulow (1847–1906), the cultivated and fastidious naturalist with a touch of impressionism. Unlike the democratic Krohg, who used his pictures to rouse the public to a social conscience, Thaulow believed art was an aristocratic pleasure for the selected few. His happy knack for choosing a subject—he was to specialize first in winter and then in river scenes—was combined with his exquisite taste as a colourist, especially with intermediate and suavely graduated tones. Studying abroad in his youth, living and travelling abroad, painting abroad at various periods throughout his life, influenced by French, Scottish, and American painters, Thaulow found both his largest public and his richest markets in Paris and London and America. Paradoxically, this least Norwegian of artists has gained a foreign reputation as a typical Norwegian. While in the museums of other countries he is most frequently represented by the works of his later years painted in his studio when he had long been out of touch with home, in Norway his pictures that are most highly regarded are those earlier ones, when he painted in the open sunlight the houses of fishermen and the snowy streets of his birthplace.

If Thaulow is considered a bit old-fashioned, there is a group somewhat younger chronologically and a great deal more modern in approach and technique. With the same joy in colour, the same passion for their native scene that has characterized Norwegian painters for more than a hundred years, they transfer to canvas the mountains, the snow, the moss, the waterfalls of one of the most scenic countries on the globe.

In the National Gallery in Oslo and in the Rasmus Meyer's Collections and in the museum in Bergen, the foreigner who has been travelling in Norway can see the whole visual panorama that passed before him recaptured. He will see the wetness of the ground around the turf-roofed cottages of Nicolai Astrup (1880–1928). He will feel the delicate palpitations in the landscapes of Thorvald Erichsen (1869–   ), as if summer had painted herself. He will stand in the windless hush of a sunny day on the *Island of Happiness* by Oluf Wold-Torne (1867–1919). Wold-Torne is mourned for dying young (fifty-two is young in Norway), but his flowers still bloom in the Rasmus Meyer's Collections, their fragility unbruised by their strong handling, his nudes suggesting a power that might have come into even greater fulfilment.

Henrik Sörensen (1882–   ) is intoxicated with the old Norwegian pigmentation and with it he fills canvases so monumental that the museums are hard put to it to house them. Ludvig Karsten (1876–1926) was also carried away by chromatic enthusiasm, although it may be debated if his colours did not come more from his palette than from Nature. Hugo Lous Mohr (1889–   ) paints the moss on the rocks in a way that is Norway to those who know it. Per Deberitz (1880–   ) still retains the originality and Jean Heiberg fulfils the promise of their youth. The summer tourist who would imagine what winter is like in this far northern land can feel the snow beneath his feet and touch it, as it is piled against the walls of the houses and on the roofs and sills, in *Röros in Winter*, as Harald Sohlberg (1869–1935) felt it. But snow is not merely a cumbersome ornament to a village street. It is a phenomenon in itself. In Sohlberg's *Winter in the Rondane Mountains* (National Gallery), the intense blueness, the empty white, are painfully dazzling. Hard as enamel, brilliant as ice, colder than freezing—thus winter looked and felt to this exceptional painter.

Even when they do not live in Norway, Norwegian painters continue to "see colour" and to transfix it on their canvases. Joronn Sitje (1895–   ), who was born in Telemark, found herself far from snowy fjords and heathery fells when she went to live in Kenya, East Africa. But she painted what she saw in true Norwegian fashion, and the tints and tones in the flesh of her half-nude Negro figures have rarely been more subtly perceived and recorded. Jonas Lie (1880–   ) has lived in the United States so long, since 1893, and identified himself so completely with its artistic institutions, that one sometimes forgets that he was born in Norway and is a nephew of the writer of the same name. Although Lie paints Maine and the Adirondacks, his American seascapes and landscapes, his snow and rivers and forests, hold in their whiteness and wetness, their verdure and their rocks, something of the pure colour and bold lines of Norway.

It is not only the walls of the art galleries that sing—and sometimes shout—with all the hues of the rainbow. It is not only offices and private homes that are enriched by truly admirable portraits and pulsing landscapes, by etchings and drawings, by sketches and still-life studies. The walls of churches and schools, of public buildings, cafés, and hotels are vibrant with frescoes, many of them so excellent that they merit a special visit and special attention.

Although the famous painters of the older period occasionally turned to decorative murals—Werenskiold in the Fridtjof Nansen frieze at Lysaker, Eilif Peterssen in his *Ascension* in Ullern Church, Hugo Lous Mohr's frescoes in the church at

Norway paints her picture upon the canvas of Nature—one of
her masterpieces.

A floating, falling fabric of prismatic tissue.

Volda, and, most notable of all, Gerhard Munthe's series in Haakon's Hall in Bergen—there is a younger group which has won its distinction primarily from this genre. Of them, three men—all still living—have animated acres of wall space with tinted ebullience.

Axel Revold (1887–   ), with his frescoes in the Bergen Stock Exchange and in the Deichman Library (in Oslo); Alf Rolfsen (1895–   ), with his ages of man in the new crematorium and his earlier illustrative panels in the telegraph office and the Artisans' Festival Hall in Oslo, testify to what rank these artists have attained. The corridors and hall and auditorium in the Seamen's School at Ekeberg, just outside Oslo, are a triumph of Per Krohg (1889–   ) in their draughtsmanship, fancifulness, and exuberant colour. On the walls of the Aula of the University in Oslo, the Arts and Natural Sciences are symbolized by Edvard Munch, that prodigious genius who does as he pleases in this medium as well as in landscape and portraiture in oils, in etching, lithography, woodcuts, and drawing.

Munch's pictures fill whole rooms in the National Gallery and Rasmus Meyer's Collections, so it is possible to follow the steadily exalting evolution of this artist, to trace how his subjectiveness has deepened and how his technique has been perfected to accommodate this deepening.

In his early portraits—such as the one of Hans Jaeger (National Gallery)—his intuition of what makes one man different from another, and how a phase may represent the generalization of an era, is already evident. In his self-portrait, in the same gallery—an enigmatic figure enveloped in blue shadows—the mood merges into the permanence of a philosophy and a personality. Even in his early paintings he subdued his virtuosity to his subjective feeling. The *Sick Girl* (National Gallery) is not the portrait of an individual—or, rather, two individuals, for the last communion and the impending separation are between a mother and child—but of sickness itself, sickness holding the seed of death. Whoever has looked at a beloved face sharpened by the touch of mortality recognizes here not a study of fabrics, not the indication of a place or a season or an hour of day or night, but the actuality of an intangible moment as brief as breath, as eternal as love. *Spring,* in the same room, for all its delineation of fact—such as the blowing curtains and the mother's knitting hands—is an embodiment of earth-scented breezes and quivering hopes.

The early landscapes, also, indicating the mystery of the northern summer night, are forerunners of the morbid dreaminess, pierced with hypersensitive perception, which is to intensify with years. The individuals are already being stylized into erotic symbols.

To follow Munch's pictures through the galleries is to read the biography of a man who was born of a Norwegian and highly intellectual family, and who studied in Paris (1885 and again 1889–1892) and travelled in Germany. At his first exhibition in Berlin the dealer was obliged to close the shop, as no one came to buy, and during his first ten years in Germany Munch sold practically nothing and was supported by his friends. He was grateful to get a hundred crowns for the *Sick Girl,* which could not now be bought for ten thousand pounds, and he offered his picture of his sister at the piano to anyone who would take it for five crowns. In England his first exhibition was ignored and he has hardly yet been introduced into America. But fifty or sixty years of insistence upon one's beliefs begin to make a dent upon the public mind. Munch's

fame permeates every house in Norway; he is widely honoured
in Germany; and his second exhibition in England (December
1936) was an enormous success. Now, the possessor of a fortune, he paints and paints and paints, not selling unless he
wishes. For the last thirty years he has been working upon
eighteen panels which are to be a frieze of life.

As Munch's coloured figures, which have been compared to
those of Félicien Rops and Henri de Toulouse-Lautrec, have
become more and more symbolic, so his black and white ones
—shadowy kin to Poe and Baudelaire—have become more and
more abstract. His external forms are mere veils of colour or
black and white, shrouding the emotions of fear and jealousy,
love and hate; paintings and etchings alike are vehicles carrying as half-concealed passengers death, lust, or despair.

Dr. Christian Brinton, who has written so ably on Scandinavian art, sums up Munch's affinity with the visible universe
when he says: "In these broadly brushed canvases and strongly
accentuated lithographs we are made to wander by dark waters,
under pale, far stars and over mountains toward the rim of the
world where we stand transfixed with tragic apprehension."

There is no such far wandering as yet in Norwegian sculpture.

Despite all the traditions of wood carving from the time of
the Vikings, the plastic arts have not reached the eminence of
painting. There is, to be sure, a short roster of names including
Hans Michelsen (1789–1859), whose twelve Apostles dignify
Trondheim Cathedral; Julius Middelthun (1820–1886), whose
portrait busts are of permanent historical value; and Stephan
Sinding (1846–1923), whose *Barbarian Mother* is extremely
effective (National Gallery). But these are of limited achievement, too often echoing Danish classicism, since they all served

their apprenticeship in Danish ateliers and what reputation they have—or had—is local. There are some promising young sculptors, of whom Emil Lie is sometimes placed first.

But there has been no one in the past, and so far there is no one discernible for the future, who can be bracketed with Adolf Gustav Vigeland, whose overleaping imagination and titanic energy have been at white heat for more than half a century. Although Vigeland came to maturity during the period of naturalistic and impressionistic painting, he did not feel himself one of that older generation. And certainly what he is performing at seventy outdistances the most muscular and the most ambitious of the younger generation and outdistances even the prodigious achievements of his own youth.

For by the time he was twenty-five he had already executed the gigantic relief of Hell, now in bronze in the National Gallery, with its two hundred figures billowing around Satan enthroned, tumbling over the bridge of good intentions, rushing beyond the hill of suicides in a maelstrom of legs and arms.

Before that he had done numbers of pieces and after that he was to turn out many more. The emaciation of his earlier figures, in marble, bronze, and wood, was to round out into fuller forms; his series of groups dealing with love in all its phases of submission, conflict, discord, and fulfilment were to express the principal motifs of his art. His portrait busts—*tours de force* of psychological interpretation and technical proficiency—were to form a veritable gallery of eminent Norwegians. But all these torrential outpourings were mere flying foam specks in comparison with the tidal wave which has carried the last decades of his life on its towering crest. For nearly forty years he has been labouring with superhuman energy on a monument which, when completed, will be a pæan, a full chorus and orchestra, celebrating philosophy, life, and art, such has never before been uttered—or attempted—by a solo performer.

In 1900 Vigeland submitted to the Oslo Municipality a proposal for a fountain in front of the Storting—a bronze basin borne aloft by six nude men. From this modest container has since overflowed granite groups of a hundred figures, bronze ones of sixty, a central monolith more than fifty feet high, representing humanity struggling for freedom, and a granite bridge over three hundred feet long. The plot in front of the Storting could hold no such colossal arrangement. It was necessary to go out to the pond and the fields of Frogner Park on the edge of the town. As the years have rolled by, tons of figures have emerged from his large studio near by, which the city presented to the sculptor in 1910, and will ultimately be the Vigeland Museum. Men, women, children, and unborn lives, singly and in groups, struggling, musing, sorrowing, under trees, under water, under the open sky, are being created, with no apparent slackening of physical or imaginative force, to inhabit this ever-expanding universe. It is impossible to judge the merits of an undertaking which is not yet completed, which is unlike any other ever before seen by the eye of the layman or created by the hand of a single sculptor, and is not likely to be duplicated in a world where few cities have space for such a *Fountain* and fewer men have the biceps, to say nothing of the brain, to attack such a giant task.

Vigeland's amazing monument may or may not be the greatest piece of modern sculpture in Europe—or in the world—but at least it refutes any accusation of anæmia in this branch of the arts in Norway.

Meanwhile, the painters are flowering in that vigorous and

glowing exuberance whose form is the form of their native land and whose soul is colour. In less than a hundred and fifty years the country has painted her own portrait, and done it superbly.

The foreigner who would like his eyes to see what Norwegian eyes see, cannot do better than to follow, through the galleries, the robust and enjoyable unfolding of an art which began with the lucid naturalism of Dahl and reached genuine splendour with the objective realism of Christian Krohg.

And if he would like his mind to share the psychic restlessness and troubled melancholy which is characteristic of the Norwegian soul, he cannot do better than to follow through the world of twilit subjectivity the figure with shrouded face of Edvard Munch.

Part II

THE CHANGING
NORWAY OF
THE MIND

CHAPTER ONE

Kings, Queens, and Princes

O N February 21, 1937, the cannon from the Fortress of Akershus, whose ancient stone walls overlook the Oslofjord, boomed forth announcing the birth of the first prince to be born on Norwegian soil in more than five hundred years. This was Prince Harald, successor to the throne, whose father is Crown Prince Olav and whose mother —the Crown Princess Martha—is the niece of King Gustav of Sweden.

If it seems curious that no Norwegian prince had been born in Norway since 1370, if it seems strange that in a world where kings are disappearing like snow before the sun, the monarchical system here should be more firmly established, more satisfactory, and more popular every year; if it is puzzling to the foreigner that the King of Norway, Haakon VII, was born a Dane; and, finally, if it seems paradoxical that one of the most democratic countries on earth—so democratic that it abolished all hereditary titles in 1814—should love, honour, and maintain a royal family—the whole situation, while interesting, is not complicated, nor is it difficult to reconcile its apparently conflicting elements.

In that long procession of the Kings of Norway, a land whose legendary leaders claimed descent from no less an ancestor than the god Frey, Harald Fairhair emerges as the first to try to conquer and rule the whole of Norway. This was in A.D. 872.

The personalities and exploits of the line of chieftains who, until the beginning of the fifteenth century, succeeded Harald are set forth in voluminous detail in the history of the early Norse kings. Although to the irreverent American their names may rather uncomfortably suggest dubious aliases—for there was Eric Bloody-Axe and Harald Greycloak and Ragnar Hairy Breeches and Ketil Flatnose and Magnus Barefoot and Rolf the Ganger, and the violence of their actions was frequently of a pattern akin to that told by present-day newspaper scare-heads—the cursory reader will not long be delayed by them. But no matter how cursory he may be, either as reader or as traveller, he will not forget that when Erik of Pomerania was crowned King of Norway, Sweden, and Denmark at the Castle of Kalmar in 1397, the histories of the three countries became connected and—to all but historians—inextricably confused.

While Sweden broke loose in 1521, Norway's union with Denmark lasted more than four hundred years, during which time Norway never lost the consciousness of her nationality or her desire for independence. The union was dissolved by Frederick VI—joint and absolute monarch of Denmark and Norway—when, by the Treaty of Kiel in 1814 he ceded Norway to Sweden. To this the Norwegians objected and, applying the theory of self-determination (one notes that this was a hundred years before Woodrow Wilson), they declared their own independence on May 17, 1814. At first they considered electing as their king that Danish prince who was already their governor. They were, however, persuaded—partly by show of arms—to accept instead, as joint monarch, the King of Sweden, at that time the former French Field Marshal Jean-Baptiste Bernadotte. The Norwegians retained their own constitution and right to local self-government. The union referred only to foreign affairs and to the king's person.

For ninety-one years Norway, winning certain concessions and continually struggling for others, chafed under an enforced partnership in which Sweden was the dominant member. In 1905 the two countries finally separated, and Norway found herself wholly free and independent for the first time in six centuries. The question of whether she should become a republic—in which case no foreign power would have had any business to interfere—was settled in the negative, as the republican party was not in the majority at that time. Since she decided to become a monarchy, her choice of a king was obviously a matter of most intimate concern to the other kings of Europe.

Allied to Sweden not only by almost a century of common—if more or less quarrelling—association, but also by the crisscross of royal intermarriage which so tangles up all European history, she asked Sweden's King Oscar II to allow a member of the Bernadotte family to accept the Norwegian crown. King Oscar, unwilling thus to make formal acknowledgment of the separation, ignored the invitation, and thereupon the friendly and familiar figure of King Edward VII of England assumed a large—and, as time has proved, a benignant—role in the unfolding of events. His third daughter Maud was married to Prince Charles of Denmark, and the idea of having her upon the throne of Norway was highly pleasing to her father. In Sir Sidney Lee's biography of Edward VII is set forth with greatest clarity not only the king's frank desire to have Norway establish a monarchy and not a republic, and a monarchy friendly to England, but also Prince Charles's high sense of delicacy in refusing to accept the newly created throne until he had been elected by the Norwegian Parliament on the basis of a plebiscite. It was not until this had been confirmed by an overwhelming majority (259,563 in favour and 69,264 against) that he came to Norway with his wife and infant son and, on June 22, 1906, was crowned in the Cathedral of Trondheim as Haakon VII of Norway. Princess Maud became the Queen of Norway and the little Prince Alexander became Crown Prince Olav.

From that cold November day in 1905 when the tall young Danish prince stepped upon the soil of Norway, carrying his small son in his arms, until the present moment, King Haakon has been not only a symbol of unification in a country prone to sectionalism but the embodiment of tact, goodwill, and intelligent co-operation. He has seen conservative, liberal, radical, peasant, and labour governments come into power, and over them all he has presided. By them all he has been trusted and liked, and during every political change he has steadfastly represented the people as a whole. Willing to talk frankly and listen attentively to the most important and the least significant of his subjects, remarkably well informed on foreign as well as domestic affairs, he has upheld the tradition of royalty with greatest dignity, helping Norway to keep up her prestige among the other northern countries, and he has done this without a single case of serious disharmony. For thirty-three of the years of his reign—until her death in November 1938—Queen Maud was closely at his side, quiet in her tastes, tactful in her manner, and, although maintaining her closeness to England by a yearly visit, unreservedly Norwegian in her loyalties.

To those democracies which elect a president with extravagant expectations of a millennium, and who bid him good-bye with relief that his period of office has not been more disastrous; to those monarchies which surround their royal dynasties with "such divinity as doth hedge a king," the personal customs and daily living of the Norwegian royal family and the attitude of the people toward that family are a source of continual amazement.

For those customs and that attitude are unpretentious to a degree. In the winter the king lives in the Royal Palace and in the summer moves to his simple residence at Bygdöy a few miles away. For many years he and the queen found sufficient entertainment in a friendly table of bridge, and while they fulfilled all the public duties of their position with grace and goodwill, such formal affairs did not in the least hinder the king from strolling down to the waterfront and chatting with sailors and fishermen, both he and they completely at their ease.

To such parents the crown prince was born at Sandringham, England, in 1903. He went to school, as a matter of course, in Norway, attended the military college in Oslo, going through the ranks with the soldiers by whom he is still addressed by his first name. He studied for two years at Balliol College in Oxford and is a colonel in the Norwegian Army. Tall and blond and strongly built, he is fond of ski-ing and takes his part in many events, among them the famous Holmenkollen jumping competition. Fond of yachting, he sails his own boats and has won his share of national and international races.

When, in 1929, he married Princess Martha of Sweden, the dark-haired and lovely sister of Queen Astrid of Belgium, the people of Norway were well pleased. They are entirely satisfied by the agreeable and unostentatious household maintained at Skaugum; they indulge in the usual popular and affectionate sentiment toward the two small princesses—Princess Ragnhild born in 1930 and Princess Astrid born in 1932. But when a son was born, that was the best of all. For, oddly enough, Norway, which was one of the pioneer countries to preach and practise the equality of the sexes, does not permit a woman to succeed to the throne, and Prince Harald makes it possible to hope for the continuance of that stable and sensible system which is so firmly established.

The Norwegians regard the royal family with a respect and friendly naturalness which is difficult to define either to the Americans, who have such an overweening curiosity about royalty, or to the English, who have their own traditions of pomp and ceremony. It is not uncommon for the crown prince and princess to motor down the streets of Oslo—he at the wheel and she beside him—leave the car at the curb, and step inside a shop to make a purchase, and come out and drive off, creating no more of a stir than any other good-looking young couple. When they attend the yachting regatta at Hankö, two hours from Oslo, they stroll about, both of them in casual white linen slacks, and are unmolested by crowds or even by staring.

This does not imply popular indifference, but merely the popular acceptance of members of the royal family as neither demigods nor demagogues.

There are, to be sure, certain gala occasions with a modest amount of pageantry. On the seventeenth of May every year —the date upon which Norway declared her independence in 1814 and which is celebrated by Norwegians everywhere— thousands of schoolchildren waving flags and singing national songs parade past the palace while the royal family stand upon the balcony. To be sure, the crown prince in the course of a year makes speeches and delivers prizes. The crown princess is a patroness of handicraft industries, and a sewing-school in Oslo bears her name. The children are duly and attractively photographed. But there is a normality about the whole royal family and their way of living which most foreigners find difficult to comprehend.

Meanwhile, the king co-operates with the present Labour Government, which becomes more and more conservative as the country as a whole becomes less and less radical. The days of Communist agitators seem to be over and the ship of state is sailing forward on a remarkably even keel.

Haakon VII is the king—as his son and his grandson are destined to be kings—and as a king he embodies the continuity and unification of Norway at home and upholds her position abroad. He is also the presiding officer of whatever political Cabinet happens to be in power and the steadfast representative of all the people. And he is an extremely well-informed man. In the monarchy of Norway this most democratic and direct of persons is permitted to function in all three roles with as little interference as possible. He is honoured as a king, respected as a statesman, and quite genuinely loved as a human being.

CHAPTER TWO

Oslo and Its Lawmakers

O SLO is not the biggest or the richest or the most "historical" or even the most "modern" capital in Europe. It lays no pretence to the ever-fascinating claim of being the wickedest. Besides a fjord of extraordinary beauty and complexity, the rather ordinary buildings and uncomplicated streets give no suggestion that a city called Oslo was founded here in 1047.

But it is a liveable city, offering the traveller who is surfeited with superlatives an agreeable breathing-place. He can live at a reasonable rate in a reasonably good hotel and stroll about discovering the most ancient ruins—those of St. Halvard's Church and Olav's Cloister in the Old Town—and examining the most modern of its public buildings—the new Town Hall. He can promenade on the wide thoroughfare of Karl Johan's Gate, with the principal hotels and shops on either side, and down its centre the widely spaced bulks of the Houses of Parliament and the National Theatre, overlooked by the Royal Palace, severe and white.

Wherever he strolls, or sits, he will be aware that the people he passes in the streets, or brushes on his way to a table in a restaurant, seem hardly foreign. Their faces are the faces one

Glass is used lavishly in modern apartment houses in Oslo.

Descendants of the intrepid Gudrid face life with direct eyes.

sees in the British Isles and in the regions of the United States
where "old American stock"—by which is meant old English
stock—still predominates. Their behaviour and their language
(almost!) are comprehensible to any English-speaking visitor.
This nearness is not merely ethnological. In these days of airplanes, the London *Times* is on the news stands in Oslo in the
evening of the morning it is published, so that the English can
exclaim in horror over the last American kidnapping and the
Americans, reading real-estate notices of Tudor mansions with
fifteen bedrooms and one bath, can puzzle over the intimate
habits of the English.

Yes, Oslo is near, in space, time, and manners, to the lands
across the sea.

The Italian sailors who came into its harbour a few years ago
and refused to leave their battleship without their rifles because they were afraid of polar bears, need have had no more
apprehension than of encountering Red Indians on the streets
of New York.

And yet Norway's capital retains its Norwegian difference.
The façades of the shops, modestly low, cautiously up-to-date;
the streets cobbled in whorled designs; the nasturtiums in the
flower boxes of the sidewalk cafés; the swept open plaza in
front of the palace—all speak quite explicitly, without under-
emphasis or overstatement, of Norway and the Norwegians.

To be sure, all cities everywhere reveal themselves through
the faces of their inhabitants and the sounds of their streets
and the outline and form of their buildings. But in Oslo what
they reveal is easier to hear because it is less confused by a
conglomeration of noises, less overlaid by a confusion of fever-
ish tempos. The air, which is so pure over the harbour and the
mountains, is not impure even in this largest of Norway's

cities. The sense of being under the open sky and not far from woods and water is immanent, even in the pavement-threaded metropolis. In the small hours of night, when there is no sound at all—not a bell, not the grating of a tram, the fall of a footstep, or the honk of a motor—then Oslo speaks most clearly of all.

She speaks of the first wooden town, nearly a thousand years ago, and all the wooden towns that followed it, to be burned, one after another, until the second half of the nineteenth century when brick and stone began to supersede wood, and until now, when building in wood is forbidden within the city limits.

She speaks of the Danish King Christian IV, who was also King of Norway, and who (1624) incorporated the city and called it Christiania. The statue of King Christian still stands in the Market Place, and the musical syllables of the name which the city bore for three hundred years still stand in all the plays and novels which are familiar to the outer world, and are still to be read in many a title over a shop or a bank.

She speaks of the great men who were familiar figures on these streets, which are now honoured by their statues, and who were habitués of the cafés of the Grand Hotel and the Continental, which now display their portraits. So many of them are buried near Our Saviour's Church that to walk through the birch-shaded, green-grassed graveyard is like turning the leaves of a family album. One black marble shaft and slab have no date and need none. For the name of Henrik Ibsen is of dateless fame. Only a hammer is engraved upon the shaft of one who, like his own miner, penetrated beyond the daylight of action into the dark fastnesses of motive and desire.

Make way for me, thou heavy hammer,
To the heart's most secret chamber.

Björnstjerne Björnson who, as Georg Brandes said, had "such
an eagerness for combat that a rumbling noise arose around
him wherever he appeared," lies quietly now. The names
and faces of others—the sensitive mobile features of Henrik
Klausen in bas-relief, the bearded bust of J. G. Conradi on a
red granite shaft, Johan Selmer's above a staff of music, the
name of Rikard Nordraak—will, just as the pictures in the
family album assume individuality while one picks up anec-
dotes of the family history, come into livelier significance as the
visitor to Norway grows acquainted with the country's development in music and the theatre. Artists and engineers,
business men, educators, and statesmen who contributed to
the progress of their country and their city, are buried here.
"For a renowned man they should build a howe [mound] as
a remembrance: and to all men in whom there was some manli-
ness they should raise standing stones."

To the reflective mind Oslo speaks constantly of the past. In
the Viking Ship Hall and in the Historical Museum she ranges
boats and grave-goods of the Viking Age, medieval and prehistoric artifacts. In Bygdöy she assembles wooden houses three
hundred years old and a stave church of eight hundred years
ago. Nansen's *Fram* has a house of its own. Akershus, the old
stone fortress and until 1719 a royal palace, is open for inspection.

But for the most part and to most people, Oslo speaks of
the present. She may be nearing her thousandth anniversary,
but she does not look or seem like an ancient city. The built-up

centre is, except for a few churches, of modern architecture. The periphery of suburbs is well splashed with modernistic villas. The splendid harbour—one of the largest in Europe—is up-to-date with docks and wharves and cranes and storehouses and shops. The schools, hospitals, and museums, the business blocks and apartment houses, embody the ideals—artistic and social—of both the present generation and the one that preceded it.

Oslo is not a strikingly beautiful city, but it is on the way to becoming a practical and well-built one. Its distinction is that it represents the mentality and temperament of the three hundred thousand people who compose its population and the three million whose capital it is.

Norway is a maritime nation and its capital is that of sea-faring folk. There are railway stations and bus lines and even a subway. There are roof gardens and art galleries. But always there is the fjord with steamers and whalers and ferry boats, with fishing boats and white-sailed pleasure craft and sculls being rowed by rhythmically moving crews. There is a twentieth-century odour of gasoline and asphalt, but the immemorial smell of the sea mingles with it. There are tourists and artists and merchant princes in the cafés, but there are also ship captains with their wives and daughters and sailor lads with their sweethearts.

Not only every fourth or fifth man in Norway has something to do with the sea, but almost every man is a Norwegian. There are twenty thousand Lapps and a few Finns in the far north. The dark eyes and hair frequently seen on the west coast may date from some Mediterranean infusion, but so long ago that historians refuse to verify it and anthropologists disagree about it. But Norway, who has lost so many of her sons by emigration (nearly nine hundred thousand in a century), has not seen her stock appreciably diluted by immigration. The majority of her people are blond and blue-eyed and tall, with an average longevity of over sixty years for men and over sixty-three for women. Their mental traits, although varying in different geographical sections and in different economic and cultural strata, are, like their physical ones, sufficiently similar to have fused a strongly homogeneous nation.

The Parliament House in Oslo and the Royal Palace, which it faces, are symbols of a government such a nation has formulated and upholds—a government whose power is divided between royal authority on the one hand and elected representatives on the other.

The Parliament stands a little lower than the Palace, but concedes no other deference. Its position, power, and functions are guarded by the Constitution of May 17, 1814, and since 1935 it has been controlled by the Labour Party and the Social Democrats, collaborating alternately with the Farmer and Liberal Parties.

As might be expected, a democratic country expressing itself through a Labour Government prefers to extend favours to the proletariat rather than to the privileged, and exhibits a sensitive social conscience in regard to the sick and the old and the unemployed, to children and working men and the poor.

Thus there is sickness insurance, compulsory for those whose annual income is under fifteen hundred dollars, voluntary for those whose incomes are above that amount, and given by the relief authorities to the unemployed. Moreover, the building of hospitals, their equipment and upkeep, the full payment of all their servants, and part payment of the nurses are met, not from the premiums of the insured but from taxes. To be sure, if a Norwegian consults a doctor, the sickness insurance department pays only two-thirds of the fee as a precaution against imposition on the doctor's time. But in case of serious illness, requiring medical or surgical treatment, the municipality pays for the hospital, nurse, and doctor. It also gives the patient a certain daily sum to support his family and a stipend during convalescence. In case of his death, the municipality bears part of the funeral expenses.

If the sick are thus handsomely treated, so are the aged. All citizens seventy years old are assured of pensions, one-half of which are paid by the State and the rest drawn from old-age pension funds and insured by an extra income tax of one percent on all taxable incomes.

The thoroughness of these two provisions is typical of the whole programme of social legislation, which, through its Labour Protection Law, extends security to office workers and manual workers. (This law excepts those in navigation, fishing, and agriculture, but a State Sick Benefit Law has, since 1837, taken care of the two former.) Besides private unemployment-insurance societies of the different labour unions, Parliament has recently enacted an unemployment-insurance law, its premiums paid at the same rate and in the same manner as sickness insurance, and collected by municipalities in the same department. At the nadir of the international depression of 1929–1935, which had its repercussions in Norway, between 5 and 6 percent of the population, not counting dependents, were unemployed.

There are pensions for the crippled and the blind, provision for the mentally defective. In fact, it is possible to be born, educated, unemployed, ill; to become old, and finally to die, and throughout this entire personal history to be supported by the government.

Such social legislation—which has been of evolutionary growth and not of arbitrary enforcement—is possible only among a small, homogeneous, and highly educated people. Even among them there is political dispute. The agrarians and the industrialists are always in a tug-of-war. The employers complain that the labouring classes are demoralized by too great support or are too tyranically controlled by the Labour Party. But even the conservatives admit that in the last twenty-five years the working man has become better dressed, better fed, and better mannered than before. The Communists number less than five thousand and have no representative in Parliament. Communistic influence from Russia grows steadily less and Moscow is said to have approved a merger with the Labour Party.

Thus, in a world increasingly totalitarian, Norway governs by reason. With a record which has its failures and a system which has its faults, she is, nevertheless, true to her conviction that governmental democracy can exist only in conjunction with economic democracy, and she progresses steadfastly toward those two allied objectives. Such a point of view rests not only upon the national instinct for equality and passion for democracy, but also upon education.

It is significant that midway between the Palace and the Parliament, on the boulevard of Karl Johan, should stand, around an open court, the three classic façades of the University. There is only one university in Norway, and it has grown so large—with over two thousand students—that the library and certain of the colleges have been forced further out. But these buildings remain in their original conspicuous location, symbols as well as centres of an educational system seven years of which is absolutely thorough and unescapably compulsory.

There are colleges and academies and high schools (gymnasiums) well scattered throughout Norway. There are navigation colleges and agricultural, normal, technical, trade, and professional colleges. There is a Labour College of the Federation of Labour and the Labour Party. There are schools specializing in forestry, in housewifery, in horticulture, in dairying, and every subject under the sun. Since 1860, over twoscore Folk High Schools for adults have grown up, and these are supported by public funds and their work is approved by the Department of Education. But the most amazing and the most important of them all are the elementary schools.

Less than three million people are scattered over a territory that extends over thirteen degrees of latitude. More than half of these are isolated in crevasses that can hardly be called valleys, marooned on lonely islands, perched on mountainsides, gathered in pockets where two or three farms make a hamlet, scattered along the water's edge where one family occupies the only habitation. Over these widely separated houses and huts the winter storms howl, and between them piles up the deep and heavy winter snow. And yet there is not one single normal child in all Norway that does not get an elementary-school education.

The mere statement that illiteracy is less than one percent does not convey the incredible difficulties of such an educational triumph. While the school term in some rural districts may be limited to twelve weeks as compared to the urban twenty-one; while, during the winter, classes may be held only every other day; nevertheless, every child gets a seven-year course of solid fundamental instruction.

To the small red wooden schoolhouse planted, with its inevitable flagpole, at a point which may look utterly uninhabitated, but is a convenient (if such a word is possible) focus for the district, the children come on their skis. Sometimes a mother will carry the littlest one in her arms through the drifts. Sometimes a father will place his small daughter on a seat at the end of a pair of runners, plant one foot on the runner, and with the other, which is spiked, push through the snow. Whoever has read Magnhild Haalke's most painful, most powerful novel, *Alli's Son,* will never forget Alli, desperately straining over the oars, as every morning she rows her strange, malign, heartbreaking little Elling mile after mile over the waves which roar between their island cottage and the school on the mainland. Elling is finally left on the mainland to finish the term, just as many children—even quite young ones—must be left. When they are lodged at the school, the expense is met by the State or the county.

Despite the terrific obstacles in rural districts of getting the children to and from school, it never occurs to anyone to regard education as anything but an opportunity or, perhaps more accurately, as a right. The newspapers gave prominence (1938) to the case of an orphan who had been adopted by a farmer and had not been sent to school. When the boy reached eighteen, he not only sued his foster father but also sued the school authorities for permitting such negligence, and he demanded a large compensation, for he said, with conviction and earnestness, that he had been irrevocably wronged.

In a country where schooling is so prized, the public-school teacher is an important member of the community. In many of the red wooden schoolhouses in rural districts an apartment upstairs is part of his salary, and frequently a husband and wife are both teachers, he taking the older and she the younger children. Frequently such a man stays all his life in one locality and becomes an influential leader in politics. Often he becomes a Councillor in his municipality and not infrequently he is elected to Parliament.

People who from childhood are accustomed to sacrifice for an education and to honour teachers continue to prize learning throughout their lives. Besides the Folk High School for adults—where students must be at least seventeen years old and where the aim is to stimulate them to independent thinking and interest in general culture rather than to give them technical training or textbook courses—there is a host of study circles, leagues, and organizations and night schools. In every valley, town, and fjord hamlet, men and women form committees, work out programmes, procure leaders to conduct courses of study, and meet together in community halls, in young people's rooms, and in Labour Assembly Houses to discuss social, political, cultural, and economic problems.

And everywhere the people are readers.

They read the newspapers. The seven hundred thousand families of Norway subscribe to one million two hundred thousand newspapers—over two per family—and the press is free to such an extent that certain heated controversies are almost as exciting as criminal trials. They buy magazines and they patronize the thirteen hundred public libraries and the forty-seven hundred school libraries which are supported by the State. There are libraries on ships, in seamen's homes, and in churches in foreign harbours. The servant girl has a shelf of books in her room and the fisher lad finds a place for a few volumes in his boat. Publishers and printers and booksellers do a flourishing business in a country where it has been reckoned that every man, woman, and child reads between three and four books a year, and where even very expensive publications reach a wide sale through the instalment plan. No valley is too small to have its library and book store, and books are the most valued of gifts.

Although the conformation of the terrain, with its deep valleys and high mountains, presents technical difficulties which make broadcasting expensive, and although the length of the country is so great that the special high-frequency channel conducting the transmission from Oslo to Finnmark is the longest in Europe, the radio is busy disseminating knowledge. Starting as a private enterprise (1924) the Norwegian Broadcasting Corporation came under government control in 1933 and its educational department is indefatigable. It arranges series of lectures with supplementary "study notes," and these are delivered to groups all over the country who, under a leader, justify their name of "study groups." Scientists at the University of Oslo and at the Bergen Museum broadcast their lectures, and the public-school curricula are now being extended to include instructive radio programmes. Some of these are mutual exchanges between schools in different sections, the country children telling of their life on the farm and the fishermen's children of life on the fjords.

With a whole nation so educated from childhood and continuing its mental interests through maturity, it is not strange that from the Parliament House in Oslo should emanate laws designed to protect not the privileged classes but the proletariat, to take care of the sick, the unemployed, and the aged;

that the members of Parliament—many of whom have come from farms and fishing villages and many of whom have been teachers—should understand the needs of rural and seaside communities and should appropriate from the National Budget a greater sum for education than for defence. (In 1938, 53,445,000 kroner for the former and 51,726,000 for the latter.) It is not mere accident that the Parliament House, the University, and the Palace should be conspicuously placed in the centre of the capital city.

Everyone who comes to Oslo sees these buildings, but not everyone happens to see, in Frogner Park, a bust of Abraham Lincoln given by the people of North Dakota on July 4, 1914, with an inscription on the pedestal that "government of the people, by the people, for the people, shall not perish from the earth."

Oslo also recognizes another American belief—that the pursuit of happiness is the right of every human being.

On the hills of Holmenkollen and Ekeberg, which overlook the city and the fjord, are pleasant inns where the moderately rich and the moderately poor (which includes practically everyone in a country where stark destitution does not exist) find that relaxation which serves as hilarity in a land not given to undue demonstrativeness. To these simple resorts the father and mother and all the children and a few miscellaneous elders come by bus, electric tram, bicycle, and on foot, on Sundays and holidays. They stroll through the woods and picnic decorously. They sit, in European fashion, for hours over a four o'clock luncheon or a nine o'clock supper, or a cup of coffee or a glass of beer.

The longer vacations are spent as innocuously. Since the charwoman as well as the bank president is entitled to a two weeks' holiday with pay, tents sprout on the islands and islets in the fjord, camps spring up by pond and river, sails are white upon the bay, and bathers are bobbing in and out of the water. There are publicly and privately supported vacation homes for the children from poorer families. There are near-by allotment gardens, where for ten kroner a year the labourer can have his cabin and patch of garden for three months' occupancy.

No matter who or what a Norwegian may be, as a rule his idea of pleasure is enjoyment of Nature. Thus the very wealthy have their fishing- and hunting-camps in remote regions, and although they may ensure privacy by surrounding themselves with thousands of acres, their regime of life, in small log cabins, is as primitive as that of the farmer or the fisherman. The two books of Gösta af Geijerstam, *Northern Summer* and *Storevik,* are sunny testaments of a Norwegian family who, in sweaty toil, find fun and refreshment on their island farm, which becomes their fountain of health and a spiritual font to sustain them all their lives.

While there is in Oslo, as in all capitals, a certain amount of formal social and diplomatic entertaining, where scrupulous attention is paid to the proper seating of guests, to the etiquette of pouring the wines and serving the food, such occasions are restricted to a limited circle. And nearly every member of that circle has his fishing-camp or hunting-lodge, which he much prefers to his large town house. He may take a trip to the Continent in the spring, but in the summer he moves his family to the mountains, where they all get into their old clothes and go fishing. And he would rather sit down to a bowl of clabber or cream pudding and freshly caught trout than to any feast of Lucullus.

There are a few smartly dressed women who manage fashionable establishments, but they are very few compared to the plain-clad, strong-limbed majority.

As the Norwegian girls are strenuous playmates of the Norwegian boys and (since 1882) co-students with them at the University, so the women are matter-of-fact companions to the men in office, factory, and home. It was this relationship of straightforwardness between the sexes which not only baffled but alarmed the romantic Jerome venturing from France into this forthright Latitude of Love under the not unmalicious guidance of his creator, Maurice Bedel.

The clinging vine is not the national ideal, nor has it ever been, judging from the sagas. Although they had to submit to polygamy and were barred from the "Thing," the Viking women could become priestesses through inheritance, could annul the marriage contract as easily as their husbands, and were entitled to one-third property rights.

Almost a thousand years ago, the red-haired Freydis planned her own expedition to the New World, collected her own crew of men and women, and fought the Indians in hand-to-hand combat like any warrior. She did not scruple even to dispatch with an axe the five weaker sisters who displeased her. The gentle Gudrid also showed what stuff Norse women were made of. Mother of the first white child born in the Americas and of three bishops, she took her part in wild voyages from Greenland to America, from Iceland to Norway. She went on foot on a pilgrimage to Rome and back again and finally returned to Iceland and took the veil—a saga in itself.

On the streets of Oslo today there are so many firmly stepping young girls and older women who could be descendants of the intrepid Gudrid, that it is hard to see why Camilla Collett, whose graceful statue spreads its draperies on a pedestal in the Palace park, should have struggled so hard for the emancipation of women. However, it was a long time ago (1855) that she wrote *The County Governor's Daughters,* the first realistic Norwegian novel on marriage.

Women are now completely emancipated, with the franchise (since 1913), with complete control over their own earnings, and with members in Parliament and in municipal councils. If their numbers in these government bodies remain small, they are greater than those of the men in the population figures. Seeing the sensible women in the offices in the city, the hardworking wives of farmers and fishermen, and the efficient housekeepers and school teachers everywhere, one must believe that if there are still Noras living in Dolls' Houses, their plight is not due to the laws of the land.

Thus Oslo seats herself besides her fjord. A plain city, where the schoolmaster and the seafaring man, the farmer, and the fisherman, and the labourer make their ideas known in Parliament and their convictions prevail; where the boys and girls at the University come from city, village, and isolated valley; and where the king lives simply and converses directly with whoever wishes to speak to him.

CHAPTER THREE

Bergen and Its Musicians

BERGEN—the chief city on the west coast as Oslo is the chief city on the eastern border, the old capital as Oslo is the new; and the first silhouette of Norway seen by most travellers from America and England and the Continent—seats itself well behind a protecting network of skerries and fjords, channels and islands.

It builds itself along the harbour, and as boats throng and crowd up into the centre of the town, so pretty houses push and clamber up into the seven surrounding hills.

There is plenty of water all around Bergen. The sea edges it in an intricate ruffle of bays and beaches; the old Hansa quay and basin accompany its principal thoroughfare to the market-place. There is moisture in the air, rain in the clouds, and a deluge may be expected any minute of every day, so that the streets are clean, the foliage glitteringly green, and feminine complexions enviably clear. It may be that the sunshine chasing the showers and the showers drowning the sunlight have had an effect not only upon the externals but upon the moods of its inhabitants. If they seem more volatile, if musicians and painters and actors have not only lived here but found ap-

Bergen thrusts out her infinitely articulated fingers of rock.

Boats crowd up into the centre of Bergen and lie in the old
Hansa Quay.

preciation here, perhaps the temperamental climate has something to do with it.

In the midst of its newly washed freshness, the ancient landmarks—for more than any other city Bergen has preserved its old buildings—are pleasingly displayed.

The early sixteenth-century Town Hall, with its thick white walls and its black tiled roof, is still the headquarters of the burgomaster. And he still stamps official papers with a seal from 1591, bearing the same castle as did the original city seal of 1200. Although the fire of 1916 destroyed nearly the whole central part of the town, St. Mary's Church and the Cathedral (once a Franciscan monastery) survive in part from the Middle Ages. Rosenkrantz Tower and King Haakon's Hall in the Bergenhus Fortress on its seven-hundred-year-old site have been meticulously restored. The old City Entrance Gate with its arched opening straddles the tram tracks; and the timber chapel, as well as the long halls and small bedrooms of St. Jörgen's Hospital, still minister to a few inmates.

Although the new boulevards are broad and handsome, there are enough crooked, narrow thoroughfares to make one realize that he is in an ancient European city, and although Bergen is a thriving commercial port of more than a hundred thousand people, its modern business blocks conform not unpleasingly to the lines of the old warehouses and offices. Always a centre of culture—self-consciously so—the numerous and extensive museums are conspicuously placed, enhancing the skyline as worthily as do the spires and towers of the old churches.

Since the city is growing at the rate of a thousand inhabitants a year, villas and factories are being built up all along the water's edge. But enough of the present generation uphold the long-established tradition of good taste by suggesting the old forms in their roof lines and proportions so that the town is expanding as an organic and attractive unit.

Sentiment—and possibly an eye to tourists, for Bergen is the first port of call for nearly all of them—has preserved on the German Quay, Tyskebryggen, a crowded block of wooden buildings from those two centuries when this was the headquarters of the Hansa League in the north. Preserved and restored—for the section has been burned down four times. But since it has always been rebuilt in the same way with the same or similar emblems over its doorways, and since it is used for the same purposes, it is possible to see the actual manner in which people have lived, worked, and traded ever since 1070.

These blocks are penetrated by alleys of medieval narrowness, darkened by crazy roofs, eaves at all angles, and overhanging wooden galleries. Doors open into small dark cubbyholes, where women are cleaning fish and men are baling papers and all of them, judging from the smell, doing something with fish oil. Other stairs lead up to other cubby-holes, doubtless as dark and malodorous. Some of the walls are supported with solid wooden ribs, like a ship. Graved into a stone in one of them is "1719."

Leather fire buckets hang here and there, and there are signs to forestall the danger of any more fires than have already taken their toll. *"Tobakks rökning"* is *"forbudt."* In some places *"strengt forbudt."* According to a chalked up warning *"Drikking"* is also *"forbudt,"* although one might think this indulgence more apt to set fire to men than to buildings. Dark and dirty as is this congeries of entrances and exists, stairs and gables, this confusion of barrels and kegs, and this ingrained soil and soot and smell of centuries, they are more vividly illustrative than any museum reproduction.

The Hanseatic Museum, a little further down the street, is merely one of the fifty-two houses which once faced Tyske-bryggen. It has been cleaned up a bit, its original furniture and equipment reassembled, and a dried king codfish has returned to his throne as a mascot and decoration.

In cramped quarters, which are dark and cold even in mid-summer, the merchant had his office, his dining-room, his airless sleeping-alcove, and, upstairs, a private suite. The ap-prentices—who were not allowed to marry lest some part of the fish monopoly held by Germany should get into Nor-wegian hands—slept two in a bunk with four bunks in a cham-ber the size of a closet. It was crowded, but it was cosy, and they probably were in no haste, on a sunless winter morning, to get up and wash, even if this obligation was performed in the most entrancing brass hand basin filled with icy water from the most superb brass ewer. In the rear of this same building are the storerooms and living accommodations for a second merchant and his unfortunate apprentices.

The Hanseatic League filled a hiatus—caused by the Black Death and by political dissension—in the cultural and com-mercial life of Norway. Norway had to sell her fish and had to buy grain. The Germans organized trade and also stamped their impress upon buildings and society, furnishing one more stratum in the successive overlays which have given Bergen a cultural depth and solidity. Shut away by mountains from the rest of Norway, the isolated and busy community early developed local self-sufficiency. Communicating readily by sea with England and Scotland, Germany and Holland, she gath-ered cosmopolitanism.

Art, however much it may flout convention or defy provinciality, has a way of growing upon soil fertilized by centuries of inherited tradition. The money-scorning artist is sustained by patrons who are economically sound. The rich museums of Bergen testify to the development of painter and craftsman, and the long history of its theatre proves the vitality of its stage.

And the music of Norway is chiefly known to the world through two musicians born in Bergen.

Like other primitive people, the early Norwegians used horns for signalling in battle, for festivals and religious ceremonies, and some of these, dating from the Bronze Age, conical in shape, powerful in tone, and of great size and weight, are now in the Stavanger Museum. Harp-playing and minstrelsy were part of the education of the Viking nobles, and the sagas mention the "dialogue songs" and the scaldic poems recited at the royal courts. But whatever there was of an indigenous music was overlaid first by the music introduced by the Catholic Church in the eleventh century and then by the Reformation in the sixteenth, with its obligatory use of hymns in the Danish language. In the eighteenth century, concert life received its impetus from visiting foreigners, as when Gluck visited Oslo with an opera company in 1749.

It is understandable that Norway, being in union with other countries for centuries, did not develop an autochthonous music. And it is understandable that, after the separation from Denmark, the nationalistic feeling, expressing itself in every phase of public and private endeavour, should have begun to find its voice in the arts.

Beating upon the consciousness of philologists and patriots, it gradually pushed its tide into music. But although Waldemar Thrane (1790–1828) had produced the first dramatic-lyrical composition of national character, there was no independent production of Norwegian music during the first half of the nineteenth century. Composers and performers were bound by the Continental classical tradition. Ludvig M. Lindeman—an organist, composer of church music, and musicologist—commenced (in 1840) collecting native folk songs, vocal and instrumental, of which a thousand were subsequently gathered up. Ballads and stev-melodies (those with alternating stanzas), lullabies, love songs, seamen's chanties, drinking songs, hymns, even cattle calls, were unearthed and examined. The ancient instruments—the langeleik, which is a sort of dulcimer, violins, horns, and shepherds' instruments—were revived to accompany the jumping spring dance, the violent *halling* dance, the quieter *gangar,* and the infectious beat of the wedding marches.

Rikard Nordraak (1842–1866) dedicated himself to the nationalistic movement and composed the national anthem. But he did his country a greater service when he communicated his enthusiasm to one who was to embody it in the purest music Norway has known. For it was not the patriotic Nordraak who familiarized the world with these characteristic intervals and progressions, but two musicians, one of them older and one of them younger, but both of them claiming Bergen as their birthplace.

In a square that bears his name, a slim and fiery Ole Bull for ever plays his violin, with green leaves above his bronze head and a fountain below his feet, a "fair youth beneath the trees," who cannot leave his song. Through snow and rain, the bow sweeps the strings, drawing forth those unheard melodies which, we are assured, are sweeter than those heard.

The intoxicating airs, the passionate poetic tempo, which so captivated listeners of many countries have grown faint upon the phonographic records of remembrance. It was in 1880, when he was seventy, that Ole Bull laid down that bow which was so long and so heavy that a man of lesser build and height could not have conveniently wielded it.

In Bergen, he was permitted as a child to take part in the family quartets; as a boy he played first violin in the public orchestra; and from Bergen he went to the University at Oslo, presumably to study theology, but actually to conduct the musical and dramatic society. And here, in Bergen, where he was born and returned after a triumphal career to die, his bronze replica is properly placed.

There are elderly people in England and Ireland and Scotland, in Europe and all over North America, who remember the flashing-eyed, flaxen-haired virtuoso, whose towering height and magnetic personality contributed to the spell created by his playing. But "when old age shall this generation waste," Ole Bull, like all musicians who leave no enduring compositions but only reputation for performance, might, except for this statue, become merely one more name in the dictionary of music. It is gratifying to sentimentalists to think that in his birthplace stands the

> Happy melodist unwearièd,
> For ever piping songs for ever new.

Serious musicians and professional critics were inclined to disparage one so largely self-taught, so spectacularly successful and beloved. His tone was bad because of the thinness of his strings. He could, on the second and third strings, play only in the lower positions and then only *piano* because of the flat bridge. He was full of tricks and his taste was uncultivated. But the enraptured thousands knew better than the critics. They did not care if it was a flat bridge that made possible the miraculous rendering of chords and passages in four parts. They did not know that his staccato was brilliant up and down and his double-stopping perfect. They merely recognized that they were listening to a performance that had never been equalled in their lifetime, a poetic charm of playing that moved them as they had never been moved before. Critics or no critics, he had a power which is above the trickster as it is beyond the charlatan. By confining himself to simple Scandinavian airs and—except for one or two movements of Paganini—to his own ephemeral compositions, he saved himself from attempting interpretations beyond his capacity, and this self-imposed restraint resulted in a popularity that mounted to idolatry.

The same headlong emotion which carried him to such success on the concert stage broke through other floodgates. He planned and established a Norse Theatre in Bergen, he founded an Academy of Music in Oslo, and, full of compassion for the poverty of many of his countrymen, he organized a colony for them in the New World. He had been in America many times, had travelled a hundred thousand miles through it during his concert tours, and he commemorated these visits in his "Solitude on the Prairie," "Niagara," and "The Memory of Washington." His first wife was a Frenchwoman, but his second was an American.

Full of patriotism for Norway and idealism for the New World, he bought a hundred and twenty-five thousand acres in Potter County, Pennsylvania, added twenty thousand more to them, arranged for a hundred and twelve thousand more in the adjoining county, and celebrated the arrival of the first settlers by a speech on "A new Norway, consecrated to liberty, baptized with independence, and protected by the Union's mighty flag."

Whatever the brilliance of Ole Bull as a violinist, none can be granted him as a speculator in real estate. The hundred and twenty-five thousand acres were not only unsettled, hilly, and forested; were not only sixty miles from a railroad; but had the further and final disadvantage of not belonging to the swindlers from whom he bought them. The Utopian bubble of "Oleana" burst, and with it disappeared its founder's dream to have not only his own summer villa there but also a great polytechnic school, staffed with European professors, a civil and military institute opened to the youth of America. With it disappeared also most of his personal fortune.

Greatly distressed over the fate of the colonists he had persuaded to emigrate and with scant concern over his own financial plight, Ole Bull flung himself back into his concert tours, accumulated another fortune, and endeavoured to compensate the few Norwegian settlers who remained in the forlorn wilderness.

By a singular coincidence, the only one of the Norwegian emigrant songs and ballads which approached the rank of a folk song was "Oleana." At one time, every one was singing:

> In Oleana, that's where I'd like to be
> And not drag the chains of slavery in Norway.
> Ole—ole—ole—oh—Oleana,
> Ole—ole—ole—oh—Oleana.

It is well that Ole Bull is commemorated in bronze, for his genius, being entirely interpretative, depended—as all such genius before the days of phonographic recording—upon his presence, and his fame could hardly outlive the recollection of his last listener.

But the most gifted of Norway's musicians, with no such dynamic physique but a slight frame beset by ills, wrought out of invisible air the artist's only enduring commemoration—an original art.

Elusive and intimate as Grieg's compositions are, they hold, amidst the crash of more heroic concepts and mightier orchestrations, a fragile perpetuity. The best and the most familiar of his piano and violin sonatas and his bewitching *Peer Gynt Suite* are such unsullied reflections of a personality delicate, candid, and gay, that whoever visits his home, Troldhaugen, a few miles outside of Bergen, and steps into his study in the woods, feels an instantaneous adjustment between his art and the artist.

The approach is as it should be: an unspoiled road winding between hedges of clipped hemlock and elm, unpretentious gates opening into front yards, paths indicating half-hidden cottages, white picket fences confining a jostle of wild flowers and garden flowers—an idyllic introduction to the more secret less pruned paths of Troldhaugen.

There is little in the house itself, with its square tower, to attract the eye or detain the visitor. In a land where Nature has piled up such overpowering effects, architects have, apparently, given up the idea of competition. Except for the log cabin—as closely a part of the landscape as a lichen—the wooden dwellings of Norway, despite the substantiality they must have in such a climate, seem curiously temporary. It is not the house but the wild and yet gently lyrical setting of forest, fjord, and cliff which make Troldhaugen. Here, where the master would not permit a tree to be cut, a rock to be moved, or a fence to be built, where the underbrush grew as it pleased, for twenty summers Edvard and Nina Grieg entertained high companions. The living was simple, but the hospitality was prodigious. The house was plain, but the conversation and the music the best the world contained at the end of the nineteenth century.

The one-room log studio, down where the trees were even thicker and the briers and bushes even more tangled, secluded the little man with the intelligent and handsome head and those blue eyes whose dancing, glancing naïveté remained undimmed even in old age. As he sat in this small birchwood armchair, with this low stool under his feet, he looked out at the fjord, shifting from blue to grey, behind the white-trunked birches; at the sunshine on the red rowan berries, glittering into crystals through the rain. But he was seeing the shift of his own moods. As he rested his easily wearied body in this quite ordinary chair beside the stove, or stretched on this old-fashioned, rep-covered sofa, he heard the birds and the waves and the wind. But most clearly he heard the voices in that ear which, quite as much as the inward eye, is the bliss of solitude. And what he wrote down in piquant phrase and in a rhythm that was airy and yet frank, with a finesse that was precise and dainty, were the vivacious accents and graceful melodies of the subjective.

He had heard these accents since he was six years old and his mother taught him the theory of music and supervised his piano practice. When he was fifteen, his parents, at Ole Bull's suggestion, sent him for four years to the Leipzig Conservatory and here he heard those accents repeated in Schumann and Chopin. The melody must have been especially clear when he met the cousin who sang the birdlike songs and who was to become his fond and closely sympathetic wife.

It was at this period, between his twentieth and thirtieth years, that the inward music was more fresh, more overflowing, than it was ever to be again, and that its transcription was caught in phrases as pellucid as gems and shaped with gemlike precision.

The country where statues of musicians and actors are as honoured as those of soldiers and statesmen does not wait until its artists are dead before acknowledging their existence. Not only is Grieg's statue in the Town Garden in Bergen, but he himself received an annuity of sixteen hundred kroner from the Government (in 1874), and this made it possible for him to resign his eight-year conductorship of the Musical Union of Christiania, which he had founded, and devote himself almost exclusively to composition. To be sure, he still travelled. He went to Germany, Holland, and Denmark; he gave concerts in England; and in Paris he played and conducted his own works.

But these years more and more often saw the small figure climbing the paths of Troldhaugen and, for longer and longer hours, closeted in the log studio. And not only in summer. The leaves of autumn, the snowflakes of winter, the bird songs of spring—all of them were part of the music he was seeking to capture. He listened to the beating feet in peasant festivals in the village and peered out to glimpse the sprites who had given their name to Troldhaugen—the trolls' hill.

From where the waters of the fjord touch the edge of the forest, rises a sheer cliff. Rowing near it one autumn day, Grieg looked at the massive imperturbable face of stone and said:

"Here I should like to rest." When, not long after, the tired heart ceased to beat, his wish was remembered and fulfilled.

No artist could be as excellent as Grieg without being sorrowfully aware of his limitations. His was not the force of epic passion or the massiveness of synthetic power. His art was so intensely personal that it was, by its very nature, restricted. As he grew older, it did not grow broader, but, on the contrary, became increasingly concerned with detail, and what had been spontaneous originality in youth tended to become mannered idiosyncrasy in maturity.

To a nature as ingenuous as a child's, the folk songs of Norway made their appeal and through it worked out their unique interpretation. Grieg, inspired by Nordraak, turned to his native tunes and found in their short-phrased melodies thematic material congenial to his taste and a straightforward, vigorous rhythm suited to his capacity. So exquisitely did he adapt these traditional tunes, so glowingly fuse them, that his compositions are hardly distinguishable from genuine folk songs.

Thus, from being exclusively personal, his music became national, not less in his popular Norwegian wedding marches essayed by every piano pupil from that day to this, than in his exotic *Peer Gynt Suite*. That it never became universal may have been due to the simplicity of his own nature, for which the simplicity of the folk song was sufficient, and may have been due to the direction and emphasis he gave his powers. Daniel Gregory Mason, in his sensitive study, *From Grieg to Brahms,* suggests that, under different circumstances, Grieg's art might have developed differently. "Charmed by the exotic quality of Norwegian music, a quality that he found also in his own nature, he adopted the native idiom with eagerness, and spent the years most composers devote to learning the musical language in acquiring—a dialect."

Whether nationalism lifted Grieg above subjective romanticism, or whether it held him back from more universal utterance, it endeared him to a country whose music had been late in acquiring a distinctive character.

Music is a singularly direct expression of the composer's temper, taste, and intention. And time, which shreds away fashions, leaves the essentials of this art and of the one who created it. Edvard Grieg has nothing to fear from time.

In the cliff he loved was hollowed out a niche—a mighty tomb for a handful of ashes. But what was vital in Grieg lives in the freshness of his musical feeling and is revealed in the graceful sweetness of his song.

CHAPTER FOUR

Trondheim and Its Cathedral

E IGHT hours north of Oslo by Diesel train, thirty-two hours north of Bergen by fast mail boat, and two hours by airplane Trondheim—the third largest city in Norway—lifts the spires of the cathedral which dominates the nation's architecture and gives balance to the panorama of its history.

The trip by rail is a long-drawn-out succession of scenes growing progressively bleaker into a climate growing progressively chillier. The fertile Gudbrandsdal Valley folds itself away between its protecting mountains. The rolling country around Dombås, with its big farms and its little ones, recedes. The long white manor houses on sun-flecked slopes, suggesting hospitality and comfortable living, are replaced by smaller houses perched on naked foundations of rock or concrete. Instead of occasional hamlets where a country road holds in a curve a white church with a black spire settled down in a nest of cottages, there are widely separated houses of vertical clapboard construction—white or dun or cheerless grey—their pinched roofs, of uncompromising slate or tin, and presenting, as their only visible virtue, a determined neatness.

The farther north, the thinner the crops in the fields, the

barer the buildings, with never a shutter, never a porch, never a vine or a bit of shrubbery to soften their starkness. The higher the altitude, the fewer the trees. The evergreens give place to small birches and the birches give place to tussocked marshes. On some high meadows snow seems to be the only crop, but wire fences enclosing stretches of reindeer moss, lichened stones, and clear rushing streams indicate that even these acres are valued.

As the train approaches Trondheim, buildings gather a little more closely on the hillsides or along the zigzag roads. Smoke rises from the distant city and against the sky can be seen the cathedral which Kristin Lavransdatter, six centuries ago, saw as "so mighty, so gloriously shining, 'twas as though all things else lay prostrate at its feet."

If one comes to Trondheim by boat, the approach is (of course!) through the Trondheim Fjord, which twists its eighty-two miles of length through sides lower and less spectacular than those of the southern fjords.

Whether one comes to it by land or by sea, Trondheim seems very far away from Oslo and Bergen to be their immediate successor in importance and population; very difficult of access to have its royal origin—for it was founded by Olav Tryggvesson in 997—still acknowledged by the celebration of all the royal coronations here. However, the harbour is sufficiently busy and the section between the waterfront and the cathedral sufficiently built up to confirm at once all claims to consideration, while the exceptionally wide streets attest an established dignity.

At the end of the broad principal avenue, shaded with birches and chestnuts, stands the cathedral, the finest in Northern Europe, referred to with reverent awe in all Nor-

wegian literature and dating from the foundation of the town
when Olav Tryggvesson, ascending the throne, "bade all men
take up Christianity and those who spoke against it he dealt
with hard: some he slew, some he maimed, and some he drove
from the land."

It is a town of Olavs and of Olavs championing Christianity.
St. Olav (1015–1030) died fighting for the Cross, and his body
was taken to Nidaros (now Trondheim) and a church erected
over the grave. King Olav Kyrre ordered a stone church built
upon the site of the first wooden one. Begun in Roman style
in the eleventh century and finished in Gothic in the fourteenth, the famous cathedral is of greenish-grey soapstone.
Five fires, a Swedish capture, a storm which blew down the
great tower, and successive restorations have changed it considerably, judging from the early pictures which are preserved.
If it has grown less and less like the original edifice, it has
grown more and more like Gothic cathedrals elsewhere, so
that now it appears to the globe-trotter who has swallowed
Canterbury, Reims, Cologne, and St. Peter's, merely a smaller
morsel of milder flavour.

But the Trondheim Cathedral was not built for the twentieth century globe-trotter, and such a visitor enjoys its complete
and distinctive significance only by realizing what this elaborate pile has symbolized to a country which was long remote from civilized Europe and into which Christianity came
late, accompanied by fire and sword.

The old pagan gods were sufficient for the needs of the
Vikings. In a world of confused mythology, omens, dreams,
warlocks, and wizards, gnomes and sprites of earth and water
and air, Thor was one of the chief gods. All public meetings
were under his patronage and held upon his especial day—

On a column in the wooden city of Trondheim stands Olav
Tryggvason.

Edvard Grieg lives not only in his music but in small kinsfolk and namesakes.

Thor's day. The first Vikings to be converted by the new teaching took the precaution of still keeping on good terms with the Thunderer. Thus Helgi the Lean "believed in Christ but he invoked Thor for all seafaring and brave deeds," and another Norseman (from Ireland) was even more canny, for, after he was baptized, he "invoked Thor in voyages and whenever he thought it mattered most."

How long this intermingling of Christian and pagan beliefs and practices persisted is illustrated in the decorations of the early churches and memorials, both in the wood carvings in Norway and in the stone carvings in Britain. In the stave church at Bygdöy, which is eight hundred years old, the pagan dragon is shown with the Christian cross, and the sculptured stone crosses on the Isle of Man are engraved with the old mythology. The Gosforth Cross in Cumberland depicts a scene of the crucifixion with Loki in chains. "Prime-signing," or being marked with a cross, was a practical convenience for those Vikings who traded in Christian lands. All that was required was to have a priest make the sign of the cross over one. After that, the Norse merchants or soldiers "could mix with Christians as well as heathens while retaining the faith they liked best."

Those days when "the bloody shadow of Christianity rested over the heathen world," when "conversion to Christianity was the highest treachery against the heathen martyrs' ideals, sufferings and fate," when "Christianity was more loathsome than leprosy"—are far away from us now. Those who would visualize the champions of the White Christ pitching their tents outside the heathen temples, ringing their bells, chanting their Latin hymns, swinging their perfumed censers, and then—gathering boldness—forcing an entrance into the sanctuaries, despoiling the altars, destroying the figures of Odin and Freya, can hardly do better than to turn to the pages of Gudmundur Kamban's *I See a Wondrous Land*.

And those who would visualize what the Christian faith and the Roman Catholic liturgy came to mean to Norway during the succeeding centuries, and how this cathedral appeared to the Faithful, can hardly do better than to reread *The Mistress of Husaby*. When Kristin Lavransdatter made her pilgrimage from Husaby to Nidaros barefoot, in ashen-grey kirtle and shift of sackcloth, carrying her baby in her arms, she saw "the mighty wall masses with bewildering riches of pillars and arches and windows, the glimpses of the huge slopes of the roof, the tower, the gold of the spire far up in the sky-ey spaces." Humbly entering the doorway carved with monsters and twisted knots, she found herself in a vast nave where "the columns were furrowed like ancient trees, and in through the forest flowed the light, many-hued and clear as song, from the pictured windows."

For five centuries the Christian Church was the Catholic Church. It was during this time that Jorsalafarers, or Jerusalem-farers, took on foot the long pilgrimage to Rome. It was during this time that Nicholas Breakspeare, spending two years supervising church affairs in Scandinavia (1152–1154), organized the new archbishopric of Trondheim—Nicholas Breakspeare who was to become Adrian IV, the only English Pope in ecclesiastical history.

And it was during this time that cathedrals and monasteries and chapels and cloisters and convents were built at various strategic points, becoming centres of culture and art. Statues of saints were carved, antemensalia painted, metal hammered with all the zeal of converts and in the full florescence of Nor-

wegian art. In 1537 the Lutheran Reformation was introduced
—or, more accurately, dictated. Today, although the cathedral
at Stavanger is still standing, the ecclesiastical buildings at
Hamar are scattered in ruins along the shores of Lake Mjösa,
and the foundations of St. Halvard's Church and Olav's Cloister in the Old Town of Oslo are grass-covered. Fragments of
the stone capitals and heads of virgins and angels from the
ruins of the Munkeliv and Lysekloster monasteries, the Non-
neseter Convent, and various churches in and near Bergen are
in the Museum of Bergen.

But in Trondheim there are still plentiful reminders of
the time when Nidaros with its cathedral, nine churches, and
five monasteries, was the centre of Catholicism in Norway.
Some of these buildings have changed their names and some
have changed their uses. The Grand Palace of the Archbishops
behind the cathedral is now an armoury. Lutheran chorals,
not Gregorian chants, sound in Our Lady's Church. The island of Monkholmen, lying in the fjord near the entrance to
the city, is no longer the site of the Benedictine monastery of
Nidarholm. The monastery had been built in the eleventh
century over the spot where, years before, criminals had been
executed. On its ruins afterward a fortress was raised (1568).
The fortress gave place to a lighthouse, and thus from punitive
to ecclesiastical, to military, to life-saving, the island reflected
the cycles of change.

Severe and simple Protestantism suited the taste and temper
of the Norwegian people. If, after the Reformation, no peni-
tent Kristins came, barefooted, saying their prayers over the
wooded trails and rocky lanes, every man and woman and
child made the Sunday journey by boat or wagon or on foot
from farm to church or chapel. They listened to the hours-

long sermon and afterward to their neighbours' equally long gossip in the churchyard, which was club and caucus of the community.

A grave and godly Pietism pervaded workaday as well as Sunday life, with mealtime grace and the pastor a reverently regarded emissary of God. Björnstjerne Björnson so understood Haugianism—which, introduced by Hans Nielsen Hauge in the beginning of the nineteenth century, parallelled Puritanism in England—that he was able, in his play *Maria Stuart* to interpret John Knox. He would probably have been surprised to know that this luxuriant production, which Brandes notes as "welling over with dramatic life, but as noisily stagy as a melodrama," is not so valuable a portrayal of the spiritual life of the country as his early and simple stories. *Synnöve, Arne,* and *A Happy Boy* are more than the idyllic loves of young peasants. They are the deeper reflections of the religious faith of the people and their scrupulously observed religious routine.

On Sunday the farmer laid down his farming-tools and, no matter how the fish might come foaming into the fjord, no man would cast a hook—a custom which has held up and through the present age. Our old friend Markus the Fisherman usually gets up before daylight and hurries to his boat, but on Sundays he takes his time. "He washes his neck and hair and ears and changes the water several times to make himself as nice as possible. And the more he washes and scrubs himself, the higher his spirits rise: his eyes get as blue as the jug. He moves about smiling quietly to himself and revelling in the Sabbath and the peace around him . . . he gets into his Sunday-best. Blue duffel, every bit of it. He puts his watch in his pocket and fastens his tie carefully . . . and last of all he puts

a cloth on the table and tidies up. The Almighty appreciates
that you make some fuss of His day, and show you are grateful
for it."

The twentieth century has perceived much of this sober illumination "die away, and fade into the light of common day."
Although nominally 96.8 percent of the population is Lutheran, with marriages, births, and funerals solemnized by the
rites of the Church, the clergy find their congregations de-
creasing. To be sure, their salaries and old-age pensions are
fixed by law, so that they are economically independent of
their congregations. To be sure, the Church is supported by
the Government, absorbing twelve million kroner of the national budget. But in Norway, as in most Protestant countries,
church attendance, church festivals, and religious fervour grow
steadily less.

However, there are still certain great celebrations, and the
visitor who chances to be in Trondheim on Midsummer Eve,
Christmas, Easter, Pentecost, or King Olav's Day on July 29,
may see as many as four thousand people gathered in the
cathedral.

On such an occasion, every pew and chair is filled, the aisles
are jammed, the doorways blocked with pressing forms. The
organ peals as two deans, in rich vestments, and ten other
deans, in black gowns with white ruffs and narrow white wrist-
bands, walk down the aisle while the congregation, firmly
seated, looks straight ahead.

The two officiating deans take their places at the altar. The
ten other deans sit in a semi-circle around the chancel, five on
either side. One dean delivers the sermon. The others kneel
at the altar, their black and white figures stylized into effective
symbols against the reredos. The service lasts nearly two hours,

and during it the congregation, not kneeling to pray or rising to sing, sits immobile.

Perhaps, thinks the shivering intruder, they are past moving, congealed by the cold. He has been given to understand that the nave of the church can be heated by electricity and the rest of it by steam, but at midsummer he is convinced that the radiators are filled with ice water.

The light comes through the pierced stonework behind the altar and lies in pale patterns on the stone floor. The choir sings splendidly in rich, well-trained voices. The congregation —seated—joins in the hymns.

The visitor, wrestling not with the devil but with premonitions of pneumonia, wonders if King Olav in his tomb is any colder. Perhaps this icy draught is from that very tomb? No. It is only the breath of the June evening.

Upward to the stones which once listened to the Catholic Mass, rises the Creed, its cadence as unmistakable in Norwegian as ever it was in Latin. The people sit motionless. Whatever else they believe, they believe the calendar, which says it is June 25, instead of the thermometer, which says it is ten degrees Celsius—a triumph of faith indeed.

It is a faith with tolerance. Norway is a Lutheran country, but Roman Catholics, Quakers, Mormons, Jews, Seventh Day Adventists, Christian Scientists, and—more recently—Buchmanites—hold their meetings as and where they please. It is even affirmed that, in a cave in Leiradalen, pagan gods still sit unmolested in the darkness.

Religion is no longer the chief concern of Trondheim. The cathedral is honoured, but so is the Royal Norwegian Scientific Society, the oldest one in the country (1767), the new Technical College (1910), and all the accompanying institutions of modern hospitals, excellent schools, and comfortable homes for old people that characterize Norwegian cities.

The cathedral at Trondheim—which was the first stone building in the country—is, paradoxically, in the midst of what is the last large wooden city. White wooden cottages, white wooden palaces, white wooden shops, hotels, and offices —unlike many Norwegian towns built of wood, Trondheim manages to convey an air of solidity and age. And unlike most others, a certain decorative gaiety. The doorways are framed with carvings of scrolls and shells and crowns and garlands. The window lintels are carefully worked. Wood carving has touched cornice and fanlight, rail and balustrade, and white paint has made it into lace. Two, three, five centuries of painting have thickened the lacework, but much of it is still admirable. Sixty-odd years ago a law was passed against any more building in wood within the city limits, and some of the oldest specimens were moved to the outdoor museum a few miles away. Fire has taken its usual toll. But enough of the seventeenth century, and even of the sixteenth and fifteenth centuries, remains to make Trondheim almost a museum in itself, with the four immense snowy houses on the four corners of the principal street as its focus.

The largest of these was built by a widow who had long cherished the peculiar ambition to own the biggest house in Norway. Her husband discouraged this notion, but at his death she took his money—now hers—and built the tremendous barracks which, since 1704, when Bernadotte came to occupy it, has belonged to the king. The King's Palace, it is called, and to it the royal family come occasionally, and through it, for a fee, the visitor may be guided through acres of rooms as white as snow caves with wooden floors painted and polished;

through miles of hallways like tunnels of ice, up white stairs into white corridors. Wood is supposed to be warmer and to make possible a more even temperature than stone in this climate. One remembers the stone cathedral and fervently hopes that this is so. But, judging from the chill at a summer noon, wood in the walls and wood in the stoves—which are the only method of heating this ancient caravanserai—must wage a losing struggle with the winter thermometer.

Except for its size, the palace is not magnificent. The few carpets are a bit worn. On the first floor—used for guests— wash-stands and pitchers suggest that modern plumbing has not yet been introduced—which is the melancholy fact—while in the plain kitchen two old-fashioned ranges cook the royal banquets.

The first King of Norway and Sweden—the Field Marshal Bernadotte who had served Napoleon—is remembered by his portrait hanging here with the black curls around a strong, small-featured face and a blue ribbon across the breast. The present king's origin is honoured by the Danish furniture and Copenhagen porcelain in his study, and the late queen's by the fireplace (the only one in the house) and the English murals in her rose and gold tea-room. And the democratic habits of Norwegian royalty are suggested by the plain severity of the palace as a whole and by the unpretentious audience chamber, where anyone can have his conversation with his sovereign.

If the present town is an extraordinary display of wood, it is nothing compared to the town which preceded it. In the Scientific Institute are ancient dishes and platters and bowls of wood, water pitchers made of wood and bound with wood, keys and candlesticks, water basins and baptismal fonts—every kind of implement and tool made of wood. Excavations under Our Lady's Church brought to light a wooden pavement and wooden water pipes from the fourteenth century. Instruments of torture and execution from old Monksholmen are ingeniously contrived from wood. In the Marine Museum—in the same building—are wooden models of wooden ships, as well as fragments of old wooden masts and rudders and wheels, from the days when the harbour was white with sails and ships glided down the fjord without the chug of engines. At their prows figures carved from wood and painted realistically, strain forward or lean back, their eyes wide open and their wavy hair neatly parted.

The harbour and the waterfront are still busy parts of the city. But further back, on either side of the canal, is another section absorbed in other activities. Here ancient gambrel-roofed warehouses thrust their piles down into the water. Over the bridge stroll unhurrying pedestrians, jostled by an occasional motor-car or, more frequently, by a horse and cart. A not unpleasant odour drifts out from the sailmakers' and ship chandlers' shops, and a metallic clink from coal and coke yards and from the sheds where boats are being replenished and refitted. There are factories canning fish, factories making wood pulp, factories making shoes from hides brought in from the country, and factories making cigarettes and cigars. These last are small, but large enough to supply a fair proportion of what Norway smokers need or, at least, what they can pay for, for the price of a package of cigarettes makes an American blanch.

Outside the city the suburbs extend with parks and apartment houses, shops and schools, bringing the population of sixty thousand up to eighty thousand. Beyond the suburbs are farms, and from the falls of Lerifoss the big electric station sends light and heat and power to them all.

On a column in a central square stands the statue of Olav Tryggvesson, who founded the city—Olav Tryggvesson, "the most wildly beautifullest man" Norway has ever seen.

Born into the royal family, he had, as an infant refugee, been smuggled across to Orkney. He had been a slave in Esthonia "bought for a good cloak," had been a ward of the Russian Court, a campaigner in Pomerania, and then the free-lance commander of a fleet. "King Olav," says the saga, "was the gladdest of all men and very playful, blithe and forgiving, very heated in all things . . . bold before all in battle, but very gruesome when he was wroth and his foes he tormented much." His first wife had died, and when he was in England he heard of a queen called "Gyda, the sister of Anlaf Cuaran, who was King of Dublin in Ireland . . . she had been married to a mighty earl in England: he was now dead, but she ruled the land after him. Messages were sent all over the land summoning a Thing, so that Gyda should choose herself a husband." Olav, with some companions, went to the Thing under a false name and "wore his bad weather clothes covered with a shaggy cape." "Gyda went and looked over every man who seemed to her manly. And when she came where Olav stood, Gyda asked, 'Wilt thou have me? So will I choose thee!' 'I will not say nay to that,' he said. Olav then wed Gyda and stayed in England, though sometimes in Ireland." Gyda, that "young and handsome woman," vanishes from the narrative when Olav returns to Norway to ascend the throne and presumably to wed a fresh consort.

Now the hero, whose name has been shouted so lustily by

choral societies for generations, stands upon his column offering the fire of Christianity in one hand while observing the precaution of gripping his sword with the other.

If Norwegian leaders today do not brandish the cross so vehemently, neither do they grip the sword. If Norway as a whole is not fervently demonstrative in its religious observances, it is remarkably consistent in its Christian standards, in its dealings within and without its borders.

Ancient Trondheim, with its cathedral, its tomb of St. Olav, and its statue of Olav Tryggvesson, symbolizes the mystical interpretation of Christianity. Modern Trondheim, with its institutions of science, education, and social service, symbolizes its modern practicability.

There have always been compromises and contradictions in men's hearts since the days when it was asked: "Hast thou heard how Thor challenged Christ to a duel?"

CHAPTER FIVE

Another Language

O SLO in the east, close to the Swedish border and to Denmark and conscious of its political eminence; Bergen in the west, looking across the North Sea to England and cherishing its traditions of Continental culture; Trondheim in the north, to which Christianity brought the first literary language the country had known—if Norway's three principal cities still, in this age of communication, retain distinctive differences, how much greater those differences must have been a few centuries ago!

To the superficial observer travelling from east to west, from north to south, Norway seems a remarkably unified country. The land is a geographical unit, the people homogeneous. Education is universal and the tastes and necessities of everyone sufficiently similar to allow for the formulation and enforcement of laws for the greatest good of the greatest number.

To be sure, there are certain paradoxes, such as snow in midsummer, sunshine at midnight, pigs eating seaweed, foxes eating whale meat, wedding rings worn on the right hand, and eggs sold by the pound. There are contrasts, climatic and cultural, between the bleak mountains of Nordmark and the smiling meadows of Telemark. But the similarities are more apparent than the differences. There is, however, one contradiction which does—and very soon after his arrival—puzzle the foreigner.

The encyclopædic bi-monthly time table—as indispensable to every house as a telephone directory—contains not only the schedules for trains all over Norway, but their connexion with the Continent, England, and Sweden, and supplements this vast aggregation of data with an intriguing variety of symbols.

Tiny crossed knives and forks indicate stops where hot food can be had, while a goblet signifies cold dishes and beverages. A frontier station with customs and passport examination is represented by the sketch of a building, sleeping-car accommodation by a bed. Motor-car, airplane, boat, and train connexions are marked by pictures of these conveyances, while wireless telephones and radio receivers on the train, an infinitesimal envelope for one class of mail and a postal horn for another, make the tracing out of a route (incidentally the Norwegian word for this time table is *rutebok*) as much fun as solving a series of rebuses.

But with all these concessions to the international language of pictures, when it comes to Norwegian itself, there is no such consistency. The same time table may spell the same place in different ways. It apparently makes no difference if a passenger buys a ticket for Hanastad or Hanestad, Marok or Merok, and the train that bears him toward Undset or Unset, Grundset or Grunnset, warns him *"Böyd deg ikkje ut"* in one compartment, and *"Laen Dem ikke ut"* in another. For more intimate moments he is classified under *"Herrer,"* *"Mann,"* *"Menn,"* or *"Maend."*

These discrepancies are not confined to printed notices to

the foreigner. Oslo makes fun of the speech of Bergen. Trond-heim is Trondhjem to certain Trondheimers or Trond-hjemers.

If these things were merely echoes from the day when Dan-ish words and spelling came in with Danish dominance, they would be readily comprehensible. But the deeper one probes, the more complicated the situation becomes. There are, briefly, two languages in Norway—Landsmaal and Riksmaal. But this is not because of different nationalities, as in Ireland, or because of two distinct races, as with the French and Flem-ish in Belgium, and the Swedes and Finns in Finland. And, says Dr. Didrik Arup Seip, Rector of the University of Oslo, it is not entirely because of the period of union with Den-mark.

There is only a single nation in Norway and the struggle is between two language forms which have closely influenced and are still influencing each other. The one is rooted partly in Danish and partly in the native tongue, and the other is a newer, literary language, founded on the archaic country dia-lects. Although comparatively few foreigners learn Norwegian, this situation is extremely interesting to whoever wants to un-derstand the country. For the origin of the cleavage is rooted in Norwegian character, and the history of the struggle is the history of Norway.

The terrain of dividing mountains, of parishes split by fjords, of districts separated into valleys, of islands far from the mainland, has not only fostered but forced an individualism which gives colour to and infuses a stubborn selfsufficiency into every group.

"Everybody knows it is the mainland that counts," writes Gabriel Scott in his *Burden of Iron,* "and, therefore, those who live on it are apt to look down their noses at the islanders, whereby much enmity and envy are created. For the islanders are no less apt to think they are human beings, too . . . they have sheep and cattle . . . and they hear the news from all the ships they board and get to know a thousand things that escape others' ears . . . the little kings pull on their water boots and go out on to their stair and spit into the sea."

Although Scott's novel depicts only South Norway and only the period around 1768, this situation remains true, in a measure, today. Each fragment of a parish vies with the other. "Each man is filled entirely with his own self-interest and no one cares the least bit for his neighbour, nor for the parish as a whole. The little kings make war upon each other—those on the mainland and those on the islands, too. Each one is set wholly on his own advantage and at the same time he is afraid to put his ounce into the scale lest someone else may have some advantage of that ounce."

That co-operation as a practical commercial arrangement between producers and consumers should have become so firmly established and, in some of its organizations, even more highly developed here than in any other Scandinavian country, is a triumph of reason over instinct. The farmers and merchants get together in business for their common advantage, but when it comes to vocal communication, each glories in his native—and of course superior—manner of speech.

The distinctions which the terrain created were emphasized by historical events. Thus Bergen, the royal residence and the most important city during the eleventh, twelfth, and thirteenth centuries, held onto her Westland speech and customs even after the king had moved to Oslo, which had been more or less outside and in loose relation to the rest of the country, and had had, through long periods, a separate government. She held on, even after the economic centre was shifted and the government bureaux transferred, and the former Provost of St. Mary's Church in Bergen became King's Chancellor in Oslo and established there his office with its archives. The official archives might be moved to Oslo, but the official language, which was formulated about 1270, was in a codex composed at Bergen in the Westland form.

The linguistic conflict was not merely between east and west. From the middle of the twelfth century the Trondheim district began to compete with the Westland as a political centre. The city of Nidaros became the ecclesiastical focus, and the language written at its chapter bears the stamp of the region. With the ravages of the Black Death, which was particularly virulent in the west and the north, and particularly disastrous to the clergy and educated classes, the scribe's craft declined and the Eastland region gained in power. All these historical shifts are reflected in a linguistic struggle the participants of which had been set apart long before by the barriers of terrain.

Superimposed upon these rivalries from inside were influences from outside. In the Middle Ages Norway included a larger portion of the Scandinavian Peninsula than it does today. The powerful district of Bohuslan, holding one-tenth the population of Norway, was on the boundary of the then Danish province of Halland—and both are now Swedish. Naturally, there was a constant intermingling of related, neighbouring tongues. Added to this borderland influence in the east, the Low German of the Hansa in the west helped to prepare the way for the Danish.

At the time when Norway became politically dependent

Alleys of medieval narrowness penetrate a block of buildings
from Hansa times.

The log house does not compete with Nature, but becomes part of it.

upon Denmark, she had no unified power to guide the growth of an official language out of her many dialects. Since her old literary language was antiquated and unintelligible to the masses, it was understandable that the Danes should use theirs in treating with the Norwegians. It was logical that by the end of the fifteenth century Danish should be the official language of Norway.

Although the language of the Church and the Law remained Norwegian (also that of the lower administrative bodies, as well as letters between individuals), these could not withstand the mighty effect of the printing-press and the Reformation. Denmark had its first printing-press about 1480—more than a century and a half before Norway got hers. Therefore, when the Reformation came to Norway, the accompanying religious literature was written and printed in Danish. The Church catechisms (1537), the translation of the Bible (1550), the altar Service Book (1556), and hymnbook (1568), were sent out from Copenhagen.

While legal phraseology was slower to admit Danicisms, while certain individuals held to the Norwegian speech, while writers drew elements from both, it was inevitable that Danish should become predominant.

It was equally inevitable that, after the two countries were no longer joined, one faction in Norway should wish to get rid of all remembrance, linguistic or otherwise, of the hateful centuries; inevitable that another faction should wish to retain the cultural advantages of the association.

While the latter made every effort to keep "the king's Danish" as the model for polite society and for the schools, the theatre, and the pulpit, the former began to emphasize the suitability of Norwegian for Norwegians, stressing the belief, recently made popular by Rousseau, that the spoken idiom of the peasant was the true, vigorous, and proper basis for any national speech.

Only philologists will today go back to trace the long and complicated struggle and measure how much Landsmaal—the spoken language of the people—owes to the poet Henrik Wergeland, to writers and editors such as Peter Christen Asbjörnsen and Jörgen Moe, to orators and statesmen, and to the reformer Ivar Aasen. What principally emerges is confusion. Landsmaal was not pure and indigenous Norwegian, and Riksmaal was not the uniformly superimposed Danish. Landsmaal was a synthetic language, compiled by Ivar Aasen from dialects in the mountain valleys and western fjords which he believed nearest to Old Norse. In his determination to get away from the Dano-Norwegian Riksmaal and from Eastland dialects, he ignored the broad Eastland highlands and the towns. Thus, his Landsmaal did not unite all patriots, but divided the eastern from the western.

Neither can Riksmaal be precisely defined. It is not only a mixed language, founded on both Danish and Norwegian speech with important contributions from the east and the southeast, but it is also in a state of constant change. Conscious Norwegianizing—the decrease of foreign elements, the increase of native ones—and the rise of the lower social orders affected it. Both Ibsen and Björnson endeavoured to bring living, everyday speech into the more static literary form, but Ibsen inclined to the speech of the town and Björnson to that of the country.

From the middle of the nineteenth century Riksmaal and Landsmaal have not only been developing and changing each along its own line, but also constantly influencing each other.

Since the end of the last century a great deal of the theoretical opposition to the Norwegianizing process has been overcome. But there is still bitterly differing opinion as to the best way of accomplishing this. As Dr. Seip points out, the Landsmaal champions are frequently ignorant of linguistic history, imagining Riksmaal to be purely Danish, and too often they fight against peculiarities which have found their way into Riksmaal but are, in reality, truly Norwegian. The Riksmaal champions, equally ignorant of linguistic history and of country dialects, do not appreciate the need from which Landsmaal sprang.

The patriotic sentiment and mental confusion of both parties have been reflected in conflicting laws, in contradictory spellings, and, most disastrously, in the different public schools. While one-sixth of the population has voted for Landsmaal in the primary schools, the rest of the country districts and the towns have Riksmaal. The matriculation examinations at the University and at the teachers' seminaries require tests in *both* forms. But while all children are supposed to be able to read both forms (and those in the higher schools to write them) the principles of orthography are different in each, so that what is correct spelling in one is incorrect in the other. Furthermore, while most of the young people's associations in country districts support Landsmaal, this does not apply to country districts on the East Coast. While the towns favouring Riksmaal are increasing and, with the urbanization of settlements around quarries and developed waterfalls, now affect a third of the population, the national youth associations in the towns stubbornly support Landsmaal.

Nationalists, educators, and linguists all profess themselves eager to reduce the differences between the pronunciation and the spelling and between the two language forms. The Riksmaal champions advise the Landsmaal champions to broaden their narrow foundation and to stop emphasizing the archaic forms. The Landsmaal champions are generous with their advice that the Riksmaal followers should Norwegianize their Danicisms.

Dr. Seip's ideal is a language uniting all Norway and not too difficult for other Scandinavians to understand, and he believes that progress towards this goal is being made. But the progress is still accompanied by a fair amount of dust. The roots of the controversy are held in Norway's geography, are nourished by Norwegian temperament, and entangled in Norwegian history. It is possible they will be most effectively untangled not by further argument but by the mechanism of steadily improving communication.

For if there is nothing like a "nationalistic movement" to split a nation into factions, there is nothing like a railway— or even a highway—to bind it together.

The differences between Bergen and Oslo and Trondheim are greater than actual mileage would indicate. Until 1933, it was impossible for a motor to go more than twenty miles outside of Bergen, and even now there are only about seventy miles of connecting roadways not broken by ferries. The only communication between the cities was by boat until 1909, when the Bergen Oslo Railway was completed—that prodigious engineering feat which had to tackle ascents of over four thousand feet, a hundred and seventy-eight tunnels, and such a series of grades, curves, and bridges, and such a problem of snow and ice, as to keep the tracks continually twisting and the passengers continually oh-ing and ah-ing.

Now there are daily trains between Bergen and Oslo, taking eleven hours for the trip, another trunk line between Oslo and Trondheim, and various smaller branch lines. The invisible barriers of Landsmaal and Riksmaal may divide East from West, North from South, and country from city, but visible iron rails are doing their best to unite them. It is for this unification and not for profit that the Government runs the railways.

Only a little over two hundred miles of railways in Norway are in private hands, and these are subject to Government supervision. All the rest are Government-owned and since 1928 have been run at a loss. In fact, they do not even pay interest on their tremendous investment. They have been built, are maintained, and are being improved—10 percent of the system is electrified—for the convenience of the people.

The locomotives are smaller than those in the United States and so are the flat cars and goods vans and carriages. These last are built in compartments and are so similar to the English model that one is a little surprised to be warned that *"sigaretter"* and *"sigarer"* are not to be *"kast ut"* of the *"vinduet."* Capacity is of course marked in kilos and metres on the outside of the freight cars, for Norway has long ago adopted the logical simplicities of the metric system.

But there are more likenesses to home travel than differences. Not only does the *konduktör* speak better English than the Cockney Englishman or the nasal American, but the passengers with their zipper bags and spectacles look entirely familiar, as do the people waiting on the station platforms, lapping ice-cream cones or sucking soft drinks through a straw out of a bottle.

Over and up and down and around those mountains, which

were so long accepted as everlasting dividing lines; along those valleys which were as separated from each other as if they were canals on Mars; skirting the fjords which sunder land and water, the trains go puffing. And if some of their printed notices still confuse the stranger, and if the adherent of Landsmaal snorts at Riksmaal spelling, nevertheless he travels from east to west, north to south, country to city, and what all the eloquence of philologists and nationalists fail to do must gradually be accomplished by the wheeze and whistle of a steam engine.

If Norway—which, so far from being small, exhibits greater distances than any other country in Europe except Russia—has less than twenty-five hundred miles (3998 kilometres in 1937) of railways, this does not imply that she is laggard in the matter of communication. Quite the contrary. Instead of completing the full circle of over-expanding her railroads and then finding herself in difficulties of finance, of competition by motor highways, and of duplication by bus lines, she never drew a full circle at all. Instead, she drew an arc here and there, connecting certain points and supplementing the principal routes by boats and buses.

While this was due to obstacles of terrain, it has resulted in a system of communication not only economical and efficient but full of variation and interest for the foreigner.

Boats are and always will be the chief transportation agents essential to a country whose communication with every other —except Sweden and, for a few negligible Arctic miles, Finland—is by water. And they are equally essential between various parts of Norway itself.

In the harbours of Oslo and Bergen dock the great freighters and passenger steamers and motor-liners and cruise ships.

They debouch Englishwomen, with luggage they must have inherited from great-uncles who came back from Mafeking, and American women, with voices they must have inherited from Comanche Indians. They debouch Scotsmen in tweeds and Frenchmen in berets. They debouch wardrobe trunks and their owners and guide books and their readers. Taxis meet and whisk away this miscellany to the fashionable, semi-fashionable, and not-at-all-fashionable hotels.

Such boats and such tourists are familiar sights in every harbour of the world. But the flocks of small local steamers which come and go, their numbers and frequency graded according to the size of the settlement, although their schedules are maintained with conscientious regularity—these are especially and delightfully characteristic of Norway.

There is a never-failing fascination in watching the fishing-boats and private yachts and particularly the small coastwise craft and the local ferries gathering, congregating, and finding their berths along the harbour fronts in Bergen, Oslo, Stavanger, and Trondheim.

They unload milk and cheese and carcasses of pigs, and wood and hay, and they load gasolene and merchandise and an occasional automobile. The crew swabs the deck, paints the deck-house, shines the brass, and scrubs the white sides to greater whiteness. Stewards set up the wicker chairs for passengers and lay the long table in the dining-saloon. People gather to see the boat come in, and the same people—or are they others?—gather to see it leave. Drays pulled by one horse, two-wheeled carts pushed by one man; a few lorries and a motor-car or two unload crates and cans, barrels and boxes, and amorphous bundles. There is no congestion, no excitement, but a steady activity. Warning-bells ring and starting-whistles blow, not too loudly, and the boats draw away, not too quickly.

They steam out of the harbour, down the fjord, out between the islands, and up or down the coast into other fjords, to other islands. And there, as each one draws up to its appointed pier in some town of eight hundred houses, or a hamlet of a dozen, or alongside a wharf where only one cottage is visible, there are people to meet it. To pretty, populous villages, to treeless islands beyond the Polar Circle, the little steamers go chugging, carrying mail and merchandise and news and passengers, picking up fish and berries and wood and other passengers, always looked for, always welcomed, always concentrating on the business in hand. Among all the modern vehicles of transportation these are likely to remain longest unchanged. There will always be need of them as long as these thousands of miles of waterways connect settlements inaccessible by land, at least until that possible day when fleets of small aquaplanes will dart like dragonflies through these watery channels.

The ocean liners, whose proportions have grown so large and whose appointments so luxurious, may—although it is hard to imagine precisely how—alter their shapes, improve their machinery, replace their modernistic decorations by others more—or possibly less—modernistic. The trains, pushing up and down the mountains, through tunnels and over bridges, may become streamlined—or some other kind of lined—or may disappear entirely, as has happened in certain parts of the United States. In any case, many places in Norway will escape the railway era.

As for the motor-cars—who can imagine what they will look like after the inventors and industrial designers and gadget-makers have let their imaginations play over them for a few more decades? At present, they look very much the same in Norway as they do anywhere else. And since they have begun to thread the highways, and in some places the byways, the Government supports a road system which supplements and does not compete with the railway. Although the expense and difficulty of building motor-roads duplicate those of building railways; although it is necessary to burrow through tunnels, bridge rivers, zigzag up mountainsides, blast ledges across the face of cliffs, and dodge waterfalls, nevertheless, it is possible to motor through the interior of Norway.

Motorists who are irked by the niggling tax charges—10 percent on lodging and 20 percent on food—may become more philosophical regarding this annoyance if they remember the tremendous Government expenditure road-building has entailed. If they don't want to be philosophical, they can—and if they are Swedish or English, they frequently do—retaliate by driving on the left side of the road. When such a visiting motorist gets cracked up, it may be because in an emergency he has automatically reverted to his national custom of left-hand driving, and it may be that he is taking a chance at side-swiping one of the Storting members who voted for the present sales tax. There really are no other excuses for accidents on thoroughfares that are astonishingly many and good.

But although motor-highways are being yearly pushed further and further, there are still hundreds of miles of country roads which have never felt the pressure of a motor-wheel; hundreds and hundreds of villages which have never seen a car or heard the honk of its horn. There are still plenty of places in Norway where the horse-and-cart offers the only method of transportation. And to many a foreign visitor it offers more than that. It offers an intimate adjustment—long forgotten or never known—of man to earth.

The ponies of Norway are sturdy and willing; the two-wheeled carts or four-wheeled carriages are rubber-tired. In those regions where no sound of a railway train has ever been heard, no dust of a motor has ever been seen, one may drive hour after hour and savour a Norway hidden from travellers behind the glass of train windows and imperceptible to even the most leisurely motorist.

At four miles an hour one smells the drying hay and the milky breath of the cows lifting their heads from the fragrant clover, and sniffs the acrid odour from the turf-roofed blacksmith shop. The grades, the curves of the road, the texture of the gravel or the sand or the clay beneath the wheels, assume interest; the dampness from the water-drenched rocks, significance. Trotting at eight miles an hour along the level stretches, it is possible to hear the click of a hoe as a blue-overalled boy weeds the precious potato plot, the snap of grasses as sheep and lambs graze on an open space sloping to the edge of the road, the clatter of their hoofs as goats come to the edge of a rocky shelf to waggle their beards. Not only the crash of the heaviest waterfall but the whispers of the lightest ones, the swish of their spray, the rattle of the pebbles they loosen—such voices are not audible above the clank of train wheels or the hum of a motor.

There is always plenty of room in the smallest cart to stand up without bending and get out without ducking. There is always plenty of time when travelling a few miles an hour, time to get out and pick an unfamiliar leaf or a flower and to define it at leisure, to buy coffee and cakes and to water the horses. To travel through rural Norway by horse and carriage is as different from motoring through it, as spending absorbed weeks turning the pages of *David Copperfield* is from seeing the story flash by on the screen as part of an evening's entertainment.

Whether one travels by train or boat, by motor-car or carriage, or, joining the sportsman, becomes a tramper with a rucksack, Norway is opening up more widely every year. While these extending channels of communication are merely added conveniences as far as the foreigner is concerned, they hold deeper significance for the Norwegians. Provincial prejudices and local jealousies grow less. If it is regrettable that certain colourful distinctions fade in the increasing illumination of such progress, perhaps this loss will be counterbalanced by the advantages of increasing unification.

Nowadays, even the most obstinate partisans find themselves, almost without knowing it, whisked by train or bus into erstwhile enemy territory, and it may not be long before Landsmaal and Riksmaal will find that they have compromised their differences.

CHAPTER SIX

Roofs and Rafters

THE eye of the stranger in Norway is always caught by the pagoda-like roofs and spires of the wooden stave churches. Their beauty may be debated, but their peculiarity is striking.

A series of shingled roofs in steeply sloping tiers are topped by an ornate wooden tower, the Oriental suggestion of the outline heightened by dragon heads rearing from the gable ends of the ridge pole.

Of the seven hundred and fifty of these stave churches existing at the end of medieval times, of the two hundred and four surviving until the beginning of the eighteenth century, there are only twenty-four left. Recalling that they are built entirely of wood—in many of them wooden pegs and "knees" take the place of iron bolts and braces—it is remarkable that even this number should have withstood eight or nine centuries of storms, snows, frosts, fires, and inevitable vandalism. But besides these twenty-four, which are now preserved as national monuments, besides fragments of many others and miniature models in the museums, the style has been so frequently reproduced—or at least suggested—in new buildings, that it has become popularly associated with the country in the average visitor's recollection.

Reluctance to admit that anything—from an architectural style to a syllable—has grown from the soil on which it now flourishes, and insistence that it must have been "transplanted" from somewhere else, seems an ineradicable human tendency. Archæologists triumphantly detect a foreign origin or influence for every column, roof, and door. Ethnologists hound a race which has been contentedly living for thousands of years on the same spot back to some other remote and dissimilar spot. Philologists pounce upon the plainest word and prove that it is trailing clouds of linguistic glory, if not from a heavenly, then from an equally remote earthly home.

Therefore, the stave church, since it resembles similar forms in Russia, Bohemia, Hungary, and Germany, is often credited to the fact that the early Norwegians were constantly sailing to the Orient, Constantinople, Persia, Palestine, and Italy, and bringing back ideas from these distant lands.

Professor Haakon Shetelig, of the Bergen Museum, however, has a different explanation. Stave means a mast, and originally the Norwegian church was merely a room without aisles and with its roof supported by columns or staves. The frame was sturdily constructed by ships' carpenters who used knees in the support of joints and locked planks together just as they did in building a ship. In order to protect the outer walls from the weather, cloisters were hung from the rafters, their roof line giving the silhouette which, by accident, suggested the pagoda.

The *svalgang*—or narrow corridor—surrounded the entire building, with an abruptly pitched roof which protected not only the main walls of the church, but the church-goers as well, as they met there before and after service to talk and doubtless to engage in a bit of Sunday trading. The part of the svalgang nearest the entrance was the weapon-house, where spears and axes and bows could be stored while the worshippers were within.

As the roof of the weapon-house overtopped that of the entrance, so did a whole series of other roofs go slanting upwards at different levels but in harmonizing angles: roofs of ambulatory and choir, of apse and nave, and, finally, the spired or one- or two- or three-tiered "roof-rider," not so much for a belfry—the bells were usually hung in a separate tower near by—as for an ornamental finish. Shingled in elaborate or curious designs, this pile of roofs suggests a stack of hats, placed one on top of the other, their shaggily textured brims growing smaller and smaller and the whole array crowned by the plume of the roof-rider.

But although the primitive unit developed into this more complex form, the stave church, says Professor Shetelig, remained absolutely functional. Solidly knit together by superb craftsmanship into an indivisible whole, it is, nevertheless, elastic, yielding to the wind so that, on those which have a bell tower on the roof, the bells will ring in a storm but will rarely be blown down.

The builders were extremely particular about the timber they used, selecting, two or three years before cutting, the trees they wanted, so that the sap would run out and the inner wood harden. This material gave opportunity to the woodcarvers to intertwine dragons and crosses and every sort of mythological and Christian symbol, creating those portals and altars, beam ends and pillar capitals, of intricate and lavish ingenuity, which are among Norway's most valued art treasures.

One would like to agree with Professor Shetelig that the stave church is indigenous to Norway, for it is interesting in both form and material and admirable in construction and, except for it, the country is but meagrely supplied with impressive or original architecture, either old or new.

The cathedral of Trondheim was the first stone building of any pretension, and while this was, and is, a splendid example of both architecture and decoration, it is young compared to ancient temples elsewhere, and it is in the conventional European tradition. The Norman and Gothic churches, monasteries, cloisters, and convents were numerous and, judging from their ruins, nobly built and handsomely embellished. But the Danes sailed off with much of the cut stone to build their own churches, and the Reformation obliterated much of the Catholic decoration. Except for fragments in museums, except for a few churches and towers—notably in Bergen— there is little left to make an impression upon the visitor.

The true, the functional, the original Norwegian architecture was the log building, and in the Outdoor Museum of Sandvig at Lillehammer and, to a less extent, but still with remarkable variety and authenticity, in the Outdoor Museum of Bygdöy at Oslo, examples of these houses from every region and from every period have been collected, repaired, and restored, furnished and fitted in their original manner, and made accessible to the public.

The oldest houses, like the newest modern apartments, adjusted all the necessary apparatus of living into remarkably small space. Like them, they had built-in furniture and used the living-room for dining. The doors were as low as those in the latest motor-cars and necessitated the same bending of the head. Although each valley had its characteristic style, they all had certain similar features. The floor was of earth and the roof was of turf. Under the turf was birch bark and tar, and upon it was grass. Wooden floors came later, so did windows with glass, and so did pewter dishes instead of wooden ones. The fireplace, which had been merely a hearth in the centre of the floor, was moved into the corner. The short beds—for they were not intended for full-length lying, but for half-sitting-up against pillows—were sometimes completely closed by two tight doors, and if the sleepers were practically without air, they had privacy and the satisfaction of knowing that the inside of their breathless cubicle was decorated as elaborately as the outside.

In the very earliest houses the only ornamentation was that of carving. And what cannot be done with wood and knife during the evenings that are twenty-four hours long! And when paint became purchasable, how the carving could be embellished! The backs of the chairs as well as the fronts were engraved and coloured; so were horses' harnesses, household and farm implements, the doors and the ceilings and the rafters.

The houses grew larger, the furnishings more elaborate, but as long as they retained the low proportions and revealed the substantial material of which they were made—and so exquisitely made—they were the embodiment of pleasing suitability. Dwellings and barns and storehouses; churches, shops, and mills, were all made of logs, and in Sandvig are ranged examples of every kind, from every district, down through the centuries.

Shingled in elaborate or curious designs, the roofs of the stave church suggest a pile of hats.

Norwegians are true to the ornamentation of wood-carving.

Outdoor museums are needed in a country that is so old that it is inclined to undervalue antiques. Unlike the English, who cherish heirlooms, or the Americans, who acquire them, the man who lives in a log house which is still as sturdy as when his great-great-grandfather built it, will not hesitate to cover the weathered logs with brand-new panel-board outside and matched board inside. And when what was a softly charming cabin has become a stiffly glaring box, the renovator surveys his handiwork and thinks that he has done well.

However, the log house, which has held its own in isolated places, is now being more generally appreciated. The smartest summer cottages, the finest shooting- and fishing-lodges, the best inns, hotels, and museums, and even a few suburban villas, are using logs, either in the round or squared, painted or stained or polished. In a country where Nature creates effects on such an overpoweringly grandiose scale, any man-made architecture is dwarfed into insignificance. The simple log building, its contours blending with field and fen and fjord, its colour harmonizing with the rocks and trees, and its texture part of the forest and the earth, does not compete with Nature, but becomes part of it. It softens the most stark and sombre scene, nor loses its unpretentious worth against the most majestic background.

It is curious that the vivid colours which the early craftsmen used with richly pleasing effect, converting the panels of doors and cupboards, as well as altar and reredos, into pictures and decoration, should have been gloomily overcast by a fashion of drabness. After the Reformation, interiors as well as exteriors of churches and chapels were brought into conformity with the chilled tenets of Pietism.

"How ugly the chapel is," thinks Markus the Fisherman,

"the walls, the pillars, and the benches all painted a mixture of brown and grey, as dismal and unfriendly as possible. And here God is supposed to dwell. . . . This is the correct colour, the chapel colour if you like; but why has it become so? The sky is not umber-coloured. The sky is blue and the sky is red. Yes, the sky has sometimes every colour, except just the colours of the chapel, and nobody finds that very offensive. God paints his own house with the colours of joy, with gold and scarlet, but men use umber and grey. It looks more pious, they seem to think; it tastes of the Spirit and does not seem to be so worldly. But how on earth have they come to that conclusion? One can read about the streets of Zion which were made of pure gold. There is not a word about umber. Where, then, have they got this idea of umber?"

If one leaps from the stone cathedrals of Trondheim and Stavanger to stave churches and log houses, it is because there is little of genuine architectural interest in between. To be sure, in the southern part, where the climate was milder and the fortunes larger, there developed a wooden architecture, not so stately as the wooden colonial in America, but of spaciousness and refinement.

The large manor houses—of which Rosendahl is an excellent example—and a number of private homes in and around Bergen showed taste and standards of dignity if not of magnificence. Their furnishings, as seen in the museums today, reflected the massiveness of the Renaissance, the elegancies of Baroque, the dainty trifles of the Regency, the elaborations of Rococo, and the smooth refinement of the Empire Period. In such houses moved ladies in brocades and laces and ribbons and men in white satin knickerbockers and swaggeringly cut and embroidered waistcoats.

And in Bergen still stand the gate tower and the two large stone halls of those buildings which King Haakon erected in the thirteenth century. One of these halls forms the centre of the Rosenkrantz Tower and the other is in the three-storied, stepped-gabled, and battlemented building which gives distinction to the city—King Haakon's Hall. The building in which King Haakon's son Magnus celebrated his wedding with the Danish Princess Ingeborg (1261) and was at the same time crowned king, to reign jointly with his father, fell into disrepair and the great hall was used for centuries as a granary.

The restoration inside and out necessitated much new material and many alterations. The walls, however, are old; so are the situation and form of the windows (although their latticing is new); and so are the dimensions of the hall—a hundred feet by forty.

It is a regal room with its oak-vaulted ceiling, its carving and gilding and wrought iron. The arras, embroidered in a design of waves, each wave with an open, singing mouth, sweeps to the polished wooden floor. On a blue-carpeted dais stand the two throne chairs, the king's a little larger than the queen's. The hall, which is used on certain festal occasions, can be lighted at night only by tapers, but it is enlivened at all hours and all times by Gerard Munthe's twelve gay and graceful frescoes, telling, with stylized naïveté, the story of Princess Christina (daughter of King Haakon) and her wedding journey to Valladolid.

First comes the legation from Spain, asking the King and Queen of Norway for their daughter's hand for the brother of the Spanish king. Then the preparations for the wedding with the sewing-maids bending over their long white seams.

Next the dowry treasure is carried in chests to the ships waiting in the harbour and the father says good-bye to his little daughter as, all in white, she takes her place in the dragon-prowed vessel that is to bear her away. Under coloured sails, guarded by men in shining mail, the ship goes sailing over a sea bright with golden fish and under a sky pierced with golden stars. The voyage lasts a long time. Maidens play on harps and lutes and a story-teller tries to beguile the white-clad princess (who, the saga confesses, was seasick). Finally the procession arrives on the flowery strand of France, where birds fly to perch on the horses' heads. Thence they set forth toward the snow-tipped mountains of Spain, where the king and queen await them at the Castle porch. In the church the little princess—still in her immaculate white despite the weeks of journeying—makes her offering of a golden cup. At Vallodolid the king, in black and white, himself leads the horse of the princess, who now has a blue cape over her shoulders, toward the scene of the great wedding feast.

The flat frescoing, the archaic postures, are precisely right for the fairylike series in which Gerard Munthe has so happily expressed, without bizarrerie, his decorative fantasy.

It is appropriate that the restored Haakon's Hall should be in Bergen, the city which has managed to retain more of the suggestion of the past than Oslo. And it is appropriate that Oslo, with its older public buildings bearing the stamp of German influence and of imported styles, should, in its new buildings, be making a definite gesture toward good present-day architecture.

This is most clearly seen in the modernistic private villas, both in wood and stucco, outside the city limits, and in the large block houses and flats of increasingly better type in the city, and in the large housing-projects in the periphery.

Since the early 1920's the municipality has been building houses for its growing population. It started as its own contractor, but it now gives a guaranty upon which the contractor can borrow up to 90 percent of the actual value of the building. Private contractors and architects, private companies, co-operative societies, and concerns organized on a co-operative basis have also erected apartment houses, frequently getting support from the city in form of a subsidy. There are several "garden cities," extensive and good-looking, placed amid courtyards, playgrounds, lawns, and trees, the oldest of which is Ullevål Haveby, built by the city in 1920. The city still owns the ground, but the buildings have been turned over to the Ullevål Garden City Society.

These apartments and flats and garden-city houses are interesting both architecturally and socially. They have many windows—an increasing number of large, unobstructed picture windows—and glass is used more and more lavishly. There are not only whole walls of glass brick but a reinforced translucent glass is incorporated in the balustrades, screens, and roofs of the balconies—a most acceptable material in a land of long dark winters. The inside arrangements are compact, convenient, and attractive, and, furthermore, house rents are reasonable because of low real-estate taxes.

The municipally owned apartment houses in Oslo are valued at about fifty million kroner. In the newest of them a fully modern three-room flat, including heat, hot water, bathroom, and plenty of sunshine, costs ninety-five to one hundred and ten kroner a month, a four-room one a hundred to a hundred and fifty. In the older, less modern buildings, a three-room flat costs from thirty to seventy kroner, and the rates in other cities are somewhat lower.

There are no slums in Oslo. Building in wood is forbidden within the city limits and there are left only a few of the old one-story wooden cottages, so picturesque and unhygienic. Whether one rents a flat or a separate villa from a private or a co-operative company, or from the municipality, one is assured a fair value and just treatment with a public committee of inspection on housing matters to which a tenant can turn in case of argument. The private landlords are more or less forced to follow the low rent rate of the municipally and co-operatively owned apartment houses.

One of the most interesting buildings in Oslo, judging by architectural, social, and cultural standards, is the Folk Theatre (Folketeater Komplexet), built by Morgenstierne and Eide.

With the idea that a people's theatre could and should be self-supporting, a large site in a convenient section of the city was selected and bought, and at the cost of 6,800,000 kroner a tremendous edifice was raised. In the large auditorium of perfect acoustics all the fourteen hundred seats are equally good. Every person can see the stage without obstruction and can see everyone else, and all the seats are the same price. Whether or not a ticket-holder gets a special seat depends upon the time order of his application. There are two boxes, one for the directors and one for the actors to study the stage from the front.

The walls, the materials of the furniture and of the fittings, are inexpensive, obtaining their pleasing effects from good taste rather than from ostentatious display, and depending upon changing light effects for much of their decoration.

However, plain as it may be, it costs money to operate a theatre seating fourteen hundred people and paying actors' salaries. This necessary four hundred thousand kronen is obtained by renting out the rest of the building. A cinema, shops, restaurants, roof gardens, and cafés are all planned and decorated with the same elegance and practicality, and rent from these is rapidly reducing the mortgage.

Ultimately the present plain walls, now covered with a neutral sacking, will be hung with finer material; the present plain seats upholstered in golden silk; the boxes lined with blue velvet. And above and across the proscenium, behind the pleasing innovation of a latticed gallery, will flicker, between the acts, the light dresses of women offset by the black and white of their escorts. Although the Folk Theatre was built privately, it has become the natural centre for the Labour Party, which has club, committee, and banquet rooms, and even its newspaper offices here, renting space on the same terms as anyone else.

It is a long distance in space and time and point of view between the Folk Theatre in Oslo, used constantly by the people for business and recreation, and Haakon's Hall in Bergen, used for occasional kingly festivals.

The architecture of any country, while it is necessarily conditioned by climate and available materials, is in a direct sense an expression of the people. The plain and substantial log house dominated by scenic grandeur is peculiarly characteristic of that Norway which must, as long as rocks and waterfalls endure, be changeless. The stone cathedrals of Trondheim and Stavanger and Haakon's Hall in Bergen are chapters in the history of the Norway that has changed from a kingdom dependent upon and influenced by other kingdoms into a firmly knit independent nation.

The new architecture in and around the capital has for its purpose not the glorification of either religion or royalty but the convenience and comfort of the people. It expresses the changing Norway following in constant and orderly progress the development of ever-widening democracy.

CHAPTER SEVEN

Ibsen Returns to Norway

HIGH on a pedestal before the National Theatre in Oslo, the broad bulk of his shoulders dark against the sky, the massive head bent forward a little in characteristic thoughtfulness, Henrik Ibsen stands in bronze.

Flashing before the Empire Theatre in New York, electric signs; drawing up to the front entrance, limousines; crowding into every door, thousands of theatre-goers. Slowly being drawn back, the curtain which removes the fourth wall for one of the greatest successes of the 1934 season and the longest American run in its history—*Ghosts.*

A tourist with a guide book peering a little disappointedly at a plain white wooden building in Bergen—the Old Theatre where a twenty-three-year-old man who had been an apprentice in a pharmacy, a student at the University, publisher for nine-weeks of a weekly newspaper without many subscribers, the author of a deservedly unsuccessful three-act play called *Catiline*—once tried his hand as stage manager.

Sinding's statue, although somewhat impressive, is by no means a great work of art. The Old Theatre at Bergen witnessed not Ibsen's triumph but merely two or three of his unpreserved attempts at playwriting, and an almost unbroken series of vexations and disparagements.

Although there is a certain satisfaction in seeing the actual places associated with his early life—the house in Skien on the southeast coast, where he was born in 1828; the pharmacy in Grimstad where for three years he worked (and wrote); the Old Theatre at Bergen and the newer one in Oslo, where his second directorship was hardly more happy than the first—and though most lovers and students of the drama will find their way to his grave in the cemetery of Our Saviour's in Oslo, it is not through these now eagerly preserved shrines that Ibsen most intimately speaks.

That voice—as stern as those of the judges of Israel—is heard in all its indignation; those passages of poetic fantasy are re-uttered; those inexorable crises, akin to the tragedies of Sophocles and Shakespeare, are enacted today in London and New York and on the Continent to audiences as deeply moved as those of fifty years ago, and bring to the box office returns that not only would have amazed the playwright but astonish even the most sanguine producers.

The material environment of Ibsen's life was never of as much importance to him as his burning thoughts. The elements of the former are preserved, as they should be, in the land where he was born and to which he returned to spend his last fifteen years. The latter lived, and will continue to live, in dynamic immortality as long as there are serious theatres and great actors and actresses in the countries of the world.

For the themes which he chose, although certain of the contemporary conditions may be "dated," are of dateless significance. The debutante of eighteen who absorbedly watched Ruth Gordon play Nora in *The Doll's House* may not have

been aware that this play was the first to proclaim the "emancipation of women," but only that it revealed the deepest rela-
tionships between a husband and wife. The man of sixty
listens to *Ghosts* and knows that he is listening to truth as
stark as death itself. The most modern playwright studies
the technique of *Hedda Gabler*. The idea of playing *Peer
Gynt* bewitches actors almost as much as playing *Hamlet*.

For, besides the universal and eternal appeal of their argument, Ibsen's plays—the best of them—are "good theatre." The
fact that they are literature, which can be enjoyably read, is
not as important in determining their survival as the fact that
they are dramas fulfilling every law of stagecraft so completely
that they can no more be outmoded than the law of gravitation.

On a hill in Bergen a large and handsome modern theatre
overlooks the old wooden one. Down by the market-place a
statue of Ludvig Holberg—ornamental in flowing curls, cock-
aded hat, and knee breeches—surveys the passing scene with
a humorous smile. The new theatre testifies to the value ac-
corded the stage and drama in Norway, for although it is
privately owned, it receives subsidies from both the municipality and the Government. The statue of Holberg—whose name
is usually associated with Denmark, of which he was the
Goethe of letters and the Molière of the stage—is a reminder
that this witty scholar was born in Bergen (1684), where his
comedies, fresh, satirical, and decent, are still popular attractions.

With more than two centuries of tradition behind it, and
gravely honoured in the present, the theatre in Norway holds
genuine importance. It was, and still is, not only a place of
entertainment and of art, but a pulpit and a political plat-

form. The Landsmaal and Riksmaal advocates early recognized it as a most potent mouthpiece, for until 1850 only Danish actors had been permitted on the stage. Social reforms, literary revivals, as well as modern plays and opera, all find on it an immediate communication with the widest, most general public. The whole history and culture of the Norwegian nation are reflected upon it with extraordinary clarity. It was in Bergen that Ole Bull founded the "National Stage" in 1850; in Bergen that the Norwegian language was first used in the theatre; from Bergen that actors were first recruited for theatres throughout the country—a tradition by no means past today.

The National Theatre at Bergen is placed upon a conspicuous eminence. The National Theatre in Oslo stands squarely between the Storting and the Royal Palace and within the shadow of the University. These conspicuous positions are not due to chance, but in recognition of the dignity and power of the stage.

It must be admitted that the playwright who sheds the greatest lustre upon the country of his birth found no such cordial acknowledgment during his lifetime. His early plays, *The Feast of Solhaug* and *The Vikings of Helgeland*—in fact, practically his entire production until he was thirty-six—dealt with national history and tradition and as such were countenanced, although somewhat uneasily, as even in these there was a premonition of the coming storm. With *Love's Comedy* (1862), the forerunner of his great dramas of contemporary life, a satire on the marriage which turns love into a hypocritical institution, such a tempest broke over his head, such personal slander was hurled at him, that, after *The Pretenders* (1863), which injected fresh fury into the hurricane, he left

Norway. Only from a distance could he follow his determination to indict his countrymen of their weakness of national will, of their cowardice, corruption, and self-deception. Not that Norway was the only country that considered him dangerous, foul, and false. In Germany *Ghosts* was—it sounds very familiar—*verboten*. In Paris, the audiences at *An Enemy of the People* not only roared in protest but engaged in fisticuffs. *The Pillars of Society* infuriated England. In America, the first and single performance of Ibsen in English (for it had been played by a Norwegian-Danish Company in Minneapolis in 1882) given by Mojeska at Macauley's Theatre in Louisville, Kentucky, was the last, for many years.

Since then, Ibsen's life has been so fully recorded, his temperament and motives so acutely analysed, his works so carefully annotated, and his plays so magnificently produced, that there is no need for his admirers to travel to Norway to gather this material. Georg Brandes's *Creative Spirits of the Nineteenth Century*, George Bernard Shaw's *Quintessence of Ibsenism*, Edmund Gosse's *Northern Studies*, are brilliant and just appraisals. Halvdan Koht's more recent *Life of Ibsen* completes the long list of Ibsen biographies.

Nevertheless, foreigners who are familiar with Ibsen only through what he wrote and through what other people have written about him, will experience a curious consciousness of their literary impressions becoming more tangible and their academic and social opinions more lively as they travel and visit in the country of his protagonists.

When they pass a house newly building, with the traditional bit of green suspended from its ridgepole, they will see Halvard Solness climbing up to the top of the scaffolding, up to the weather vane of the house that he, the Master Builder, had planned. He carries a wreath hung with ribbons and flowers, and as he reaches the top, he turns to wave his hat at the people standing below—before he falls!

Or if, through the dusk, a train or a car carries one past a wooden bridge above a mill race, one strains to see the two figures—a man and a woman, Rosmer of Rosmersholm and Rebecca West—clasped in each other's arms in just such a spot while the river swirls below.

Wherever, against the side of a mountain, is left the mark and legend of an avalanche, one looks at the tomb of Brand.

In a small watering-place on a fjord moves a lightly stepping lady, her hair wet from her swim, her eyes the colour of the changing water. It is the Lady from the Sea listening as a bell rings and a steamer glides out of the fjord headed toward the ocean which will never claim Ellida now.

That dignified country house above a gloomy fjord, with the rain beating on the windows of its garden room—does the widowed Mrs. Alving sit there reading?

On the level sward of Ostraat, stretching along the Trondheim Fjord, does a dark figure pace? It is Lady Inger, the intellectual aristocratic ruler, the frightened and sinning woman.

On the city street George Tesman, with his open cheerful face, passes with his portmanteau, and Judge Brack carefully dressed and with an eyeglass. Ibsen's men and women people every village, every town, while behind the walls of the houses are handsome drawing-rooms such as the one in which Hedda Gabler stretched her idle and lovely limbs in boredom.

These people, these scenes and settings, seem more real to the reader of Ibsen than Sinding's statue before the theatre, and quite blot out the other statue, by the same sculptor, which balances it—of Björnstjerne Björnson.

This latter magnificently muscular bard and orator, politician, poet, dramatist, theatrical producer, and moralist was one of the most electrifying powers of his day. With his striking physique, buoyant and brilliant temperament, and his endless talking, lecturing, and haranguing, he was the exact opposite of the short, silent, unsociable Ibsen. He had his enemies, as radicals must always have, but not one of them could have been cruel enough to prophesy that after his death (1910) his name in foreign lands would be relegated to dignified notation in literary and historical summaries. Björnson will always be remembered in Norway, as he deserves to be. His home at Aulestad in the Gudbransdal Valley is a national shrine. But not an international one. The ruddy giant with a lion's mane is dust in the Oslo Cemetery.

But there is a figure who still flings himself upon the back of a wild buck and cleaves a passage through the air along the Gendin Edge. Ragged and reckless and romancing, Peer Gynt snatches the bride from the wedding and with her on his shoulder clambers upward like a goat to the sheerest mountain top. The Dovre trolls swarm around him—brownies, nixies, cantankerous hobgoblins, some with pigs' heads, some with silk ribbons on the end of their tails. He breaks away. He dashes home. He whirls his mother on the mad drive to the castle west of the moon and east of the sun. The sledge bells ring, lights blaze from the castle windows and doorways, St. Peter pours out the wine, the Dean's wife prepares coffee and dessert, and Åse closes her eyes as the wild journey comes to an end.

Legend has it that there was in Norway an actual man named Peer Gynt. Near Vinstra his farm and grave are pointed out and at the railway station there is a small book shop made from the logs from his cottage. The name, whether of Ibsen's hero or of his flesh-and-blood prototype, is now exploited to the utmost as a trade mark for everything from caps to cookies.

But there is no note in the railway guides to show over which stretch of heath it was that the Button Moulder came with his casting-ladle; no sign post to indicate the trail through the dark fir forest where, in the door of her hut, stood Solveig, erect and mild, her arms held out to the returning Peer.

Allegory, satire, or sheer fantasy; drama, poem, or headlong story—whatever the scholars' interpretation of this play, it does not whirl around a possibly actual character who lived in the Gudbransdal Valley, but around the most capricious and iridescent creation conceived by a writing genius.

Ibsen returned to Norway, just as Peer Gynt found his way back to the cottage in the forest.

Hundreds of foreigners approach Norway familiar only with these names. As they travel through and across that remote and impressive land, they will see it as the birthplace of Ibsen, as the material of his plays, and as the sad and glorious background for the laughing, weeping, ever-escaping, ever-returning Peer Gynt.

CHAPTER EIGHT

Norway Writes Its Life

PEER GYNT was not the last of the Norwegians to be transported by his own gifts of narrative speed and vivid imaginings.

From his day until our own the fabric of fiction has been enlarging beneath the rapid shuttle of many weavers of tales, and that fabric has been thrown from the wildest north to the mildest south, from the skerries of Bergen in the east to the copper mines of Röros in the west. There are few countries foreign to the English-speaking visitor which are better known to him through fiction. The same sublimity of terrain, the same elemental forces of Nature, the same sternly hewed faces which have offered material to the painters have offered it, also, to the novelists.

If one can recapture, in the galleries, the panorama of sea and sky, waterfall, heath, and cottage that has passed before his eye as he travelled along the fjords and down the valleys, so can one—either in anticipation of such a journey or in its retrospect—approach an understanding of a people who are more articulate through the speech of their interpreters than through their own conversation with a stranger.

The bleak stretches of Nordland, with its handful of houses

by the edge of a fjord, with its isolated farms on mountainsides, with its gossipy villages strung along narrow, uptilted streets—these places, and the human beings who inhabit them, retain not only the three dimensions of tangibility but also an intangible fourth quality through the rushing, vivified pages of Knut Hamsun.

The stranger might spend many months in Nordland and never be able to press his ear against the heart of a farm like Sellanraa, despite the fact that the basic health and the rhythm of the nation derive from the strong and regular heart beats of many such homesteads, wrung from the wilderness by a man and woman who accept toil as part of life, and who accept suffering, sinning, loving, and hoping also as part of a life that comes to its natural close in death, which is not to be escaped or even dreaded. In *The Growth of the Soil* Hamsun pours forth a prodigious river, glistening with rude humour and darting off into half-hidden streams of tenderness, which revivifies not only a group of individual lives but a whole countryside.

From the first page, where Isak comes trudging the long road over the moors up into the pathless forest to find a place on some high slope where there is sun and a spring, solitude and safety, until the last page when he—still a stump and a barge of a man but a "Margrave" now—is at his sowing, clad in wool from his own sheep, boots from the hide of his own cattle, "all is majesty and power—a sequence and purpose of things."

The foaming, cascading river of Hamsun's genius had, during its earlier subjective period, in his novel called *Hunger,* burrowed frantically down below the pavements of the city into the bitter subterranean caverns of a starving man's physical and mental frenzy. It had swirled erratically, in the eddies of *Mysteries,* with the paradoxical sincerities of Nagel, who bewilders himself as much as the reader. In the love story of *Pan,* it churned through the forested hills above a fishing village, tossing on its madcap crest the irrational wilfulness of Glahn. The river of subjectivity pitched into a pot hole of unescapable, unresolvable conflicts with *Victoria,* to reappear on the plane of a dramatic trilogy (*At the Gate of the Kingdom, The Game of Life,* and *Sunset*), and then to branch off as a delicious twisting brooklet in *Mothwise.*

To follow this last small digression is sheer frolic. For it plays about the feet of young people strolling down the country roads in the white summer night, singing and waving branches of willow. It splashes on the seal thrusting its dripping head from the sea, looking around and diving down again into its own world below. It lies in a glistening pool around Rolandsen, the telegraph operator, serenading with song and guitar the gay, innocent, untidy wife of the priest. The fishing-boats come and go. People gather in church. Damp moss and juniper are flung on midsummer fires to make the smoke properly thick and scented. Here, for an interval of foolery twinged with pleasant pangs of longing, one may stop over in a Nordland village of lesser magnitude and more laughable futility than those to which Hamsun usually gives us the key to the gates.

This amusing divagation apparently pleased Hamsun himself sufficiently for him to send somewhat the same currents coursing through *Benoni* and its sequel *Rosa.* Here again we are in another small Nordland community, a microcosm of clumsy villagers set forth for our entertainment by a writer who has for the time eschewed tragical-romantic for comical-pastoral. The river by which one traverses Nordland here ripples into more lightly traced estuaries. But next time the artist blends the flowing tints. Something of the old irresponsible vagary is caught in *Under the Autumn Star,* something of the old tragic pessimism in *The Wanderer with the Mute,* but something, too, of the fun of the comedies. With *The Last Joy* the river of genius seems seeping into grey sands, and then, suddenly, it gathers fresh force and exultation. *Children of the Age* and *Segelfoss Town* make the sweep of a complete and vital circle, crackling with the malicious gossip, the avarice and suspicion and sudden benevolences, of a small coast town, which, gathering momentum before our eyes, starts as a semi-feudal estate and comes to its completion as an industrial centre.

Segelfoss has been called the most celebrated town in Norwegian literature. Certain it is that its reader, standing on the quay to watch the boats off for Lofoten, looking at the white flag which is being raised and wondering what steamer is coming in, lounging in the village store and irresistibly sucked into all the interminable convolutions of small lives in a small place, reaches the last page with more of a feeling of intimacy with such lives than many a tourist who merely walks—or more usually rides—through an actual seacoast counterpart. To be sure, the lawyer is bombastic and the doctor is an ass and the servant girls are sadly promiscuous. To be sure, there are an unconscionable number of spiteful tongues and stolid faces, failures, fools, and vagabonds. But there is responsiveness in the lawyer's wife, generosity in the lord of the manor, goodness in the mill-owner, and philosophy in the brilliant, feckless, drunken, quixotic, ne'er-do-well of a telegraph operator whose name happens to be Baardsen, but whom we have met before as Nagel or August or Glahn or Rolandsen, and whom we have come to recognize as Hamsun himself.

Segelfoss Town and *Children of the Age* are the most captivating and illuminating guide books to the northern coast towns that the reader is likely to find, as *The Growth of the Soil* is the star which hangs above each lonely mountain farm, gilding its roofs, its fields, its animals, and its labouring human forms.

Hamsun wrote *The Growth of the Soil* when he was sixty. Much of the tempestuous revolt of his youth had been resolved by then; the savagery of his satire had softened. But he was not to stop with what will probably be his supreme achievement. The man who had been a farm labourer, coalheaver, schoolteacher, road-mender, surveyor's assistant, and free-lance writer in Norway; a clerk in Wisconsin, a cobbler in Colorado, and a street-car conductor in Chicago; who had been threatened with tuberculosis, won the Nobel prize, and now lives on his farm in Grimstad in South Norway, where he ploughs and scatters seed with his own hand—is still writing. *The Women at the Pump* and *The Ring Is Closed* are buffeted by the old waves of bawdiness and brutality and tossed high on the crest of exaltation in life and the affirmation of the right of each man to live that life according to his own nature.

Hamsun does not, like Ibsen, try to reconstruct society. He observes it, sometimes with fury, usually with humour, and more and more with compassion. A human being may be thick-headed, warped, or dwarfed, but again he may be brilliant and magnanimous, and always he is fascinating. Always he is both insignificant and precious. "Small things and great occur. A tooth falls out of the jaw, a man out of the ranks, a sparrow to the ground."

If Hamsun is a river of prodigality and momentum, Johan Bojer is a waterfall, dropping clear and sheer from height to depth. The leap between man's sky-ey birth and his earthy grave gives the force to his direct and powerful novels. Here is none of Hamsun's amoral overbrimming, but the painful persistent pull between the divine and the base, the eternal and the ephemeral. In *The Great Hunger* Per passes from poverty to wealth to destitution; stripped of every worldly honour and every human consolation, he at last stretches out his hand to God—and finds Him. In the *Power of a Lie,* which was crowned by the French Academy, the same burning torch of absolute truth illumines the same dark confusion of human hearts. The flame twists and sears them, the smoke defiles them, but the light of pure ethics is not obscured. In the most recent of his novels to be translated into English *By Day and by Night,* Leif Sund, the successful inventor of a machine-gun, is confronted by scientific achievement and enormous monetary remuneration on one hand and horror at the effects of his invention on the other. Racked between them as he seeks for peace, he is finally given strength to make the sign of the cross. Bojer's other less known but perhaps not less admirable works travel on the same exalted trajectory between the senses and the spirit. In *Life,* the sin which briefly tints drab existences with colour, inexorably blacks them out. In *The House and the Sea,* financial rectitude wars with family affection. In *The Everlasting Struggle* the loving heart of Mother Lisbeth is ground to dust—precious dust, indeed—against the wheel of circumstance.

These are mighty themes and they are mightily handled, not heavily but swiftly, not didactically but with pity and affectionate humour. Although the waterfalls are harnessed to turn a wheel, their limpid majesty still thunders against the background of black and purple and golden rock; their falling spray tosses back to the sky the light of the rainbow.

While this is true of all Bojer's novels, it is particularly so of the one by which he will be longest remembered—*The Last of the Vikings*. The time when the brawny fishermen waved good-bye to their wives and children standing mutely on the mainland and, unfurling their sails, beat their way to the Lofoten Islands, battling with cold and storms, hauling in fish like madmen, or desperately seeking them over black waves; when they brawled on shore or stood, each one before his provision chest, his back to his neighbour as he bent over to eat the flat bread, the cheese, the butter, the salt meat, sausage, and brawn the womenfolk had packed to carry them through the long siege—these times passed with the passing of sail. The Lofoten fisherman today goes thither in a motor-boat. Weather reports are wirelessed to warn him of storms; trade unions succour him. But the sea still howls and ravens, and the wives and sweethearts still wait at home for a letter, hardly daring to hope for the first sight of the returning boats.

What Hamsun did for the coastwise village and the mountain farm, Bojer has done for the Norwegian Sea. As Hamsun's are handbooks for Nordland, Bojer's is the manual for Lofoten. There have been changes in the life of the fishermen along the Banks, but certain things are changeless. Lars Myran, looking at an old man with a white heard in the light of the bonfire on the shore, thinks how, "many hundred years before, such an old man would have been the sacrificing priest, and the bonfire the sacrificial fire, and the people drinking to Thor and Freya before the Lofoten boats set sail. The shore was the same, and the fjord was the same, and the mountains and the boats were as they are now, and the people were probably very much the same, too." As these mountains and these men still remain in Norway, so through *The Last of the Vikings* they will remain in her permanent literature.

Hamsun and Bojer move with the dash and drive of living waters. While they crush flimsy craft and submerge even the bravest of vessels, with equal gusto they rollick in the wind and air. But there is a third Norwegian who has, through the written page, brought life to a heroic land.

Sigrid Undset loosens no boisterous waters. She sails no seas and leaps no precipices. But slowly, with painstaking labour, she has created—by methodically planting one tree after another—a vast dim forest which "clothes the wold and meets the sky" of a whole epoch of Norway's history that previously had neither a road nor map, for it had never been recorded in writing. The roots of this forest are in the deep rich soil of medieval time, its verdure in the psychological ozone of the present.

Sigrid Undset, born of a Norwegian father and a Danish mother in Denmark (1882), with a childhood spent in Oslo, has long lived in Lillehammer, not far from the ruins of the twelfth-century Hamar Cathedral and near the antiquities of Sandvig. Although she has, as a woman, been pre-eminently concerned with the subject of love and, as a Norwegian, she has found the subject full of woe and conflict, as a scholar she has reconstructed the past with such fidelity that it is on this last achievement that her rightfully acquired fame will rest.

The characters in *Kristin Lavransdatter*—or at least their

emotional experiences—although they lived in the thirteenth century, are analysed according to the methods of twentieth-century psychology. But the background, the *décor,* are unique and of incalculable value to whoever would look at Norway not merely as scenery but as a venerable and still evolving nation. In the immense, carefully arranged forest of facts, architecture—both of stone cathedral and log-built farm-house, with its open hearth in the centre of the main hall and its score of scattered outbuildings—is seen through the vista of proper perspective. Customs, ecclesiastical, domestic, and legal, bloom on the branches to persist or perish through suc-ceeding seasons. Folklore and legends fill their appointed space in the shadows.

Sigrid Undset has planted many trees since her first novel *Marthe Oulie* (1907). From the days of *The Happy Age* and *Jenny* and *Mrs. Waage* up to her recent *Faithful Wife,* she has dug and watered and pruned with ardour and increasing artistry. With the exception of one idyll, *The Spring,* which flowers into happiness through the author's determination rather than by the sap of growth, they all bear the fruit that lost Eden to Adam and Eve. The harvest of religion is almost as hard to gather, since the only ladder to reach it is that of duty. Even symmetrical and handsome trees can be depress-ing when they exist only to cast a shadow and their leaves un-fold for the sole purpose of withering and falling. But the gleaming forests of *Kristin Lavransdatter* and *The Master of Hestviken* are lasting memorials quite sufficient for one life's work. Such a labourer, such a creator, such an artist is en-titled now to homeward plod her weary way and leave the world to darkness.

Meanwhile, in the south, Gabriel Scott has been writing,

as has been said of W. H. Hudson, "as naturally as the grass grows." A happy sweep of grass it is, warmed by the sun, freshened by the breeze, and kept green by contentment whose perennially renewing seeds spring from pure religion undefiled.

It must be admitted that Gabriel Scott (1875–   ) first made himself known by a fearsome tragedy. In *The Burden of Iron,* the eighteenth-century peasants, enslaved by Denmark and powerless in disunion, are by famine, wolves, and murderously freezing cold lashed from their lethargy to heroic revolt, although not until they have wrecked their superstitious sadism on two young girls accused of witchcraft. But after Scott had paid this tribute to the racial penchant for suffering, he turned himself to the idyll, and here he found a place not likely ever to be crowded in a land where, even when they joke and romp, people—at least those whom the reader is able to meet in English translation—cannot forget that life is very difficult.

Markus the Fisherman does not find it so difficult. On the contrary, he finds it engrossing and delightful, and even if in the end he must leave it, he is merely casting off the dust which settled around him at birth and has moved with him through the years since then. It has sometimes choked him a little, that dust, and made his eyes sting till the tears came. But it has also given strange and lovely colours to the sunrise and sunset. But now he has learned that "the gift of being pleased with little things is the cradle of happiness," and now he is ready to fling off the dust and to return to the embrace of the heavens.

"Art thou poor, yet hast thou golden slumbers? Then, O sweet content!" might be the song of *Christopher with the*

Twig, the crippled herdsboy on a lonely plateau. Even Our Lord and Saint Peter, visiting the earth in *The Golden Gospel,* can "drink the waters of the crisped spring" of Scott's imagining and find them sweet.

There is another spot in Norwegian fiction where the reader may see reflected in the pellucid waters of a small fjord the faces of five happy children and those of a loving and indulgent father and mother, and the form of the old servant in a black knitted cap and big wooden shoes and "skin like old bark with thousands of tiny lines"—Marthe.

It is a tranquil and a cheerful spot, that island farm which Gösta af Geijerstam has so quietly revealed in his *Northern Summer* and *Storevik.* Haying-time and milking-time, evenings with fairy tales, family expeditions to the woods, family celebrations of birthdays and Christmas—the joys are simple ones, the griefs are transient, and affection shines as serenely as the sun sheds its light on the first cowslips of spring.

The traveller who has paid his tribute to Magnhild Haalke —paid it in horror for her story of *Alli's Son* and in anguished acknowledgment of this new writer's undeniable ability— turns from the dreadful tension of that tragedy, from the cruel rocks of its bleak setting, to bless the idylls of *Storevik.* Now he can look out upon the skerries and the islands and the mountains that make the coast of Norway so divinely fair, and believe that, although life must always be stern in such a land, it may also hold exquisite joys.

The Norway of Hamsun and Bojer and Undset is almost as well known to English readers as to Norwegian. Familiar also to many in America are Trygve Gulbranssen's woods that sing and his wind that blows from the mountains. Gulbranssen does not plant a forest of such sweep and majesty as Undset. Critical Norwegians are inclined to say he does not plant real trees at all, but merely arranges stage scenery in a pretty screen. But it is an extremely pretty screen, and the feudal homestead of the Björndals, which is placed before it, and the actions of bear-hunting and bargaining and love-making, which are staged within doors and out, are lively with excitement and sentiment.

Gulbranssen is young as years go—he was born in Oslo in 1894—but he does not belong to the modern school whose older generation included Hamsun, Bojer, and Undset and whose younger includes Christiansen, Hoel, Egge, and Falk-berget.

Sigurd Christiansen, who followed his rather heavy trilogy *The Kingdom* by the absorbing prize-winner *Two Living and One Dead,* and followed that by *Chaff before the Wind,* has learned how to keep psychological analysis from halting an exciting story. Peter Egge, with his warm and sympathetic *Hansine Solstad* and his prize-winning *Guests,* speaks for the stubborn farmers of Tröndelag, and Jacob Breda Bull for his native valley, Osterdal, dark with forests and vocal with rushing rivers. Johan Falkberget has dug from the rough and often sordid matrix of the copper mines a precious and durable metal. Olav Duun, with his monumental cycle of six novels, *The Juvikings,* traces the fortunes of a peasant family through generations.

The vitality of these modern realists extends across the Atlantic to claim Ole Edvart Rölvaag, whose *Giants in the Earth* is one of the truly great novels of the pioneer West. Its sequels, *Peder Victorious, Pure Gold,* and *Their Father's God,* and his last book, *The Boat of Longing,* have established his place in American letters.

Among the living and modern realists high place is given to Sigurd Hoel, whose terseness of style is honoured—or defamed, according to one's point of view—by being compared to that of Ernest Hemingway.

Hoel, who first won attention by *Sinners in Summertime,* is a young man and a city-dweller. The Oslo that Sigrid Undset used as a background for her early sociological novels was a place of "dirty and humid streets, with worn sidewalks, bordered with cramped unfurnished lodgings and cheap shops." Oslo, and every city for that matter, has always been to Hamsun the concentration of evil and a violator of the soul's integrity. "No one," as Björkman says, "has so mercilessly denounced the very principle of urbanity." But the Oslo of Sigurd Hoel's *One Day in October* is neither a nightmare of horror nor an argument for social improvement. It is a metropolis of today, like other cities everywhere, but distinctively itself, with its sounds and odours, its streets and cafés, its flats and offices. Even the weather is so characteristic that one closes the book with the feeling that he has been, during the tense recital, warmed by the summerly breeze of the afternoon, drenched by the cold autumnal storm of the evening, and emerged, after the dreadful blackness of night, into a temporarily clear morning.

One Day in October is a cross-section of a few lives within the confines of a small area during a limited twelve hours—a pattern similar to a number of American and English and Continental novels of the last decade. But the characters, although their strengths and weaknesses are those of human beings everywhere, could exist only in Norway—or at least only here could they get themselves into this particular set of miseries. The tourist who strolls down Karl Johan Gate may or may not see a Hedda Gabler or a twentieth-century Kristin Lavransdatter. But he will pass Fru Welland and Fru Gabrielsen and the ill-fated Fru Raven. He cannot escape the newspaper woman or avoid bumping into Andersen's handcart loaded with potatoes. And, rubbing shoulders with them in the street, he will find himself accompanying them to their respectable homes and finally find himself distressingly intimate with their sluggish or frustrated or rebellious hearts.

The Oslo is that of today. The style is as fresh as tomorrow. But the tug-of-war between love and duty, the ideal and the real, is as much of a draw as it has ever been. The fact that Hoel writes so well merely confirms the impression of these readers who are familiar with only such Norwegian fiction as has been chosen for translation, that most of his countrymen find life a toilsome trudge from the cradle to the grave. To such readers it seems that in the whole procession, from Hamsun to Hoel, the faces are melancholy, the figures defiant or bowed in defeat or, at best, in resignation. Sometimes "the maid forlorn and crowned with rue" will, in Bojer's books, fly for a few tingling moments over the snow on skis, or draw a deep breath on some mountain seter. Sometimes, in Hamsun's, jokers will dance in a mocking ring around the victim of their own vice or others' malice. Only the serene eyes of Gabriel Scott's humble folk and the laughter of the children of Storevik redeem, in part, the sombre pilgrimage.

Oddly enough, the culminating effect is more impressive than depressing. If the men and women in that procession suffer, nevertheless, they have strength and will to survive, and to survive with all the dignity that may become a man. The gloom seems blacker because it is contrasted with the unquenchable torch of the ideal. People are tormented not be-

cause they are stupid but because they are passionately conscious of social injustice and furiously indignant with their
own and other people's frailties. Even when their literary
creators convict them of triviality, they refute their own accusation by denying them the painless light-heartedness or the
easy surrender of the trivial soul. They are mediocre because
they are seen against a background of unparalleled majesty.
And they are redeemed by their fierce refusal to despair.
Weak or wicked or wretched, they struggle manfully, sometimes almost divinely. They struggle against the overwhelming forces of exterior Nature, such as tempests and cataclysms
and harvests lost by drought or frost, or a disastrous fishing-
season, and with equal anger and scornful determination
against their own hatefulnesses, emotional contradictions, and
limitations. This is the stuff from which strong lives and
strong literature are made.

The admirable fiction which so interprets Norway to the
traveller who is also a reader is not confined to the past half-
century. As Peer Gynt was not the last of the story-tellers,
neither was he the first. In a land of long winter nights, story-
telling has, since earliest times, mingled its breath with common speech. Kings and chieftains engaged troubadours and
scalds, not only to recount the past, but to record the present.
Earl Thorfinn the Mighty of Orkney kept a Boswell close
beside him to chronicle his every deed and saying. Before
Olav the Holy went into the fatal battle at Stikklestad, he
ordered three scalds into the shelter of the shield burg so that
posterity might have a true record of the fight, and all three
versions of these war correspondents of a thousand years ago
are quoted in the subsequent saga.

But the great mass of the people could not afford scalds

and troubadours. They retailed their own exploits and elaborated their own fancies by their own hearths, piling up deep overlays of the tradition of telling stories and listening to them, remembering them and repeating them.

A literature which began with the swift movement, trenchant dialogue, and sharp characterization of Edda and saga, continued through homely narratives, epigrams, fables, and legends—a rich and mellowed accretion which was in the 1840's to be gathered up and sifted by Jörgen Moe and P. C. Asböjornsen in their collections of folk tales. This same elusive stuff was to be pressed into solid ammunition by Ivar Aasen when he began his war for a literary language based upon the native dialects.

Björnson was to utilize it, too, consciously reapplying the brevity of the saga style to his early romances after warming it up a bit by his own youthful optimism. *Sunny Hill*—his first and by many considered his best story of Norwegian peasant life—and *A Happy Boy* came from this period and are still popular in Norway. But Björnson became increasingly didactic and inclined to generalization of types, so that *The Kurt Family,* which preached morality, and *The Gauntlet,* which attacked the double standard, have gone the way of most "problem" novels.

It is Jonas Lie (1833–1908), whose first book, *The Visionary,* appeared in 1870, who is the forerunner of the modern Norwegian novel. Lie condensed description and eliminated debate. His characters spoke and saw and felt quite in the manner of characters today. Although he had no stomach for the cruder brutalities, he was, nevertheless, a realist. Although he had the firmest grip on the actual lives of the seafaring

In a Square that bears his name a slim and fiery Ole Bull for ever
plays his violin.

Before the National Theatre Henrik Ibsen lives in bronze.

people whose family life he so graphically delineated in *The Pilot and His Wife, Rutland,* and *Go Ahead,* he brought the same qualities to his writing about the professional and official class, to which he himself belonged, and it is by these latter—particularly *The Family at Gilje*—that he is best known in translation. The mysticism, which was part of his nature, shows at its best in his collection of short stories called *Trolls.*

Lie introduced the impressionistic manner of building up character and effects by an accumulation of details, and Alexander Kielland (1849–1906) added to this the frankness which remains as a characteristic of Norwegian writing. A sophisticated and cultivated man, who gave up business to become a writer, a patrician who devoted himself to social justice—Kielland wrote with the power which many Norwegians possess, but with a polish few have acquired. Today his novels, which are set in the old town of Stavanger, with its few fine families and its many fishermen and sailors and tradesmen, have value to the student of Norwegian letters as his polemics against the inanities of the educational, the tyranny of the bureaucratic, the injustice of the economic systems of his day have to the sociologist.

Arne Garborg (1851–1924) was spokesman for the peasant class to which he belonged, even writing much of his low-keyed and lyrical works, as well as his more radical denunciations, in the Landsmaal which was based on his native dialect. To him may be partly due the large place continuously occupied by the peasant in Norwegian fiction.

If these men were the literary fathers of the present generation of novelists, Amalie Skram (1847–1905), with her in-

vective against the unhappiness of marriage and her indict-
ment—in the four volumes of *The Hellemyr Folk*—of laws
which create poverty and spread disease and perpetuate crime,
was the mother.

These names have interest for whoever surveys the literary
history of Norway.

It is an invigorating history.

Norwegian writers have never been afraid to deal with
tremendous subjects: man's conquest of himself and of the
elements, his duty to his neighbour, his reconciliation with
God. These passionate arguments are saved from abstractness
by the inherited talent for telling a story and by the breathtaking glory of the setting and by the fierceness of the action.
From Undset's characters of the thirteenth century to Hamsun's and Bojer's of the twentieth, from Rölvaag's pioneers in
the New World and back to Christiansen's and Hoel's city-
dwellers of today, they all live with an intensity that is almost
frightening.

For this is a land not of mirage but of reality and awful
grandeur, of heights that are snow-capped even in summer, of
abysses that slash through mountain rock, and seas that howl
through storms. It is a land where, in the fight for existence,
men have been forced to keep their elemental physical powers
while their emotions have been driven below surface expression as the waters sink into the profound and soundless fjords.
There are flowers, but their blossoming-time is brief. There
is sunshine, but it is too soon blotted out in rain. And in human hearts "the whiteness of the lily dies with spring, and
summer slays the freshness of the winds, and autumn stills the
laughter of the woods."

These are the changeless elements of the Norwegian scene

and of the Norwegian character, and about them the changing generations of writers tell and retell their sagas of prowess and ephemeral love, and pain that is the spear which pins man to the earth.

Part III

SPITSBERGEN— THE FROZEN RIM OF THE WORLD

Spitsbergen—the Frozen Rim
of the World

ABOUT half-way between the North Cape and the North Pole are scattered the islands of Svalbard, the largest of which are those of Spitsbergen.

Without a tree, with glaciers sweeping down between the mountains—snow paths for the winds to ski upon—white with sunlight day and night for nearly four months, glittering in starlight day and night for another four, with ice floating in its bays in midsummer and gales cutting the air into knives regardless of season—who would journey to Spitsbergen? And why?

Many hundreds of people journey to Spitsbergen. There are fishing-boats, mail boats, colliers, freighters, and, every season, more and more cruise boats, well loaded with that ever-increasing tribe of travellers who are curious to see the lesser-known parts of the globe, so long as they can see them from cushioned deck chairs, if the weather is lenient, or from behind plate-glass windows of a heated salon if it chances to be inclement.

The trapper, looking out from his hut, may grunt resentfully at the sight and sound of a passing or anchoring steamer intruding upon his solitude. The geologist, the meteorologist, the botanist, and all the dedicated brotherhood of scientists may look down their noses at these soft-living ignoramuses who do not know Jurassic rock from cretaceous, or a fungus from a moss. The workers in the coal mines doubtless have their opinions also of the laughing, camera-carrying crowd which comes trooping up from shore to exclaim over a chained Eskimo dog and to tramp over the hills to peer into a black shaft.

The tourist is not abashed by any such implications. He does not think it is necessary to be an oceanographer or an ethnologist or a mining engineer to enjoy a trip to Spitsbergen. He experiences a sense of space, freedom, and freshness as he leaves the cliffs of Norway and sets forth upon the open sea, while the sun, shining through the night, makes a daylight softer than day. He may not care about the movement and oblation of glaciers. He may not even know that glaciologists keep measuring some of these seemingly motionless bodies as meticulously as beauty specialists measure the girth of their clients. But he is profoundly impressed as he looks at them and realizes that in travelling to Spitsbergen he has travelled into the Glacial Period, that when he arrives there he is actually in the Ice Age, that it is existing here as it existed in prehistoric time over the face of the globe.

It is fun to get within five hundred miles of the North Pole, even if one doesn't care to struggle further on a dog sled, carrying pemmican and a sleeping-bag. It is no grim business but a queer novelty to stand upon the deck of the *Stella Polaris* as this daintiest of yachts approaches the surging, heaving barrier of packed ice. The *Stella Polaris* is no ice-breaker like the old Russian *Krassin,* nor is it a wooden *Fram,* built to yield to ice pressure and to slide up on a floe. The *Stella Polaris* is fleet and graceful as a cat, and like a cat in its deftness and reserve. It marches straight up to the growling, monstrous pack ice and audaciously dabs at it and backs away, and that is quite sufficient. It is only play, and it does no harm to tweak the whiskers of the polar dragon, which has, for far too long, lashed its icy coils around the northern top of the world.

In Magdalena Bay one may be imaginative as well as statistical. To be sure, a white cross marks the grave of some whaler and white bones the skeleton of some whale, and there is a monument erected by the Norwegian Government to commemorate those Dutch sailors of the sixteenth century who found their way to this far coast. But in the summer sun it is more agreeable to turn one's eyes from these bleak mementoes to the glacier-girded mountains of a gentle mauve, patterned with a snow so closely speckled with microscopic algæ that it is apple-blossom pink. Where the glaciers creep down to meet the sea, they pile up in tumbled heaps of white and blue. This white is like that of clouds, or smoke, or snow, or ashes, but the blue is like nothing else in the created world.

There are sandy amethystine coves, and beaches cobalt and russet, as well as glacier fronts and caves around Magdalena Bay. One can stroll across the lower slopes of the mountains, over green and golden moss, red saxifrages and heathlike andromeda tetragona with drooping waxen blooms. One can rest upon rocks furred with black lichens and gather Arctic buttercups and poppies. If one cannot lie beneath arboreal shade, that is not because there are no trees. There are polar willows everywhere, all complete with trunk and branches and

leaves. They are two inches high and their tips alone are
visible in the vivid green cushions, but they are trees nevertheless, and are honoured with the name of salix polaris. But
one can see trees elsewhere on the globe. In Magdalena Bay
it is better to watch the small icebergs sparkling and floating
and half-believe that this one is a long-necked crystal swan,
and that one is a chunky polar bear, while yonder forked tail,
in the water and out of it, is a dolphin of clearest ice. The
whole bay is a play shop of fanciful forms. A great aquaplane,
its glossy wings outspread, rocks on glassy pontoons. A tiny
galleon, all sails set, billows before the wind until, without
warning, it vanishes like a submarine. Near the shore a huge
armadillo is drifting sluggishly, his dark blue carapace etched
by the waves into symmetrical scales. Mythological beasts and
birds—green, lemon-yellow, and ivory—a duck bigger than a
Cyclops, a spired city smaller than a fist; castles and caves of
hollowed ice—they form and float, they are submerged and
reappear in other metamorphoses. Now and then a sharp report or a cracking blast roars forth from some glacier, which,
shaking its fist at such human foolery, has flung a thousand
tons or so of ice into the sea as a gesture of indignation. After
all, even on the sunniest of summer days, Magdalena Bay is
not a play shop of aquatic toys. There are other white specks
than those of flowers upon these slopes. All the bones are not
of whales and seals. The monument to the Dutch sailors does
not blanket all those who have perished here.

These sailors were by no means the first.

The sagas mention a country called Svalbard, and in the
Middle Ages the Norwegian kings claimed sovereignty not
only over this but over all the polar lands—a sovereignty that
was lost when Norway was united with Denmark (1389). Two

centuries later (1596) a Dutch expedition under Willem Barents rediscovered the islands and Henry Hudson saw them in 1607. In 1620 an English ship's crew wintered here. Then, like one of its own icebergs, Spitsbergen floated into the unrecorded mists. Historians knew of it, but it was, in actuality, a *terra nullius,* a no-man's land. In 1920, by a treaty signed in Paris, it was given back to Norway.

That casual traveller, whom scholars snub and tourist agencies woo and without whom the writers of travel books would perish, may puzzle why Norway—or any nation—should be so eager to claim an area a little less than Scotland's, a little more than West Virginia's—24,290 square miles of ice and treeless, frozen mountains. He will admit that Cross Bay is like a coign of the moon with the Midnight Sun sharpening its peaks and the fogs smudging them out. The glaciers curve down on every side, highways from heaven, ramps whose landings are suspended clouds. Where they meet the sea, the snowy shapes and crystal forms of icebergs drift, disintegrate, and disappear. That the Norwegians are not oblivious "to this bow-and-string tension of beauty and silence a-spring" is proved by their poets and painters. But scenic phenomena are not the only reason why there was rejoicing over the Treaty of Paris. Another cove dotted with waiting colliers, other mountains blackened with coal dust, present another reason.

Sloping up from Advent Bay are sooty tracks and muddy paths not in the least like highways from heaven. The scaffoldings that mark the entrances to the coal mines do not suggest ramps whose landings are suspended clouds. The clank of iron baskets, carrying coal along overhead wires to the waiting colliers, violates the Arctic hush. But Longyear

City, yearly mining about three hundred thousand tons of excellent-quality coal, has its very tangible value. There is more coal in Spitsbergen than in Norway proper, where two and a half million tons are needed annually.

As early as 1610 the sailors discovered and burned "sea-coales," and the succeeding generations of whalers dug it for their use. A cargo was shipped to Norway in 1894. But coal-mining as a commercial enterprise was not started until 1905 with the arrival of an American, John Munro Longyear. The coal is of a high heating power with little ash, and the mining of it is simplified since there is no danger of water flooding in a region where the earth, from a few feet below the surface, is always frozen solid for a depth beyond which no mine has ever penetrated. Furthermore, no timber is necessary to support the "working face." And since the deposits are not only near the sea but on hillsides, colliers can be loaded with a minimum of labour by self-working, overhead tramways from mine to pier.

The coal mines are blackened testimonials of that time when alders, firs, and ferns, pines and cypress, flourished luxuriantly in a sub-tropical climate similar to that of Southern Europe today. They grew rapidly and decayed rapidly, and in their deposits, heated under great pressure, are still found perfect impressions of that long-distant period. Fossils of the gingko biloba, the deciduous tree which is the ancestor of our conifers, are especially well preserved.

Longyear sold his claims to Norway in 1916, but the city which bears his name has continued to grow, looking black and untidy and unshaded to the summer visitor picking his way up the muddy road and wandering among the log houses, frame buildings, barracks, and sheds. But the six hundred men and sixty women who live here are proud of Longyear City, with its church and school and hospital, of their tightly built houses, of the cows who furnish fresh milk for the half a hundred children, of the tiny cold frames where lettuce and radishes can be coaxed to grow. They regret that visitors come only in summer, when the grimy mud is soft under foot. In the winter, when the snow covers all the soot and coal dust, when the moonlight and starlight flood the frozen bay and silver the mountain tops, and the Northern Lights illumine the sky, then Longyear City pleases them best. The Governor's House, the officers' mess, the cottages of the married men, the barracks of the single men are well warmed, for there is plenty of coal, and all well lighted, for there is plenty of electricity.

Although in the summer there is little to delight the eye in this settlement, with its family resemblance to many another frontier mining community, there is nothing to offend the social conscience. The faces of the inhabitants are self-respecting Norwegian faces, the houses are decent habitations, the children clean and well clothed.

But the Russian mining-settlement of Barentsburg, a few miles away by boat in summer, or a few hours by ski in winter, is a nightmare of decay and disrepair. There are still a few substantial buildings left from the time when the Dutch owned and occupied it. But since they sold their mining rights to Russia, all traces of Dutch cleanliness have disappeared. There is grime on the faces of the heavy-featured labourers who huddle in crowds to stare at visitors, dirt on and in the dismal buildings, filth in the open sewers, and misery over it all. One hundred and seventy-seven thousand tons of coal go down the chute to waiting ships, most of it to be carried to Siberia.

The straggling streets of Longyear City may not suggest a popular centre to cruise passengers from London, Paris, and New York. But they are decent highways compared to those of Barentsburg, and they must be metropolitan boulevards to the man who for months has seen no living face but those of seals, foxes, or bears.

The most northerly people in the world today getting their living from the country, are the Norwegian sealers. The Scotsmen gave up sealing long ago, and although the Newfoundlanders seal around their island, and the Russians in the White Sea and on their own coast, and the Americans and Japanese in the Pacific, the Norwegians are the only men left who still make a living by sealing at large. Up from Hammerfest and Tromsö they come in the spring to roam all over the Arctic from Novaya Zemlya in the east to outside Greenland in the west and as far north as ice permits. The seals lie on the ice, the old ones in a slothful heap with their "eyes closed in a mindless, senseless, dreamless slumber," the yearling pups "with a soft velvety puppy coat and round sad eyes like saucers." The sealers bring their big boat as close as they dare and then push further in small boats and creep quietly out on the ice with clubs. On a lucky day they can sometimes kill a thousand.

> The sun is brave, the sun is bright,
> The sun is lord of love and light;
> But after him it cometh night.
> Dim anguish of the lonesome dark!—

Winter is the time to trap the white and blue fox and to shoot the polar bear or, rather, set the bait and gun so cunningly that he shoots himself. The over-winterer usually lives alone and keeps to his allotted area, since few districts are rich enough to support two men. His solitary hut is large enough only for himself, his bunk, and his stove, but there is room enough outside to stretch his legs. Leagues and leagues of room—frozen mile after frozen mile—glittering under the winter moon. Daily, upon his skis, he makes the long journey to his trap lines, and if he can get from thirty to forty foxes in a season, his year's living is assured. Perhaps two over-winterers can together get a hundred or more bears in a season, and if the price they fetch seems small, the labour is always great and frequently dangerous. The over-winterer is his own man and that is his compensation. His physical needs are few and his passion for independence prodigious, and he has no desire to change his career or his address.

When, in April, the sun begins to pay out its beams sparingly and briefly, there is hardly a hint of warmth in them. But tenuous as they are, they are threads upon which a million shuttles begin to weave a design of life.

The birds return. Millions and millions of them! Guillemots, singly, in pairs, in companies and battalions; strings of quaint little auks in black and white uniforms; snow buntings in summer plumage, the only song birds of these northern latitudes. The air is pierced by the sharp cry of the Arctic terns and by the high-pitched notes of the auks as their wings beat rapidly a few inches above the water's surface. The barnacle geese honk and the gulls scream. Only the fulmar, wheeling past, rarely utters a sound when in flight.

Wings flash against the sky. Beaks shatter the water like a

hail of bullets. Mountains pulsate with sound and stir. On ledges and in crevices of cliffs that seem as bare and steep as walls of city masonry, the female lays her eggs and hatches them and tends her clamouring young. The male swoops out into space, dives, fishes, gobbles, gorges, and brings home food to his family.

The lone trapper gorges, too. Now he can have eggs, large and fresh, and plenty of them for the mere gathering. He can have juicy roast duck and brent goose and pancakes stiff with egg. One of the phenomena of the Arctic is the amount of fresh eggs and fresh fowl the trapper is able to consume. He knows where to find the eggs and he knows where the eider duck sat upon her nest while the handsome drake stood near, and in this nest, after the young have been hatched, he finds the freshest eider down—that airy stuff whose equivalent is solid cash. Egg-gathering and down-gathering, fresh eggs and fresh meat—the spring sun filtering through the Arctic air penetrates into the trapper's hut and lays a feast upon his table and piles up feathers in his bag. Now he may return to Norway for a holiday and exchange his furry and fluffy merchandise for clothes and equipment and stores.

All through the light of summer days and nights the birds wheel and scream, floating, flapping, flying, transformed from real to unreal tints. For when the under side of white wings catch the reflection of the water, they seem pale green. When the upper side of brown wings catch the shadow of the clouds, they seem lavender. The purple sand pipers court upon the beach; the skuas chase the kittiwakes; and a pair of graceful grey phalaropes ride buoyantly upon the waters of the bay.

To the hungry hunter these birds swooping down to the sea, rising effortlessly into the air, drifting with the wind or breast-

At Temple Bay the glaciers build a mile-long façade of sunny
domes and caves of ice.

To Spitsbergen—the frozen rim of the world.

ing it, may chiefly signify a change in the monotonous menu of winter. But since the days of Icarus, such motion has tantalized whoever has believed that man, too, should be able to lift himself from the ground and travel through the air. These gulls and guillemots—their propellers are never out of order and no ice freezes on their ailerons. Perfect take-off and perfect banking to a landing are achieved without fail. Altimeter and compass are invariably correct. There is no hitch in the combustion of the fuel. So must these fliers, combining in their feathered fuselage all virtues of airship, airplane, aquaplane, glider, and balloon have seemed to those men who built the huge hangar whose framework still criss-crosses the sky at New Alesund on King's Bay.

The North Pole—the mythical North Pole, the symbolic North Pole, the actual North Pole! The North Pole that is so unmistakably situated on every schoolroom globe and mentioned vaguely, explicitly, casually, and universally—only a few individuals of all the teeming millions of the earth have ever reached that geographical axis.

The nearest most of us will ever come to it will be this hangar.

For from out this now empty chrysalis of wood once emerged the *Norge,* the first airship and the last to pass over the northern apex of the globe.

The three men who conceived and achieved this spectacular adventure—Roald Amundsen, Lincoln Ellsworth, and Umberto Nobile—must have stood, just where we are standing now, by this hangar—its gaunt bones covered by two and a half acres of canvas—and imagined how the giant dirigible which they had flown from Rome would soon float over its final and uncharted course.

But not entirely uncharted, for even while the *Norge* was waiting to start, Richard Byrd had in his Fokker plane, the *Josephine Ford,* made a dash from this very landing-place, reached the North Pole, and returned in just over fifteen hours (May 9, 1926).

Although this flight by the American took away a certain novelty from the projected attempt of the *Norge* in the minds of the world public, Amundsen did not so regard it. Byrd's object had been to fly to the Pole and back, while the Pole was to be merely one station on the trip of the *Norge* across the Polar Sea from Svalbard to Alaska.

In the evenings, in the warmth of the director's house, around a table strewn with maps and charts, Amundsen, Ellsworth, and Nobile must have discussed their final arrangements. The Italian had planned and constructed the ship; the American had produced much of the money for its purchase from Italy; and the Norwegian, with his polar experience, had mapped the route.

They hoped, but could not know that their hopes would be fulfilled; that the *Norge* would rise from New Alesund at 9:55 a.m. on May 11 and that at 1:25 p.m., thirteen and a half hours later, the Norwegian, the American, and the Italian flags would be so dropped that their standards would fix themselves into the ice and they would unfurl and float upon that very point which instruments determine to be the North Pole. They hoped, but could not know that forty-six hours and twenty minutes after it had left the ground at King's Bay, the *Norge* would come in over the land at Alaska, and thus the Polar Sea would have been crossed for the first time.

As they sat around the table in New Alesund, it may be that they paused in their looking forward to look back a little and talk of Amundsen's more youthful plans for a seven-year drift to the North Pole in Nansen's old *Fram,* plans which he abandoned when he heard that Peary had already reached the coveted spot by sledge (1909); of his two attempts from Seattle (1920) to get to the Pole by ship; and of his almost successful essay of the previous year. At this time, with Ellsworth and two airplanes, one of them piloted by Captain Riiser-Larsen, he got within one hundred and sixty miles of his goal (87′ 43″). Both planes had been forced to land in an open lane of water, one had been left behind, and the double crew had returned in the other, defeated in achievement but not weakened in determination.

It was well that the three men sitting around the table could not look forward and see Nobile two years hence in another and a new airship, the *Italia,* coming down in disaster northeast of Svalbard. Well that they could not foresee that worse disaster when Amundsen, rushing forth to rescue his friend in the airplane *Latham,* placed at his disposal by the French Government and piloted by the French Captain Guilband, would disappear north of Tromsö, never to be traced, although Nobile would return to an unfriendly world.

It is possible their talk touched the Swedish Andrée, who (1897) with two companions, Fraenkel and Strindberg, had gone up in a balloon from Dane's Island, not far from here. Even then his bones were lying on the shore of Franz Josef Land, but it would not be until 1930 that those bones would be found and, after thirty-three years, the photographic films near them developed and the diary, close at hand, deciphered. They may also have recalled the three Norwegian marine aviators, Leif Dietrichson, Sven Brun, and E. W. Eliassen, who in the summer of 1923 had flown above Svalbard, and Count

Zeppelin himself, who had gone up in the air to make observations.

But most often they must have spoken of Nansen.

Everyone who dreamed of going to the North Pole spoke of Nansen, for he, in his athletic prowess, in his intellectuality, and in his burning belief in an ideal, was the living symbol of bravery and brilliance.

Amundsen had, in imagination, lived every hour of the first and most famous voyage of the *Fram* (1893–1896), that unique ship designed not to crash through the ice but to slip out of its grip and be hoisted free of the pack; that unique route not against the current but drifting with it across the Polar Sea. The *Fram* had not reached the North Pole and neither had Nansen, who, with Hjalmar Johansen, left her to make the final dash on skis. But he got within two hundred and seventy-two miles of it (86′ 14″) and his exploit had rung all over civilized and uncivilized creation.

He had been famous before the trip with the *Fram*. A handsome and well-born young man, who had already won recognition for the earnestness and originality of his research in zoology, oceanography, biology, and histology; who had crossed Greenland from east to west on ski and sled, something which had been considered utterly impossible—such a sailor-hunter-sportsman-scholar could hardly fail to be famous. And since these attractive qualities of physical and mental power were fused in a personality affectionate, frank, and gay, their possessor could hardly fail to be loved.

Fridtjof Nansen was by inclination and training a scholar, and his professors always mourned that he did not devote himself sole-heartedly to science. But he was, equally, a man of tremendous energy—a virtuoso in action, strenuous sport, and daring adventure. And he was, potentially, an artist.

Whoever has spent absorbed hours over the two heavy volumes of *Farthest North*, gripping the covers excitedly as the *Fram* drifts forward, turning the pages apprehensively as she drifts backward, must recognize that it is not merely because the events are set forth vividly but because of the narrator's sensitive response to outer and inner experience, his intro-spection and aspirations, that the book is literature. Nansen wrote prodigiously. Books on sport, adventure, travel—many of them illustrated by his own sketches and paintings—diaries, lectures, articles on international relations—he had fluency and good taste in expressing himself through the written word.

In personal contact he was equally effective. His striking appearance, his straightforwardness and impartiality, made him a figure in London when he was Norwegian Ambassador, and in Washington when he was wartime Minister Plenipotentiary on Special Mission. Part of this special mission was the negotiation of trade relations to ensure Norway's supplies, particularly of foodstuffs.

All these honours had been his at the time when Amundsen, Ellsworth, and Nobile sat around the table at New Alesund, and it is probable that they, with the rest of the world, assumed that the activities of the great Norwegian had, now that he was sixty-five, reached their fulfilment and end. It is probable that the greatest of those achievements seemed to them, as to the majority of people, his Polar exploits. But it was the last decade of his life which was to hold the most immense and heroic labours of this passionate and practical idealist.

In 1920, when he reluctantly left his laboratory and study to accept the position of High Commissioner of the League of Nations, he was confronted with half a million war prisoners to be returned to their thirty respective homelands. With energy and astuteness, he not only organized and engineered this prodigious feat, but, since there had been no provision for it in the Treaty of Versailles, he personally, from public and private sources, raised the necessary funds.

Nor was this all. The following year he raised funds and directed relief work for millions of famine sufferers in Russia. One cannot raise funds without first gaining the sympathy of those who may contribute. To have won such support for Russia at a time when she was particularly unpopular, was a task requiring exceptional persuasiveness and energy.

Nor was even this the end. In 1922, after the Græco-Turkish War, a million and a half panic-stricken refugees rushed from Thrace and Asia Minor without money, without tools, without provisions of any kind, without even a destination. To rescue this starving mob, to settle them in Greece, to move half a million Turks out of Greece to Turkish soil and help them all to self-support, was Nansen's task. By painstaking manipulation of countries, organizations, and individuals, by wise choice of colleagues and superb financing, he accomplished it. It was a migration of almost two million people— the largest known to history. "One has to go back to the age of Cæsar or Augustus," it has been said, "to see similar world problems laid in the hands of a single individual."

And even now he had not finished. His hair perfectly white from the horrors he had witnessed, his face lined with strain, having resigned from the League of Nations in indignation over that body's policy toward the Armenians, he again assumed the burden of High Commissioner and the labour of saving that unhappy race.

While in the long perspective of history the name of the man whom Romain Rolland has called "the only European hero of our time" will gather greatest lustre from its final decade; while he received the Nobel prize and "there is not a country on the Continent of Europe where wives and mothers have not wept in gratitude for the work that Nansen did," yet always, whenever anyone thinks about the North Pole, there will be a special and romantic remembrance of this versatile young adventurer. Of his many loves, Polar exploration was one of his first and certainly his last. The very year of his death, still bewitched by the unknown, by "the peaks and glaciers which no human foot had ever trod . . . glistening beyond the drift ice," he was planning a scientific expedition with Hugo Eckener across the North Polar region.

Of the three men planning the flight of the *Norge,* Amundsen was the one who was most closely Nansen's friend. Their friendship had been sealed when the older man had (in 1910) let the younger one take the *Fram* for the trip which started for the Arctic and ended at the Antarctic.

And of the three men it was around Amundsen that the clouds both of acclaim and criticism had most closely gathered.

It is Amundsen's picture, with its extraordinary eagle-like features, that is, like Nansen's, still seen all over Norway.

Amundsen had determined in boyhood on a career of exploration, and definitely directed his energies, his studies, and his life to this end. He had (1906), with six men and the little fishing boat *Gjoa,* discovered the Northwest Passage, taking three years to find his way through that perilous and utterly unknown route between the Atlantic and the Pacific. He had

(1911) placed the flag of Norway on the South Pole and named the plateau where it stood for Haakon VIII. He was the third man to navigate the Northeast Passage (1920). This flight with the *Norge,* if successful, was to be the culmination of his career. It was successful and it may be that Amundsen accepted it as his last adventure, although posterity will not fail to lay a leaf of laurel on his final flight, by which he hoped to rescue Nobile.

The achievements of Amundsen are catalogued in many books, including his own, *First Crossing of the Polar Sea.* But unlike Nansen, he could not express himself in words, and his personality is more winningly conveyed in *Voyages of a Modern Viking* by Helmer Hanssen. Reading this affectionate and informal record by one who sailed with Amundsen on the *Gjoa,* went to the South Pole with him, and was captain of the *Maud,* one of the only two ships that have ever succeeded in the Northeast Passage, one is quite sure that no one would have been more pleased than Amundsen when the Russians from Moscow succeeded (1937) in making their station at the North Pole before they drifted south with the Polar Stream.

New Alesund, where the hangar stands, is a desolate spot when the winds from off the glaciers howl from all directions at once, each direction more bitterly cold than the other. Yet here are houses, shops, a "hotel," if you please, and the inhabitants strolling about without overcoats, for it is summer, and if one is ever to doff winter garments, it must be on a summer's day. Sometimes in summer it is warm, so that coat-doffing is a recognition of that possibility. That a hangar should be built here is comprehensible, for where else can an airship or plane take off more suitably for the North Pole? But what are these houses? Why these pipes and tracks? And why should there be a concrete power house on that hill?

At the turn of the century, two Norwegians, who had made a fortune in the Klondike, came to New Alesund (naming it after their home of Alesund in Norway) to make another in coal. Men were brought here, houses built for them, the mine was opened, tracks were laid to carry the coal to the water, and wires were strung to carry electricity. Pipes, insulated and electrically heated, brought water to the houses. Since 1929, when explosions made it necessary to flood the mine, it has been closed, but New Alesund has not been deserted. There is a shop where boats can be repaired, the Government keeps a station here where fishermen can get salt and ice, and there is the possibility that oil and benzine may be extracted from the coal. In the summer, there is a regular mail service from Norway and a fair amount of coming and going. In the winter, one man and his wife keep watch over the machinery.

It may be that in the not too distant future a sanitarium will be opened here, for in an air where the only germs and bacilli are those brought by boats in summertime, tubercular lungs heal as rapidly as wounds. And that is rapid, indeed, as many a trapper, who has sewn up a cut with his sail needle, can testify. The uncannily preservative purity of the air was remarked in 1691 by Friedrick Martens, a surgeon on a Dutch ship, who wrote: "Bodies do not decay or fall into dust in this country: this was proved by a corpse which we found there and which had been buried ten years before. There was no change either in the face or in the clothes. The cross erected over the grave gave the date when the burial took place."

There may be a sanitarium offering its patients the diversion of dog-sledding over the glaciers, but today the most interesting thing at King's Bay is the old hangar.

Realizing what it represents in the history of man's adventures into the Arctic, it is impossible not to wonder what he may attempt—and accomplish—in the future. The old legends of Norway that tell of lands under the sea where men farm and fish and sail, and where the grain is richer than any grain on land, bear a certain kinship to Sir Hubert Wilkins's great plans to reach the North Pole by submarine. He even went so far as to purchase his submarine and name it the Nautilus, in honour of Jules Verne, and fit it out with gadgets that would bore up through the ice for air and fresh water, and with a pair of skis on her deck. These were not intended to run over but under the ice, thus protecting the top hamper from the possibly jagged undersurface of the frozen fields.

We are not much nearer reaching the North Pole by submarine than Sir Hubert was when he abandoned his project. But we are a good deal nearer reaching it by air than when, in 1922, Vilhjalmur Stefansson predicted a regular Arctic air route. It is easy to believe that it will not be long now before planes will be passing over the Pole as casually as over a city skyscraper.

Passengers in such a future transport, looking down on Spitsbergen, will see a wider expanse than do those who look out from the deck of a steamer. But Temple Bay, when viewed from a height, will lose something of its curious detail.

This symmetrically hollowed bay is entered between crags of limestone and Silician rock, whose walls are so evenly stratified, so level across the crests, so upheld by buttresses uniform in size, shape, and spacing, that they suggest the architectural form which gives the place its name.

These twin ranges half enclose a watery surface at whose eastern end six glaciers, pushing down between separating ridges, meet in a gigantic frozen mass. Surging together, with a movement that is imperceptible and a pressure that is irresistible, they build up another temple, not of rock but of glacial ice, whose façade curves for a frozen mile and rises from the water for a hundred perpendicular feet. From the deck of the *Stella Polaris* it seems merely an abrupt snow bank. From a smaller boat, at closer range, the complication of its structure appears.

Columns of fractured ice stand free before it. Spires of splintered ice rise above it. Caves, dark as death, are hollowed in its base. The pavement of its entrance steps and court is a mosaic of ice and water. Behind its detached towers, set back from step and court, the mile-long front suggests, in form and fancy, such stuff as dreams are made on. Yonder is half a recessed arch; here opens a broken portal; there hangs the fragment of a twisting stair; further above clings a ruined gallery. Behind clerestory windows, mullioned in frost, one pictures choirs and cloisters spanned with icicles, naves and aisles carpeted with snow.

Solomon's Temple was raised without the sound of a hammer or a saw, but human hands fashioned it nevertheless. This edifice is constructed of frozen water and carved by the chisel of the elements. It changes with the seasons, with the sun and the wind, and continuously, without haste and without hesitation, steps down into the sea. Its pinnacles crumble; its arches disintegrate; its caves are sealed. Constantly it flakes and falls. Constantly it is rebuilt. The glaciers buttress up new walls. The winds sharpen new pinnacles. The frost engraves pristine and translucent fretwork. The sea hollows other caverns in fresh foundations.

There are no worshippers in this temple unless one so reckons the gulls, perching like gargoyles on the ridge, or the seals that thrust their heads up among the mosaics of the floating pavement. Its only bell is the boom of a loosening ice block and its crash as it topples into the sea.

But the temple has its votaries.

These are the scientists.

When B. M. Keilhau, Professor of Geology at Oslo University, made his geographical, palæontological, and botanical investigations in Svalbard in 1827, he was entering the first items in those long columns of scientific data which are still being scrupulously and intelligently compiled.

Many years were to pass before other Norwegians followed Professor Keilhau. Swedes, Austrians, Frenchmen, Germans, and Russians explored the country, verified or disproved each other's findings, discovered and noted their own. The Englishman Sir Martin Conway investigated the interior in 1896 and his *No Man's Land* remains the basic source for the history of Spitsbergen from its discovery in 1596 to the beginning of the scientific exploration of the country. Such captains of sealing-vessels as had an eye for geographical observation contributed facts not less important for being gathered on their own initiative, as when Skipper Elling Carlsen of Tromsö circumnavigated Spitsbergen for the first time in his small fishing-boat. Although these sealing-captains sent in much geographical information, nevertheless, when Captain Gunnar Isacksen induced Prince Albert of Monaco to direct his annual oceanographic cruise to Spitsbergen (in 1906), it was high time for organized exploration. Isacksen was offered, and accepted, the leadership, and three topographers, a geologist, and two engineers—one mining and one civil—set to work in earnest.

Every year since then there has been a scientific expedition to Svalbard, since 1922 financed by the Norwegian Government, and since 1928 organized under the name of Norwegian Exploration of Svalbard and the Polar Regions (N.S.I.U.). The Institute, which co-operates not only with other Government agencies and departments, but also with organizations and individuals of every country, has its headquarters at Oslo and its publications in the scientific libraries of the world. But its laboratory is on these treeless mountains, under and in these icy waters, below this mossy soil.

No ocean bank is too deep or too shallow for sounding; no moss or lichen, fungus or flower, too humble for classification. The discovery of a fossil plant or fish is as respectfully recorded as the discovery of a post-glacial volcanic cone; the velocity and oblation of glaciers measured as scrupulously as the mileage and minutes of a horse race. Certain enthusiasts have brought musk oxen from Greenland and there has been some talk of bringing penguins from the Antarctic. The few pairs which were carefully carried only as far north as the Lofotens have not yet had time to show if these amusing creatures will deign to adapt themselves to further transplanting.

While all the workers in this laboratory are sustained by the purest ray serene of scientific research, some of them have the added satisfaction that goes with immediate utility. They have not only discovered the present coal deposits but hope for more and possibly other minerals and metals. Copper, iron, and oil have been located, although in quantities too small to be worked, and there is some zinc of good quality. Since meteorological conditions in the Arctic influence the weather in Norway—in fact, in the whole of the temperate zone of the northern hemisphere—the establishment of meteorological stations, with their warnings by radio and wireless, have saved the lives of thousands of fishermen.

Not all this laboratory work is done in the field. In Oslo, men leaning over desks compile data from diaries of wintering hunters, make plans of hunting-stations and maps of hunting-areas. Lantern slides, films, and photographs from aerial surveys, flying routes—all these must be classified, catalogued, and filed.

And as the geologist lays bare and interprets the piled-up stratifications of rock, so the philologist peels off layer after layer of the jumbled names which have accumulated through the centuries.

It was natural that the Dutch discoverers should give names to various localities; Spitsbergen itself is Dutch for "sharp mountain peaks." And it was natural that the various explorers who followed should add new names and change old ones. By slow accretion the nomenclature piled up. Swedish words, personal and geographic terms on top of those left by Dutch and English whalers, and the descriptive titles given by Norwegian hunters were overlaid by others—German, Austrian, Russian, Polish, French, Italian, Gaelic. Names were perverted, misunderstood, replaced, translated, and mistranslated, and often the same locality had several which were entirely different. When the N.S.I.U. started to publish its final editions of charts and maps, it was obvious that some order must be brought into this linguistic chaos. Practically all maps, books, and papers dealing with Spitsbergen and Bear Island from 1596 had to be examined; ten thousand names had to be analysed to find out when and why they had been given and the identity of people commemorated by them. It took until 1934 for about thirty-three hundred final names to be agreed upon—merely one filament in the web of science by which Svalbard is being netted.

As the *Stella Polaris* heads south, Spitsbergen recedes and finally fades from sight. But it may be that before the coast of Norway appears, Bear Island will be visible, beginning with a crumpled end like a piece of pie crust, sloping up into a complexity of planes and profiles, some rocky, some sandy, and some grassy, and ending in a bastioned plateau topped with velvet verdure. Since, in this vicinity, the Gulf Stream and Polar Current meet, there is often fog over the big island—it is ten miles long—and its wireless and meteorological stations are of especial value. In 1934 such numbers of cod and haddock were caught off its banks that they furnished sensational headlines in newspapers across the Atlantic. Over it, as over Spitsbergen, swarm the geologists and hydrographical and geodetic surveyors. Although its mines are not being worked, there is always hope that coal may add its revenue to cod.

By now the traveller who, a few days ago, puzzled why Norway was so eager to regain control of her old Arctic possessions, begins to realize that it was not merely because of a sentiment surviving from the Middle Ages. Economic reasons, legal reasons, scientific reasons, all contributed to her eagerness and influenced the decision of the Treaty of Paris (February 9, 1920) by which Norwegian sovereignty over Svalbard was definitely established.

Such decisions must be definite today. The time has passed when the Pope could claim that, since the earth was the property of God, he, being the representative of God, had the right to the disposal of those parts of the globe which had not been taken possession of. It is more than four centuries since Alexander VI, on the return of Columbus from his first voyage, conferred on the King of Spain and his descendants all lands lying to the west of an ideal line drawn from the North Pole to the South. This line passed one hundred leagues to the west of the Azores and included the regions already discovered as well as those not yet known!

Present international law rules that a State does not gain sovereignty over no-man's land merely by discoveries, by colonization, by sending scientific expeditions, or by establishing wireless or other stations. Any State which wishes to acquire sovereignty over territory must bring that territory under its control, maintain order, organize and administer justice, and permit subjects of other States to enter the territory and assure them of legal protection during their stay. This Norway has done in Svalbard.

Svalbard is no longer no-man's land.

Looking out at Bear Island and seeing Spanish, Russian, French, German, and British trawlers and a Faeroes cutter; glancing at the record of scientific expeditions from England, Austria, and Sweden, and the visits of American entomologists, Danish historians, Latvian astronomers, British ornithologists, Polish physicists, and a host of others, one might call it an everyman's land.

But it is part of Norway, and a valuable part. It not only balances its own budget with a surplus—thanks to taxes raised in Svalbard and duties on coal exported from there—but contributes 40 percent to the revenues of Hammerfest and Tromsö. It will always be alluring to some men who have made one fortune and are hoping to make another, to labourers who must find a livelihood, to trappers who prefer their mode of existence to any other. It will always attract scientists.

If it seems incredible that anyone with a round-trip ticket can travel in comfort to within five hundred miles of the North Pole, it seems credible that in a few years more there may be a permanent trans-Arctic air route from Europe and North America to Japan and China and Russia, and that there may be excursion planes from Spitsbergen carrying passengers over the North Pole as prosaically as they now carry them over the English Channel. Such a jaunt will require no laborious years of planning, no months of accumulating equipment, no painful and protracted struggle with the elements. One will merely step aboard, settle into a comfortably upholstered chair, and be borne through space. From a huge safe ship in the sky we will look on the ships in the sea far below: on colliers and freight boats, on small motor-boats and large cruise ships. We will look back on the long history of Norwegian Arctic exploration, sweeping from the North Pole to the South, through dangers and death, to achievement and glory.

Methods of transportation will change as men become increasingly ingenious. But it will take more than man's ingenuity to change the face of Spitsbergen. Only cycles of geologic time, only a shift in the Gulf Stream, will alter that icy profile.

Until that unpredictable future period, birds will continue to float through the crystal air, two-inch willows will grow from the frozen ground, glaciers will flow between mountains of snow, building temples of light. The whale will seek the safety of the most distant wastes, and the white polar bear and the seal with weeping eyes will flee before the hunter to the farthermost ice rim of the world.

BRIEF CHRONOLOGICAL OUTLINE
OF NORWEGIAN HISTORY

PART I: PERIOD BEFORE CHRIST

12,000 B.C.

Ice Age still covered Scandinavian Peninsula.

6000

Norway became habitable for man.

4000

Stone Age.

2000

First parish settlements.

1500

Bronze Age.

500

Iron Age.

300

First authentic written record relating to Norway.
Pytheas, of Massilia (Marseille), visited the country.

PART II: THE VIKING PERIOD

(*Eighth to Eleventh Century*)

A.D. 790

Norwegian Vikings raid Dorchester in England.

793

Sack Lindisfarne.

795

First of twenty years of forays on Dublin.

825

Extensive raids inland from Dublin.

832–42

Half of Ireland in subjection.

850–65

Attacks on Frankish Empire.

851

Wintered in Isle of Thanet, England.

852

Invaded London and Rochester.

853

Olav the White made King of Ireland.

855

Wintered in Isle of Sheppey.

859

Active in Spain, Morocco, and Balearic Islands.

860

Sailed up the Rhone to Valence.

861

Captured Pisa and Luna in Italy.

862

Invaded the Seine and the Loire in France.

865

Engaged in siege of Constantinople (Byzantium).

866

Harried Northumbria, Mercia, East Anglia (England).

871

Wessex saved by Alfred from the Vikings.

881

Engaged in Cologne, Bonn, Coblenz, and Metz (Germany).

882

Besieged Paris with 700 vessels and 40,000 men, sailing up Seine.
Besieged Flanders, Brabant, Picardy, and Louvain.

890

Invaded Germany.

900

Colonized Iceland.

911

Dukedom of Normandy founded by Rolf the Ganger, son of a Norwegian earl, who received a fief from the French king.

982

West Greenland discovered by Erik Raude.

985

Norwegian colonies established in West Greenland.

1000

Leif Ericson discovered American continent.

PART III: THE EARLY NORSE KINGS

(Part of this contemporaneous with Viking Period and Saga Period)
A.D. **872**

Harald Haarfager (Fairhair) acknowledged absolute monarch of Norway. This marks entrance into the world of Norway as one kingdom. In 866 Harald determined to attack the smaller kings of Norway and three years later began a series of battles terminating in sea victory of Hafsfjord. He ruled until he divided his kingdom among his twenty sons.

930

Erik Blodökse (Bloody-Axe), his favorite son, installed as over-king. The other kings grouped themselves into three parts. The Trondheim district, the Valleys of Sogn and Hallingdal, and the southern slopes of Lake Mjösa and Oslofjord were autonomous states.

935

Erik deposed by Haakon the Good. Haakon had been educated in England at the Court of King Aethelstan. He was engaged in wars with Erik's sons until he was killed in battle and leadership passed to a triumvirate of Erik's sons, headed by Harald Graafeld (Greycloak) who controlled the western districts.

961

Harald Graafeld and the two other members of the triumvirate killed Earl Sigurd, who ruled in the north. Sigurd's son, Earl Haakon, enticed Harald to Denmark and there murdered him.

970

Earl Haakon ruled all Norway except the southwest, which was held by a vassal king. Overthrown by his feudal lords, Earl Haakon was killed by his own thrall in 995.

995

Olav Tryggvesson entered upon his reign, accomplishing Christianization of Norway.

1000

Olav Tryggvesson jumped into the sea at battle of Svolder, and the conquering Danes—Earl Erik and his brother Svein, sons of Earl Haakon—ruled country.

1000–1100

Stone churches built. Also stone cathedrals at Trondheim and Stavanger.

1015

St. Olav, son of Gudröd, who was nephew of Tryggve, continued Christianizing of Norway. After a few years, King Knut the Great of England and Denmark invaded and claimed Norway. Olav fled to Russia (1029) and returned to die at battle of Stiklestad (1030). Became St. Olav later.

1030

Knut installed his son Svein as king. His rule was so chaotic that people summoned Olav's son Magnus from Russia. Svein fled to Denmark.

1035

Magnus the Good became king. He also held disputed right to

the Danish throne and invited his father's half-brother Harald Haardraade (Hardruling) to rule jointly with him.

1046

Magnus's death left as sole monarch Harald Haardraade. He fought to retain Danish rights, but lost them. He conquered in England from the Tyne to York, but was defeated by the Saxon Harold II. Harald the Hardruling was killed, but his son Olav escaped.

1066

Olav Kyrre (Peaceful), with his brother Magnus, shared kingdom of Norway. Magnus died (1069) and Olav Kyrre founded Bergen and established cathedrals at Trondheim, Bergen, and Oslo.

1093

Magnus Barfod (Barefoot) succeeded Olav Kyrre, but, unlike his father, he loved warfare and engaged in three expeditions to Scotland and one to Sweden. He was killed fighting in Ireland.

1103

Magnus Barfod succeeded by his three sons, Eystein, Sigurd, and Olav. Sigurd lived longest. He was a Crusader and travelled to Jerusalem.

1130

Sigurd died and his only son Magnus was ousted by Harald Gille (born in Ireland), who claimed to be a natural son of Magnus Barfod.

1136

Harald Gille killed and his son Inge ruled. Inge was a weak cripple, ruled by strong aristocrats, and was killed by his nephew, Haakon Herdebred.

1161

Haakon ruled for a year and was killed by Erling Skakke.

1163

Magnus, son of Erling, crowned in Nidaros (now Trondheim) Cathedral.

1184

Sverre (illegitimate son of the Sigurd Mund whose son Haakon reigned for a year) defeated Magnus's father Erling in 1179, and Magnus in 1184. He ruled unconquered till his death in 1202.

1202

Haakon III succeeded his father Sverre. Died 1204.

1204–1217

Inge Baardson (son of Sverre's sister) ruled.

1217–1263

Norway at height of her political and cultural power under Haakon IV Haakonson. Iceland and Greenland become dependencies.

1263

Magnus succeeds his father, Haakon Haakonson. Sells Hebrides and Isle of Man to Scots King.

1280

Quarrels between Church and State throughout reigns of Magnus's sons, Erik and Haakon, each of whom was king in turn.

1299–1319

Haakon V brought Norway greater independence. At his death the throne went to his three-year-old grandson Magnus, whose father was Duke Erik of Sweden. Thus two countries were united through this child.

1319

The Black Death ravaged Norway, destroying great numbers of population, particularly the educated class.

1343

Haakon VI ruled. He married Princess Margrete of Denmark, daughter of King Valdemar Atterdag. Valdemar died in 1375 without male issue. Therefore Denmark elected Olav, son of Haakon VI and Margrete, as King of Denmark.

1380

Haakon VI died, and Olav, already King of Denmark, succeeded to his father's throne, ruling both countries.

1387

Olav V died, and his mother Margrete ascended the throne.

1389

Erik of Pomerania, great-nephew of Margrete, was elected Regent.

1397

Erik crowned King of Norway, Sweden, and Denmark at Castle of Kalmar.

PART IV: THE UNION OF THE SCANDINAVIAN PEOPLES

The Kingdoms of Norway and Sweden had been united in 1319 when Magnus (whose father was Duke Erik of Sweden, and whose grandfather was King Haakon of Norway) ascended the Norwegian throne. The Kingdoms of Norway, Sweden, and Denmark were united when Magnus's grandson (whose maternal grandfather was King of Denmark) succeeded to all three thrones.

1450

Reconstruction of union—Norway holding her position as a separate kingdom within the union.

1658

Tröndelag and Baahus lost to Sweden.

1660

Trondheim restored to Norway.

1718

Incessant wars with Sweden.

1788

Repealing of Danish law, forbidding importation of grain except from Denmark. Timber becomes source of wealth to Norway.

1807

Rising nationalistic movement, leading to separate administration for Norway.

1811

Founding of University of Christiania, Oslo.

1814

Union between Norway and Denmark dissolved by Treaty of Kiel. By this Treaty Frederick VI (joint and absolute monarch of Denmark and Norway) ceded Norway to the King of Sweden. Norwegians did not acknowledge this, and in May 1814 a National Assembly declared Norway an independent constitutional kingdom. It elected Prince Christian Frederick of Denmark as King of Norway. The Holy Alliance would not permit this, and Christian Frederick was forced to abdicate. However, the free Norwegian constitution was recognized, and on November 4, 1814, Norway entered voluntarily into a personal union with Sweden.

When Norway was ceded to Sweden Frederick VI excepted the then Norwegian dependencies of Iceland, the Faeroes, and West Greenland.

1821

Continual conflict with Sweden resulted in Norway getting her own maritime flag.

1844

Norway given her own naval flag, although union sign appeared on both this and maritime one.

1844

Abolition of Councillors of State and responsibility of Ministers to Storting (Parliament) recognized.

1873

The office of Governor abolished and adoption of Norwegian Prime Minister.

1898

Union sign removed from mercantile flag.

1902–1905

Negotiations on question of consular rights for Norway.

1905

Dissolution of union with Sweden, by the Karlstad Agreements (October 6).

1905

Plebiscite (voting for a monarchy) elected Prince Carl of Denmark as King of Norway (November 18). He took the name of Haakon VII. His son, the Crown Prince, was named Olav.

1920

Land areas brought under Norwegian sovereignty after this period included Svalbard, Jan Mayen, Bouvet Island, and Peter I Island.

1931–32

Land areas annexed by Norway but declared Danish by Hague Tribunal included Erich Raude Land and Southeast Greenland.

1933

Greenland awarded to Denmark by International Tribunal at Hague, although it had been a Norwegian possession until 1814.

SALIENT FACTS AND STATISTICS

Area

Norway proper has an area of approximately 124,556 square miles, including some 150,000 islands and skerries. If Spitsbergen and Jan Mayen are included, the total area amounts to about 148,990 square miles. Norway is the most northwesterly country in Europe, long and narrow, extending from 58° to 71° N. and forming the western and northern part of the Scandinavian Peninsula. Surrounded on three sides by the sea, its coastline is exceedingly complex and of great length. The average altitude is considerably higher than that of Europe; only one-fifth of the entire country lies lower than 650 feet above the sea. The rivers are numerous, but short in length, being interrupted by many waterfalls and rapids.

Climate

The climate, in general, is comparatively mild. The coasts are washed by the Gulf Stream, which explains the high temperatures as compared with similar latitudes elsewhere.

Form of Government

Norway is a limited and hereditary monarchy. Executive power is vested in the king, legislative power in the Storting, and judicial power in the Judicature. The king exercises his power in the Council of State (Cabinet). He has no power to dissolve the Storting. Women are admitted as members of the Cabinet. All Norwegian subjects, men and women, have the right to vote upon attaining the age of twenty-three, provided they have lived in Norway for five years, are still resident there, and have not had the right to vote suspended or cancelled.

Religion

The Evangelical Lutheran is the established church of Norway. The inhabitants professing this faith are required to bring their children up in this church.

Population

The total population of the kingdom, according to the 1935 census, was 2,881,605. Of this number 1,330,217 resided in towns and rural townships and 1,438,977 in rural districts proper.

Occupation

Agriculture and forestry support over 800,000 of Norway's inhabitants, fishing and hunting nearly 200,000, industry and handicrafts about 775,000. Commerce and transport occupy over 500,-000.

Division of Land

Three-quarters of the surface is in mountains, marshes, and skerries. Rivers and lakes occupy 5000 square miles, forests 27,500 square miles. There are 264,784 registered farms, 94 percent of which are owned by their occupants.

Currency and Weights and Measures

The coinage, measures, and weights are based upon the decimal system. This was adopted for the coinage in 1876 and for weights and measures in 1882. The monetary unit is called a krone, divided into 100 öre.

BIBLIOGRAPHY

HISTORY

Carlyle, Thomas: *The Early Kings of Norway*. Harper & Brothers, New York, 1875.

Falnes, Oscar J.: *Norway and the Nobel Peace Prize*. Columbia University Press, New York, 1938.

Gade, John A.: *Christian IV, King of Denmark and Norway*. Houghton Mifflin Company, Boston, 1928.

Gathorne-Hardy, G. M.: *Norway*. Charles Scribner's Sons, New York, 1925.

Gathorne-Hardy, G. M.: *The Norse Discoverers of America*. Clarendon Press, Oxford, 1921.

Gjerset, Knut: *History of the Norwegian People*. The Macmillan Company, New York, 1915.

Gray, Edward F.: *Leif Eriksson, Discoverer of America, A.D. 1003*. Oxford University Press, London, 1930.

Heckscher, E. F., Bergendahl, K., Keilhau, W., and others: *Sweden, Norway, Denmark, and Iceland in the World War*. Yale University Press, New Haven, 1930.

Hovgaard, William: *The Voyages of the Norsemen to America*. The American-Scandinavian Foundation, New York, 1914.

Kendrick, T. D.: *A History of the Vikings*. Charles Scribner's Sons, New York, 1930.

Larson, Laurence M.: *The Earliest Norwegian Laws, Being the Gulathing Law and the Frostathing Law*. Columbia University Press, New York, 1935.

Lawrence, A. W., and Young, J.: *Narratives of the Discovery of America*. Jonathan Cape and Harrison Smith, Ltd., New York, 1931.

Nörlund, Poul: *Viking Settlers in Greenland*. Cambridge University Press, London, 1936.

Olrik, Axel: *Viking Civilization*. The American-Scandinavian Foundation, New York, 1930.

Shetelig, Haakon, and Falk, Hjalmar: *Scandinavian Archæology*. Oxford University Press, London, 1937.
Williams, Mary W.: *Social Scandinavia in the Viking Age*. The Macmillan Company, New York, 1920.
Willson, T. B.: *History of the Church and State in Norway*. Constable & Company, Ltd., London, 1903.

NORWEGIANS IN THE UNITED STATES

Andersen, Rasmus Björn: *The First Norwegian Settlements in America within the Present Century*. (Proceedings of the State Historical Society of Wisconsin, 1898, pp. 149–167.)
Blegen, Theodore Christian, and Ruud, M. B., editors and translators: *Norwegian Emigrant Songs and Ballads*. (Songs harmonized by Gunnar J. Malmin.) University of Minnesota Press, Minneapolis, 1936.
Blegen, Theodore Christian: *Norwegian Migration to America 1825–1860*. The Norwegian-American Historical Association, Northfield, Minn., 1931.
Flom, G. T.: *A History of Norwegian Immigration to the United States, from the Earliest Times to the Year 1848*. Privately printed, Iowa City, 1907.
Gjerset, Knut: *Norwegian Sailors in American Waters. A Study in the History of Maritime Activity on the Eastern Seaboard*. The Norwegian-American Historical Association, Northfield, Minn., 1933.
Larson, Laurence M.: *The Changing West, and Other Essays*. The Norwegian-American Historical Association, Northfield, Minn., 1937.
Norlie, O. M.: *History of the Norwegian People in America*. Augsburg Publishing House, Minneapolis, 1925.
Qualey, Carlton C.: *Norwegian Settlement in the United States*. The Norwegian-American Historical Association, Northfield, Minn., 1938.
Strand, Algot E.: *A History of the Norwegians of Illinois*. John Anderson Publishing Company, Chicago, 1905.
Sundby-Hansen, H., editor: *Norwegian Immigrant Contributions to America's Making*. Norwegian News Bookstore, Brooklyn, N. Y., 1921.

GUIDE AND TRAVEL BOOKS

Beckett, Samuel J.: *A Wayfarer in Norway*. Robert M. McBride & Company, New York, 1936.

Bernatzik, Hugo A.: *Lapland*. Constable & Company, Ltd., London, 1937.

Clark, Sydney A.: *Norway on $50*. Robert M. McBride & Company, New York, 1936.

Hammer, S. C.: *Norway*. A & C. Black, Ltd., London, 1928.

Laughlin, Clara E.: *So You're Going to Scandinavia!* Houghton Mifflin Company, Boston, 1937.

Lingstrom, Freda: *This Is Norway*. Gerald Howe, Ltd., London, 1933.

McBride, Robert M.: *Norwegian Towns and People*. Robert M. McBride & Company, New York, 1927.

Slingsby, W. Cecil: *Norway, the Northern Playground*. D. Douglas, Edinburgh, 1904.

Vidnes, Jacob: *Norway*. Oslo, 1935.

A New Handbook on Norway. Robert M. McBride & Company, New York, 1929.

The Norway Yearbook. Third Year of Issue, 1938. Edited by Per Vogt. Oslo.

OLD NORSE LITERATURE AND MYTHOLOGY

Adams, Julia Davis, editor: *The Swords of the Vikings. Stories from the Works of Saxo Grammaticus*. E. P. Dutton & Company, New York, 1928.

Boult, Katharine F.: *Asgard and the Norse Heroes*. E. P. Dutton & Company, New York, 1926. (Everyman's Library No. 689.)

Boyesen, Hjalmar Hjorth: *Norseland Tales*. Charles Scribner's Sons, New York, 1894.

Capper, D. P.: *The Vikings of Britain*. George Allen & Unwin, Ltd., London, 1937.

Craigie, William Alexander: *The Icelandic Sagas*. G. P. Putnam's Sons, New York, 1913.

Edda Sæmundar (The Poetic Edda). Translated with an introduction by Henry Adams Bellows. The American-Scandinavian Foundation, New York, 1923.

Edda Snorra Sturlusonar (The Prose Edda). Translated by Arthur Gilchrist Brodeur. The American-Scandinavian Foundation, New York, 1916.

Four Icelandic Sagas. Translated by Gwyn Jones. The American-Scandinavian Foundation, New York, 1935.

Hollander, Lee M.: *Old Norse Poems.* Columbia University Press, New York, 1936.

Jamieson, Peter A.: *The Viking Isles.* Heath, Cranton, Ltd., London, 1933.

Koht, Halvdan: *The Old Norse Sagas.* The American-Scandinavian Foundation, New York, 1931.

Laxdæla Saga. Translated by Thorstein Veblen. B. W. Huebsch, New York, 1925.

Munch, Peter Andreas: *Norse Mythology; Legends of Gods and Heroes.* The American-Scandinavian Foundation, New York, 1926.

Olrik, Axel: *The Heroic Legends of Denmark.* The American-Scandinavian Foundation, New York, 1919.

Olrik, Axel: *Viking Civilization.* The American-Scandinavian Foundation, New York, 1930.

Phillpotts, Bertha S.: *Edda and Saga.* Henry Holt & Company, New York. 1932. (The Home University Library.)

The Saga Library. Edited by William Morris and Eiríkr Magnússon. 4 vols. Quaritch, London, 1893–1905.

The Saga of Grettir the Strong. E. P. Dutton & Company, New York, 1913. (Everyman's Library No. 699.)

Snorri Sturluson: *Heimskringla; the Norse King Sagas.* Translated by Samuel Laing. E. P. Dutton & Company, New York, 1920. (Everyman's Library.)

Snorri Sturluson: *Heimskringla, or the Lives of the Norse Kings.* Edited by Erling Monsen. Appleton Century Company, Inc., New York, 1932.

Snorri Sturluson: *Heimskringla: the Olaf Sagas.* Translated by Samuel Laing. E. P. Dutton & Company, New York, 1930. (Everyman's Library No. 717.)

The Story of Burnt Njal. E. P. Dutton & Company, New York, 1911. (Everyman's Library.)

Volsunga Saga. The Saga of the Volsungs, the Saga of Ragnar Lodbrok, together with the Lay of Kraka. Translated by Margaret Schlauch. The American-Scandinavian Foundation, New York, 1930.

Volsunga Saga, with Songs from the Elder Edda. Translated by William Morris. The Walter Scott Publishing Company, London, 1888.

THE ARTS

Mason, Daniel Gregory: *From Grieg to Brahms.* The Outlook Company, New York, 1902.

Moore, Mrs. Aubertine Woodward, and Anderson, Rasmus B.: *Norway Music Album.* Oliver Ditson Company, Boston, 1900.

Scandinavian Art: A Survey of Swedish Art, by Carl G. Laurin; *Danish Art in the Ninetenth Century,* by Emil Hannover; *Modern Norwegian Art,* by Jens Thiis. The American-Scandinavian Foundation, New York, 1922.

Stub, Mrs. Valborg Hovind, editor: *Songs from the North. Representative Songs of Norway, Sweden and Denmark.* Oliver Ditson Company, Boston, 1907.

Vreim, H.: *Norwegian Decorative Art Today.* Albert Bonnier Publishing House, New York, 1937.

FOR WHALING AND FISHING

Melville, Herman: *Moby Dick.* E. P. Dutton & Company, New York, 1907. (Everyman's Library.)

Ommanney, F. D.: *Below the Roaring Forties* (English title: *South Latitude*). Longmans, Green & Company, New York, 1938.

Scott, Gabriel: *Markus the Fisherman.* George Allen & Unwin, Ltd., London, 1931.

Watson, Angus: *My Life.* Ivor Nicholson & Watson, London, 1937.

SPITSBERGEN AND THE ARCTIC

Amundsen, Roald: *Hunting and Adventure in the Arctic.* Duffield & Green, Inc., New York, 1924.

Amundsen, Roald, and Ellsworth, Lincoln: *First Crossing of the Polar Sea.* With additional chapters by other members of the expedition. Doubleday, Doran & Company, Inc., New York, 1926.

Amundsen, Roald: *My Life as an Explorer.* Doubleday, Doran & Company, Inc., New York, 1927.

Andrée, S. A.: *Andrée's Story: the Complete Record of His Polar Flight, 1897.* The Viking Press, New York, 1930.

Bibliography 281

Binney, George: *With Seaplane and Sledge in the Arctic.* Hutchinson & Company, Ltd., London, 1925.

Brown, R. N. Rudmose: *Spitsbergen.* Seeley, Service & Company, London, 1920.

Christensen, Lars: *Such Is the Antarctic.* Hodder & Stoughton, Ltd., London, 1935.

Conway, Sir Martin: *No Man's Land. A History of Spitsbergen from Its Discovery in 1596 to the Beginning of the Scientific Exploration of the Country.* Cambridge University Press, London, 1906.

Conway, Sir Martin: *With Ski and Sledge over Arctic Glaciers.* J. M. Dent & Sons, London, 1898.

Dole, Nathan Haskell, editor: *America in Spitsbergen. The Romance of an Arctic Coal Mine.* Marshall Jones Company, Boston, 1922.

Ellsworth, Lincoln: *Beyond Horizons.* William Heinemann, Ltd., London, 1938.

Glen, A. R.: *Under the Pole Star.* Methuen & Company, Ltd., London, 1937.

Glen, A. R.: *Young Men in the Arctic.* (The Oxford University Arctic Expedition to Spitzbergen, 1933.) Faber & Faber, Ltd., London, 1935.

Gordon, Seton, F.Z.S.: *Spitsbergen Archipelago.* Cassell & Company, Ltd., London, 1922.

Hanssen, Helmer: *Voyages of a Modern Viking.* George Routledge & Sons, Ltd., London, 1936.

Mittelholzer, Walter, and others: *By Airplane towards the North Pole.* George Allen & Unwin, Ltd., London, 1925.

Nansen, Fridtjof: *Farthest North.* Harper & Brothers, New York, 1898.

Nansen, Fridtjof: *In Northern Mists.* Frederick A. Stokes Company, New York, 1911.

Nansen, Fridtjof: *Hunting and Adventure in the Arctic.* Duffield & Green, Inc., New York, 1925.

Rasmussen, Knud: *Across Arctic America. Narrative of the Fifth Thule Expedition.* G. P. Putnam's Sons, New York, 1927.

Sörensen, Jon: *The Saga of Fridtjof Nansen.* The American-Scandinavian Foundation, New York, 1932.

Stefansson, Vilhjalmur: *Unsolved Mysteries of the Arctic.* The Macmillan Company, New York, 1939.

Worsley, Commander F. A.: *Under Sail in the Frozen North.* Stanley Paul & Company, Ltd., London, 1927.

JUVENILE

Aanrud, Hans: *Sidsel Longskirt and Solve Suntrap, Two Children of Norway.* John C. Winston Company, Philadelphia, 1935.

Carpenter, Frances: *Our Little Friends of Norway, Ola and Marit.* American Book Company, New York, 1936.

Dunlap, Maurice: *Stories of the Vikings.* Bobbs-Merrill Company, Indianapolis, 1923.

Dunlap, Maurice: *Viking Knights; a Tale of the Pagan North.* Moray Press, London, 1933.

Falkberget, Johan: *Broomstick and Snowflake.* The Macmillan Company, New York, 1933.

Hall, J. O.: *When I Was a Boy in Norway.* Lothrop, Lee & Shepard Company, Boston, 1921.

Hamsun, Marie: *A Norwegian Family.* J. B. Lippincott Company, Philadelphia, 1934.

Hanson, Lida Siboni: *Eric the Red.* Doubleday, Doran & Company, Inc., New York, 1933.

Hosford, Dorothy: *Sons of the Volsungs.* The Macmillan Company, New York, 1932.

Martineau, Harriet: *Feats on the Fiord.* The Macmillan Company, New York, 1928.

Perkins, Lucy: *Norwegian Twins.* Houghton Mifflin Company, Boston, 1933.

Schram, Constance Weil: *Olaf, Lofoten Fisherman.* Longmans, Green & Company, New York, 1929.

Wade, M. H.: *Our Little Norwegian Cousin.* L. C. Page & Company, Boston, 1903.

FICTION

Classical Literature

Björnson, Björnstjerne: *Sunny Hill.* The Macmillan Company, New York, 1932.

Björnson, Björnstjerne: *A Happy Boy.* The Macmillan Company, New York, 1931.

Björnson, Björnstjerne: *The Gauntlet; Beyond Our Power.* (From his Plays. First series. Translated with an introduction by Edwin Björkman.) Charles Scribner's Sons, New York, 1913.

Björnson, Björnstjerne: *Three Comedies: The Newly-Married Couple; Leonarda; A Gauntlet.* Translated by R. Farquharson Sharp. E. P. Dutton & Company, New York. (Everyman's Library.)

Björnson, Björnstjerne: *Arnljot Gelline.* The American-Scandinavian Foundation, New York, 1917.

Ibsen: *The Works of Henrik Ibsen.* With an introduction by William Archer and C. H. Herford. Charles Scribner's Sons, New York, 1911.

Lie, Jonas: *The Family at Gilje.* Introduction by Julius E. Olson. The American-Scandinavian Foundation, New York, 1920.

Modern Fiction

Bedel, Maurice: *Jerome, or the Latitude of Love.* The Viking Press, New York, 1928.

Bojer, Johan: *The Last of the Vikings.* Appleton Century Company, New York, 1936.

Bojer, Johan: *By Day and by Night.* Appleton Century Company, New York, 1932.

Bojer, Johan: *The Everlasting Struggle.* Appleton Century Company, New York, 1931.

Bojer, Johan: *The House and the Sea.* Appleton Century Company, New York, 1934.

Bojer, Johan: *The Great Hunger.* The Century Company, New York, 1925.

Bojer, Johan: *The Emigrants.* The Century Company, New York, 1925.

Bojer, Johan: *The Power of a Lie.* The Century Company, New York, 1920.

Bojer, Johan: *Life.* The Century Company, New York, 1920.

Bojer, Johan: *The Face of the World.* The Century Company, New York, 1919.

Bojer, Johan: *Pilgrimage.* The Century Company, New York, 1924.

Bojer, Johan: *The Prisoner Who Sang.* The Century Company, New York, 1924.

Bojer, Johan: *Treacherous Ground.* Moffat, Yard & Company, New York, 1920.

Christiansen, Sigurd: *Two Living and One Dead.* Liveright Publishing Company, New York, 1932.

Christiansen, Sigurd: *Chaff before the Wind.* Liveright Publishing Company, New York, 1934.

Duun, Olav: *The People of Juvik.* Alfred A. Knopf, Inc., New York, 1930–1935.
  v. 1. *The Trough of the Wave.*
  v. 2. *The Blind Man.*
  v. 3. *The Big Wedding.*
  v. 4. *Odin in Fairyland.*
  v. 5. *Odin Grows Up.*
  v. 6. *The Storm.*

Egge, Peter: *Hansine Solstad.* Doubleday, Doran & Company, Inc., New York, 1929.

Fangen, Ronald. *Duel.* The Viking Press, New York, 1934.

Geijerstam, Gösta af: *Northern Summer.* E. P. Dutton & Company, New York, 1937.

Geijerstam, Gösta af: *Storevik.* E. P. Dutton & Company, New York, 1938.

Gulbranssen, Trygve: *Beyond Sing the Woods.* G. P. Putnam's Sons, New York, 1936.

Gulbranssen, Trygve: *The Wind from the Mountains.* G. P. Putnam's Sons, New York, 1937.

Haalke, Magnhild: *Alli's Son.* Alfred A. Knopf, Inc., New York, 1937.

Hamsun, Knut: *August.* Coward McCann, Inc., New York, 1930.

Hamsun, Knut: *Benoni* and *Rosa.* Alfred A. Knopf, Inc., New York, 1932.

Hamsun, Knut: *Growth of the Soil.* Modern Library of the World's Best Literature, 1935.

Hamsun, Knut: *Hunger.* Introduction by Edwin Björkman. Alfred A. Knopf, Inc., New York, 1935.

Hamsun, Knut: *Mysteries.* Alfred A. Knopf, Inc., New York, 1933.

Hamsun, Knut: *The Ring Is Closed.* Coward McCann, Inc., New York, 1937.

Hamsun, Knut: *The Road Leads On.* Coward McCann, Inc., New York, 1934.

Hamsun, Knut: *Vagabonds.* Coward McCann, Inc., New York, 1930.

Hamsun, Knut: *The Women at the Pump.* Alfred A. Knopf, Inc., New York, 1928.

Hamsun, Knut: *Victoria.* Alfred A. Knopf, Inc., New York, 1929.

Hamsun, Knut: *Children of the Age.* Alfred A. Knopf, Inc., New York, 1924.

Hamsun, Knut: *Segelfoss Town.* Alfred A. Knopf, Inc., New York, 1924.

Hamsun, Knut: *Pan.* Alfred A. Knopf, Inc., New York, 1921.

Hamsun, Knut: *Mothwise.* Gyldendal, London, 1919.

Hoel, Sigurd: *One Day in October.* Coward McCann, Inc., New York, 1932.

Kamban, Gudmundur: *I See a Wondrous Land.* G. P. Putnam's Sons, New York, 1938.

Larsen, Hanna Astrup, editor: *Norway's Best Stories.* The American-Scandinavian Foundation, New York, 1927.

Rölvaag, O. E.: *Giants in the Earth.* Harper & Brothers, New York, 1927.

Scott, Gabriel: *Markus the Fisherman.* George Allen & Unwin, Ltd., London, 1931.

Scott, Gabriel: *The Burden of Iron.* Hutchinson & Company, Ltd., London, 1935.

Undset, Sigrid: *Burning Bush.* Cassell & Company, Ltd., London, 1935.

Undset, Sigrid: *Faithful Wife.* Alfred A. Knopf, Inc., New York, 1937.

Undset, Sigrid: *Gunnar's Daughter.* Alfred A. Knopf, Inc., New York, 1936.

Undset, Sigrid: *Ida Elisabeth.* Alfred A. Knopf, Inc., New York, 1933.

Undset, Sigrid: *In the Wilderness.* Grosset & Dunlap, New York, 1933.

Undset, Sigrid: *Kristin Lavransdatter.* (A Trilogy.) Alfred A. Knopf, Inc., New York, 1929.

Undset, Sigrid: *The Longest Years.* Alfred A. Knopf, Inc., New York, 1935.

Undset, Sigrid: *Master of Hestviken.* Alfred A. Knopf, Inc., New York, 1934.

Undset, Sigrid: *Saga of Saints.* Sheed & Ward, Inc., London, 1935.

Undset, Sigrid: *Son Avenger.* Alfred A. Knopf, Inc., New York, 1930.

Undset, Sigrid: *Stages on the Road.* Alfred A. Knopf, Inc., New York, 1934.

Undset, Sigrid: *Wild Orchid.* Cassell & Company, Ltd., London, 1935.

Undset, Sigrid: *Winding Road.* Alfred A. Knopf, Inc., New York, 1936.

Undset, Sigrid: *Images in a Mirror.* Alfred A. Knopf, Inc., New York, 1938.

Wildenvey, Herman: *Owls to Athens.* Poems translated by Joseph Auslander. Dodd, Mead & Company, New York, 1935.

Fiction Dealing with Norwegians in the United States

Ager, Waldemar: *I Sit Alone.* Harper & Brothers, New York, 1931.

Bojer, Johan: *The Emigrants.* The Century Company, New York, 1925.

Ostenso, Martha: *Wild Geese*. Dodd, Mead & Company, New York, 1925.
Ostenso, Martha: *Dark Dawn*. Dodd, Mead & Company, New York, 1927.
Peterson, James A.: *Hjalmar; or, The Immigrant's Son*. Holter, Minneapolis, 1922.
Rölvaag, O. E.: *The Boat of Longing*. Harper & Brothers, New York, 1933.
Rölvaag, O. E.: *Giants in the Earth*. Harper & Brothers, New York, 1927.
Rölvaag, O. E.: *Peder Victorious*. Harper & Brothers, New York, 1929.
Rölvaag, O. E.: *Their Fathers' God*. Harper & Brothers, New York, 1931.
Rölvaag, O. E.: *Pure Gold*. Harper & Brothers, New York, 1930.
Rud, Anthony M.: *The Second Generation*. Doubleday, Page, New York, 1923.
Salverson, Laura Goodman: *When Sparrows Fall*. Thomas Allen, Toronto, 1925.

BIOGRAPHY AND CRITICISM

Brandes, Georg: *Creative Spirits of the Nineteenth Century*. The Thomas Y. Crowell Company, New York, 1923.
Brandes, Georg: *Henrik Ibsen, Björnstjerne Björnson. Critical Studies*. William Heinemann, Ltd., London, 1899.
Brandes, Georg: *Reminiscences of My Childhood and Youth*. Duffield & Green, Inc., New York, 1906.
Campbell, Oscar James, Jr.: *The Comedies of Holberg*. Harvard University Press, New York, 1914.
Falnes, Oscar J.: *National Romanticism in Norway*. Columbia University Press, New York, 1933.
Gosse, Edmund William: *Henrik Ibsen*. Charles Scribner's Sons, New York, 1915.
Gosse, Edmund William: *Studies in Northern Literature*. C. Kegan Paul & Company, London, 1879.
Hammer, S. C.: *Ludvig Holberg, the Founder of Norwegian Literature*. Basil Blackwell & Mott, Ltd., Oxford, 1920.
Johansen, David Monrad: *Edvard Grieg*. Princeton University Press, for the American-Scandinavian Foundation, New York, 1938.
Jorgenson, Theodore: *History of Norwegian Literature*. The Macmillan Company, New York, 1933.
Koht, Halvdan: *The Life of Ibsen*. The American-Scandinavian Foundation, New York, 1931.

Larsen, Hanna Astrup: *Knut Hamsun*. Alfred A. Knopf, Inc., New York, 1922.

Larsen, Hanna Astrup: *Scandinavian Literature*. (Reading with a Purpose, No. 54.) American Library Associaton, Chicago, 1930.

Larsen, Hanna Astrup: *Sigrid Undset*. The American-Scandinavian Foundation, New York, 1929.

Lillehei, Ingebright: *Arne Garborg*. Society for the Advancement of Scandinavian Studies, Urbana, Illinois, 1914.

Shaw, George Bernard: *The Quintessence of Ibsenism*. Brentano's, New York, 1913.

Topsoe-Jensen, H. G.: *Scandinavian Literature from Brandes to Our Day*. The American-Scandinavian Foundation, New York, 1929.

Undset, Sigrid: *The Longest Years*. Alfred A. Knopf, Inc., New York, 1935.

Weigand, Hermann J.: *The Modern Ibsen: a Reconsideration*. Henry Holt & Company, New York, 1925.

Zucker, A. E.: *Ibsen the Master Builder*. Henry Holt & Company, New York, 1929.

EDUCATION AND LANGUAGE

Educational Yearbook. Columbia University Press, New York, 1938.

Haugen, E. I.: *Beginning Norwegian. A Grammar and Reader*. F. S. Crofts & Company, New York, 1937.

Haugen, E. I.: *Origin and Early History of the New Norse Movement in Norway*. University of Illinois, 1933.

Jensen, Arne Sigurd: *The Rural Schools of Norway*. The Stratford Company, Boston, 1928.

Jorgenson, Theodore: *Norway's Relation to Scandinavian Unionism, 1815–1871*. St. Olaf College Press, Northfield, Minn., 1935.

Loftfield, Gabriel E.: *Secondary Education in Norway*. United States Office of Education, Bulletin 17, 1930.

INDEX

171